MAEVE McCLENAGHAN

NO FIXED ABODE

Life and Death Among the UK's Forgotten Homeless

PICADOR

First published 2020 by Picador

This updated paperback edition first published 2021 by Picador
an imprint of Pan Macmillan
The Smithson, 6 Briset Street, London ECIM 5NR
EU representative: Macmillan Publishers Ireland Ltd,
Mallard Lodge, Lansdowne Village, Dublin 4
Associated companies throughout the world
www.panmacmillan.com

ISBN 978-1-5290-2375-6

Typeset by Palimpsest Book Production Ltd, Falkirk, Stirlingshire
Printed and bound by CPI Group (UK) Ltd, Croydon, CRO 4YY

MIX
Paper from
responsible sources
FSC® C116313

Visit **www.picador.com** to read more about all our books
and to buy them. You will also find features, author interviews and
news of any author events, and you can sign up for e-newsletters
so that you're always first to hear about our new releases.

'Investigations into dark and difficult areas of society give a presence to people who usually remain invisible. Journalist Maeve McClenaghan's *No Fixed Abode: Life and Death Among the UK's Forgotten Homeless* is a vital exposé of the crisis on British streets'
Guardian

'An indictment of modern Britain . . . [it] shows time and again how national safety nets have been eroded. McClenaghan neatly captures the right-thinking person's bewilderment at the state that we as a society find ourselves in, but she also seeks answers . . . *No Fixed Abode* couldn't be more illuminating, timely and urgent'
Helen Davies, *Sunday Times*

'Maeve McClenaghan compassionately brings to life the human tragedies behind the statistics . . . This adds a depth of humanity to the storytelling often missing in more standard journalistic accounts . . . *No Fixed Abode* is a powerful book. It tells a very important story in a human way and in doing so motivates the reader to demand change. It is a campaigning book of the very highest order, always advocating but never didactic'
Eoin Ó Broin, *Irish Times*

'An urgent, searing examination of our homelessness crisis . . . Crucially, McClenaghan offers solutions to a very complicated and nuanced problem . . . The result is a much-needed antidote to the apathy that can often surround homelessness. It is movingly told, passionately argued and totally engrossing'
Rory Sullivan, *iNews*

'I sat down and wept . . . A challenging and compassionate investigation into British homelessness . . . McClenaghan writes with the pace and clarity you'd expect of an award-winning investigative reporter chasing a lead . . . It can feel unbearable . . . But it is worth it, to stare down despair and bring hope where you can. For McClenaghan, this journey ends with her peeling potatoes at a soup kitchen; for someone else, it could start by reading this book'
Liz Dodd, *The Tablet*

'The story this book tells, the work of Maeve and the Dying Homeless project, the lives and, most importantly, the deaths it contains, matter. These souls may have felt, at times, invisible but they were not. They mattered . . . This is a story that desperately needed to be told'
Michael Sheen

'A sensitive exposé that illustrates the complexities of modern homelessness. Moving, poetic and as rousing as Orwell'
Cash Carraway, author of *Skint Estate*

'An incredible journalist. Her work on homelessness in the UK is vital and urgent. Maeve's book gives space to the stories of those at the sharp end of the housing crisis. She treats them as people, not numbers'
Vicky Spratt, Refinery29

'Maeve's impeccable, dogged research gives a voice to those who are not usually given one, and asks tough questions of the authorities which failed them . . . A vitally important book'
Jane Bradley, UK Investigative Correspondent for the *New York Times*

'Profoundly moving . . . A damning indictment of the austerity years, an inspiring testament to remarkable individuals working to help the vulnerable and a call to arms to give humans their most basic of rights – a place to call home'
Marisa Bate, author of *The Periodic Table of Feminism*

'A vital and entirely original book that both gathers missing numbers and humanizes the people who comprise them. Moving and insightful, this is a masterclass in the best of investigative journalism'
Jenny Kleeman, author of *Sex Robots & Vegan Meat*

'McClenaghan goes where few have gone before. Telling rich and varied personal stories of the path to homelessness while keeping a steady gaze on the societal structures and government policies that make homelessness part of the UK's socio-economic fabric. It's hard to celebrate homelessness, but *No Fixed Abode* deserves an ovation'
Leilani Farha, UN Special Rapporteur on adequate housing (2014–2020)

No Fixed Abode

Maeve McClenaghan is an award-winning investigative journalist and founder of the critically acclaimed podcast *The Tip Off*. Now working at the Bureau of Investigative Journalism as part of the Bureau Local project, Maeve has previously produced investigations for BBC radio, the *Guardian* and BuzzFeed UK. She has won numerous awards for her journalism and has been nominated three times for the Orwell Prize.

This book is dedicated to all those who lost their lives while homeless, and to those who fought so hard to prevent more unnecessary deaths

Contents

PART THREE There Are Lessons to be Learnt

PART FOUR Change

Preface to the paperback edition

After any great disaster comes a time of reckoning. A moment for reflection. An opportunity for change. Do we learn lessons from the chaos? Do we aim for a return to the old life, or reach for something even better?

The Covid-19 pandemic has brought us to this moment. It has shone a piercing light through the cracks that have permeated our society for years, unseen by many. Perhaps most clearly, it has shown the gulf of inequality when it comes to homelessness and poverty.

Overnight, the concept of home took on a new, elevated significance. Government after government started to impose lockdowns, asking their citizens to go home and stay there – but how can you go home if you have no home to go to? How can you stay safe and self-isolate if you're stuck in a hostel, or crammed with numerous others in one-room apartments?

'Housing has become the frontline defense against the coronavirus. Home has rarely been more of a life-or-death situation,' declared Leilani Farha, UN Special Rapporteur on the right to housing. This was fact, not hyperbole.

Those experiencing poverty, housed in cramped shared accommodation or tiny bed-sits, suffered catastrophic losses.

Black, Asian and minority ethnic people were hit the hardest,[*] and women from that cohort were found to be suffering the greatest financial and psychological consequences from the pandemic.[†] People with precarious immigration status missed out on services.[‡] Violence against women increased.[§] The virus revealed to us what many of those experiencing homelessness already knew: the safety net we assume will catch us if we fall is an illusion. It has been hacked away by years of cuts to every support service imaginable.

When the first lockdown hit in early 2020, I watched as people whose stories I had followed for years tried to keep pace with the rapid changes. Those sofa-surfing found their options ran out: families and friends were no longer able or willing to put them up. Youth homelessness skyrocketed.

One woman I spoke to, who had fled domestic violence with her two sons only to end up in a homeless hostel, suddenly found that the grim, decrepit bathroom they shared with dozens of other tenants was less of an unpleasant inconvenience but now a potential death-trap for her young children. (Approximately half of all hostel residents in London shared bathroom facilities.) She was eventually offered an alternative by the council: a flat in a block that previously had been

---

[*]   Office for National Statistics, 'Why have Black and South Asian people been hit hardest by COVID-19?' (2020), https://www.ons.gov.uk/peoplepopulation andcommunity/healthandsocialcare/conditionsanddiseases/articles/whyhave blackandsouthasianpeoplebeenhithardestbycovid19/2020-12-14

[†]   'BAME women and Covid-19' (2020), https://www.fawcettsociety.org.uk/coronavirus-impact-on-bame-women

[‡]   Eve Dickson et al., 'Local Authority Responses to people with NRPF during the pandemic' (2020), ICRD, University of Wolverhampton, https://www.researchgate.net/publication/343774922_Research_report_Local_Authority_Responses_to_people_with_NRPF_during_the_pandemic

[§]   Office for National Statistics, 'Domestic abuse during the coronavirus (COVID-19) pandemic, England and Wales: November 2020' (2020), https://www.ons.gov.uk/peoplepopulationandcommunity/crimeandjustice/articles/domesticabuseduringthecoronaviruscovid19pandemicenglandand wales/november2020

condemned because it was deemed completely unsafe for habitation. One man I heard from was stuck in Heathrow airport's departure lounge for weeks. He usually slept rough in central London but had moved to the airport. Then as the shops and amenities around him began to close one by one, he was not sure where to go next. He and the dozens of other people sleeping out at the airport were moved into hotels, in rooms block-booked by councils. But he was soon replaced; weeks later there were dozens more people sleeping at the same airport. They had nowhere else to go.

Many more people remained on the streets and others joined them. Some were those who had never experienced homelessness before – pushed into crisis through loss of jobs or evictions.

Similar stories played out around the world. In Belgium and France, people found themselves starving, the usual food-aid supplies having dried up. In Italy police handed out fines to those sleeping rough. In Las Vegas, scores of people found themselves sleeping on the streets after their shelter was shut down. They were advised to sleep in a car park, using the parking grid squares as markers for how far apart to lie. Those in crowded homeless shelters in New York died in tragic numbers.

We can no longer avert our eyes from these hard truths. The narrative we have been fed for so long has been proved unworthy: it is not only the wealthy who deserve a place to call home, we all do.

But this simple lesson is all too easy to forget. How soon before we slip back to our old habits – where hard-working twenty- and thirty-year-olds struggle to scrape together a deposit to meet the astronomical cost of the housing market? Where councils again find ways to turn away those facing homelessness, limited by their ever-shrinking social-housing stock? Where we walk past people sleeping on the streets without a second thought? It is up to all of us to remember.

Not since the end of the Second World War have we faced such a point of reckoning as a society: a moment when we can decide how we are going to build back our world in a fairer, kinder, more just way. Because it is not enough to just return to 'normal'. Normal was not working for the refugee women I met in bed-sits and church-hall shelters. It was not working for the elderly man bouncing between hospital stays and the streets. It was not working for the men and women who died in doorways, tents and squats.

We can start by taking lessons from the emergency, Blitz-spirit response to the pandemic. Many homelessness outreach groups adapted amazingly quickly, setting up spaced-out cordons to stop people bunching up too close, handing out food parcels to those now sheltered in temporary accommodation.

At the same time, we witnessed an extraordinary push in official homelessness policies and action. Outreach schemes scrambled and joined up services in ways previously unimaginable. Dr Al Story, one of the authors of the national Homelessness Sector Plan, said, 'We've achieved in the last week what we've been trying to achieve for a decade.'

The government, which for years had insisted there was 'no magic money tree' to support society's most vulnerable, changed tack overnight. A government decree told councils they had forty-eight hours to house all those sleeping on the streets. Whole hotels were booked to house people temporarily. The sheer number of people supported through the 'Everyone In' scheme was impressive, but also showed just how shockingly far from reality the official figures on homelessness had been: government data logged nearly 4,300 people sleeping rough before the pandemic; more than seven times that were supported by the programme.* Modelling by academics showed that the efforts to bring people in from the streets saved hundreds of lives.†

And yet at least 976 people experiencing homelessness still died in 2020, an increase of 37 per cent on the year before. Despite all the efforts, something was still going very wrong. And, as quickly as the help came, so too did doubts about how long it would last.

It has become clear that without a major overhaul of support services we are facing a tidal wave of homelessness. Millions of people in the UK have been financially pummelled by the crisis; the global economy is in tatters. In Britain, half a million people have fallen behind on their rent, and one in four of those has been threatened with eviction or cancellation of their lease. Local councils, responsible for the bulk of home-lessness support, are in dire financial straits. We could see a huge increase in those experiencing homelessness as the reality of that financial downturn hits. The fall-out from the pandemic on people's physical and mental health will reverberate for years to come.

So now is the time to think big, to reimagine how things could work. Now is the time for change. The need for a viable, well-funded social safety net has been proved to even the staunchest libertarian – the vast reach of the illness has perhaps revealed to some that misfortune is not always a choice or a punishment for foolish decisions. We now know that unimaginable dangers can hit us all, even the Prime

---

*   National Audit Office, 'Investigation into the housing of rough sleepers during the COVID-19 pandemic' (2021), https://www.nao.org.uk/press-release/investigation-into-the-housing-of-rough-sleepers-during-the-covid-19-pandemic/

†   Dan Lewer et al., 'COVID-19 among people experiencing homelessness in England: a modelling study' (2020), *Lancet Respir Med*, 8, pp. 1181–91, https://www.thelancet.com/journals/lanres/article/PIIS2213-2600(20)30396-9/fulltext#seccestitle170

Minister. We now know that having a safe and secure place to retreat to, to recover in, to keep us alive, is not a luxury, it is a basic human right.

This book charts a time before Covid-19. A time when insidious cuts to vital services had crept in slowly and quietly, a country asymptomatic but riddled with disease. For many, the effect of years of austerity policies and tightened belts was invisible. It was easy to pretend it wasn't there, wasn't happening. But this pandemic has taught us that the invisible catches up with us, and when it does we can either turn our gaze away or face up to the truth.

If we are going to move forward, let us look to the mistakes of the past – let this book be a record of all the ways we failed and a guide to all of the ways we can improve.

I hope things will never be the same. I hope we won't go back to the old 'normal' that was failing so many. I hope the frustrations and injustices laid out in this book can be consigned to history. But unless we stare them down, understand how they happened and why, we will never learn how to build back better.

April 2021

Author's Note

This is a work of non-fiction. Most of the events in this book took place in 2018 and the stories are drawn from more than two years of research, hundreds of interviews and days and weeks spent shadowing those involved. Data and figures are accurate as at that time. Where appropriate, names have been changed to protect the privacy of those involved or to keep people safe, and these have been marked with an asterisk. Many of the events described in the book were witnessed first-hand but other descriptions were pieced together through documents (including police and council reports) or through in-depth interviews with those who were there.

The original count of deaths was part of a project undertaken at the Bureau of Investigative Journalism, called Dying Homeless. This was a collaborative project with local journalists across the country, and I am indebted to colleagues and editors for their invaluable assistance in this unenviable task. The Dying Homeless Project won the Royal Statistical Society's prize for Investigative Journalism, the Expert Citizen's Insight Through Journalism Award and was short-listed for the Orwell Prize, the Amnesty International UK Media Award, Drum Online Media Awards and the Global Editors Network Data Journalism Awards, and for Campaign of the Year two years in a row at the British Journalism Awards.

PART ONE

Who Counts?

CHAPTER 1
It started with a death

The temperature hovered around freezing as the darkness started to give way to another late-December day. The small Suffolk town of Lowestoft, perched on the most easterly coast in the UK, was, like all mornings, the first to see the sun rise, hazy and red against the freezing mist that hung in the air.

As light licked the icy fronds of grass in the quiet gardens of the quiet town, it fell too upon a strange shape. There was something terrible where the day should be. Something casting its shadow on the morning, silent as a secret: a body.

Tony pulled up his hood as he walked along the hushed main road, the whisky in his stomach keeping him warmer than the thin, olive-coloured jacket he had on. Christmas had come and gone, two days past, and while the holiday had remained stubbornly snow-free, the days before and after had compensated with freezing rain and sludgy ice. The chill still remained. It bored deep into the skin, as deep as the bone.

The roads were empty and around him the warm glow of windows framed the happy gatherings of families sitting down to the last of the leftovers, children sifting the remaining, inferior chocolates from rattling tin boxes. This walk was etched in Tony's muscle memory – he was heading home.

Except he wasn't.

Tony no longer owned the compact, semi-detached house on Priors Close. Number 1. A house he had called home for twenty years. Set on a quiet street, the windows of the six houses on one side reflected back the twinkling Christmas lights of their mirrored partners on the other. This was a place where families came to settle, where pensioners nested the fortunes of a lifetime's work into the surety of sand-coloured brick. As the building developers had categorized them, these were not homes but 'Professional Rewards', the privilege of 'experienced professionals in successful careers enjoying financial comfort in suburban homes'.

Tony hadn't lived there for three months, not since the police and bailiffs had come and kicked him out, pulling him from the building, changing the locks.

He turned off the main road and into his old street. A haggard, wild-eyed man, out of place among the Christmas lights and neatly trimmed hedges. Was that a curtain twitching? The residents here kept an eye on each other. Months later, walking down the same street, I had felt the itching sensation of eyes on my skin – turning quickly, I had spotted a face, frozen and placid, behind a double-glazed window.

Had anyone seen Tony as he entered his old driveway? Was he watched as he slipped down the weed-lined path that ran along the side of his house, into the back garden?

The decking in the backyard was cold and wet, and yet, incongruously, the garden chairs were still out, a hangover from better, summer days. He settled himself down in one, his thin frame pressing against the icy plastic, twisted the cap from the deep-blue bottle of Haig Club whisky he had brought with him and raised it to his lips like a silent prayer. No one was telling him he wasn't allowed home.

*

The next day Tony's younger brother, Jeremy, drove over to their mother's house to check in on her. She had called the day before, her voice thin and terse on the line. Tony had gone out wandering again and she was worried. Jeremy had sloped into his four-by-four and driven around the neighbourhood looking for his brother, as he had done so many times before. Tony would wander off so often that Jeremy had taken to sticking lengths of cotton thread across the doors so he would know if his brother had been in or out that day.

Once, driving into town, he had noticed a cluster of people on the side of the road gathered around a prostrate figure. He knew immediately who it was: Tony, passed out on his way back from the off-licence.

That day he had found him. This time he didn't.

It was the next morning, just as he was helping his elderly mother out of her house to get to a doctor's appointment, that the police car swung into the drive. Jeremy sighed, wondering what his brother had done now. The policeman's voice was flat and grave: 'I think we'd best have a talk.'

That was it, then. It had happened. Something had gone terribly wrong.

On the afternoon of 27 December, one of the neighbours from Priors Close had peered between their curtains and seen Tony staggering wildly in the direction of Number 1. Tony cut a sorry sight, the light rain painting constellations on his thin green jacket, his jogging bottoms sodden as dank puddle water seeped up from the cuffs. Something in his stumbling steps gave the impression of a man in distress.

As the neighbour watched Tony stagger down the narrow path that ran beside his old house and into the back garden, which lay in sight of the neighbour's window, he pulled himself away from the glass and made for the telephone. He knew Tony had been sick and had a stoma-bag fitted, but also knew he struggled with alcohol addiction and could be a violent drunk. Before he'd been evicted from the house, Tony had had run-ins with the neighbours and with the police, who had logged him on their system as a 'Vulnerable Person'.

The neighbour called social services first but they suggested he was better talking to the police. It was the day after Boxing Day; resources were stretched.

Forty miles away in the sterile control room of Suffolk Constabulary, the call handler picked up the 999 call. The clock on her screen flashed 3.46 p.m. She was a trainee, new in the role, and her usual trainer was not in that day so a colleague was standing in, helping support her where he could. On the other end of the line, the neighbour tried his best to describe what he'd seen. 'He went out the back, to the garden. He's been out there for two . . . maybe three hours. He's . . . He's just . . . not moving,' the neighbour rattled down the phone. 'He's in some sort of light coat . . . The weather's horrendous.' The call handler noted down the details. Outside the control-room building, the rain lashed against the windows.

'He's in his late forties, I think, but he looks seventy,' the man continued. 'He looks awful, he obviously needs someone to go and check on him.' The call handler blinked at the screen. 'OK, I'll see if we can get someone out to have a look,' she said. She didn't ask the neighbour if he knew Tony's name because, if she had, the police records would have shown a history of concerning incidents like this, events which often resulted in Tony needing hospitalization. Neither did she ask the neighbour to go and check on his condition. The neighbour rang off. The call handler tried to pass the call on to the ambulance team, who said they were too busy and turned it down. With the decision that it wasn't a police matter, the call was dropped.

Hours slid by. The light dipped, the night fell. Tony prised open a second bottle of whisky. The waxing moon hung behind the clouds. Around midnight the temperature dropped below freezing.

The next morning, at 10.20 a.m., another neighbour, whose house overlooked Tony's former garden, looked out of their window and saw something strange. He too had noticed Tony sitting in his old garden chair the day before. Now, squinting, he could just make out some white trainers, seemingly laid out on the ground. Worried, this man also called the police. 'He's just sort of lying down on his side, with his face down,' the neighbour said.

The police arrived a short while after. Tony was dead. He lay just metres from his former back door. His clothing was frozen solid and covered in frost. When the police tried to move him they noted his body was 'very stiff and his limbs would not bend'. The police report put it bluntly: he died 'having frozen to death overnight'.

I first read Tony's name a few weeks later when it popped up on my Twitter feed. Something about the scant details in that article had grabbed my attention and, days later, I was still fixated on the sorry story. A man dying homeless metres from the door of the house he had lived in for decades – it was too bleak to be true.

For weeks I had been thinking about homelessness in the UK. It was hard not to. Every day, walking around London, it seemed more and more people were sleeping rough. Encampments had sprung up in the unlikeliest of places: a cluster of sleeping-bag beds like weeds in the undergrowth around Finsbury Park; cardboard-box beds blooming like mould under a railway bridge. My daily walk from the Underground station to my office was marked by the sight of a solitary one-man tent, sat incongruously outside a Prêt a Manger, a strange image at a busy city-centre crossroads.

Every day I was confronted with this inconvenient evidence, and every day I felt the pang of guilt from not knowing what to do. I felt like a coward. Too many times I rattled some spare change into a proffered cup, a deft move that allayed guilt without requiring eye contact. But then I would walk away troubled by the rumours that some might be fake beggars, exploiting people's generosity before heading back to wide-screen TVs and game consoles. I had no idea if that was true but at times I found myself clinging to the idea like a comfort blanket, an easy excuse to keep on walking.

Who were all these people? Were the numbers really growing and, if so, where were they coming from? How could so many be making such wrong turns in life to come to live like this?

The questions kept coming, day after day, until I could avoid them no longer. I am an investigative journalist; it is not in my nature to push down my curiosity. Reading that news article about Tony had sparked something in me. I needed to know what was happening, to understand better.

Which is how I found myself stepping out of a taxi to knock tentatively on Jeremy's front door. Bracing myself, not entirely sure what I was doing there, I waited as the footsteps approached on the other side. A wave of uncertainty hit me – was this a fool's errand? Just what was I hoping to get out of this?

I was jolted from my free-wheeling doubts as the door swung open.

I had managed to get in touch with Tony's brother through

a journalist at his local paper, who had passed on my imploring message asking to meet. The wait had been agonizing but finally Jeremy had agreed that I could travel out to Lowestoft to hear more. He had his own questions about what had happened to his brother.

A healthy, well-built man in his mid-fifties, Jeremy was affable if a little blunt. After I gratefully accepted a cup of tea, we settled down at opposite ends of a large, L-shaped leather sofa. Jeremy lent back, his legs wide, feet firmly planted in tan-brown boots.

'Firstly, I just want to say I'm so sorry for your loss,' I stammered.

'It was a long time ago,' said Jeremy, brushing it off. He must have seen the confusion on my face as I did the mental calculation. *It wasn't that long*, I thought. 'It had been waiting to happen for a long time – the last five years,' he explained. 'We all expected it to happen, really, though not in that way, not how it happened.'

The brothers' lives had taken very different routes, playing out just a mile down the road from each other. Jeremy had bought his own house, a grand detached place surrounded by large gardens to the front and back. He'd drawn on his carpentry skills and fixed it up with raised decking outside and a pleasing open-plan interior, the living room elevated, giving it a ski-chalet feel. He had worked hard, invested his money, raised his kids and now delighted in his grandchildren, plastering large, studio-posed photos of them on his walls and filling his large back garden with a swing-set and outdoor toys.

Tony, on the other hand, had taken a different direction. He had always liked a drink, Jeremy explained. Decades earlier, he had been the self-appointed master of ceremonies at the holiday site the family owned, propping up the bar or leading the site's club in a night of karaoke. Neil Diamond was his go-to, and he'd swagger out a tune, drink in hand as holiday-makers clapped and whooped.

The men's parents had bought the site, a jumble of 124 chalets – 'a bit like a mini-Butlins', Jeremy said – after the death of the family's youngest son from leukaemia, aged twenty-three. While Jeremy had laboured hard, helping his parents stock the shop, clean the pool and keep the place running, Tony instead holed up in the bar, waiting for the young women looking for a holiday romance. He grew his hair long, giving him a rakish air, and was careful to dress to impress: a nice suit, expensive cologne, nothing out of place. 'Mr Poseur', Jeremy called him. But behind the jibes, Jeremy had started to worry. Tony was taking to the party life a little too easily. He was in his late thirties but was stuck in a kind of arrested development. He was beginning to forget the real world.

When the family sold up the holiday site at the turn of the millennium, Tony spiralled. His share of the profits, about £300,000, was enough to buy him one house outright, which he rented out, and another on a mortgage. With no worries about income, he kept up the partying. Jeremy watched from afar as Tony would gather groups of friends in the pub, drawn by his random offers to buy rounds of drinks. When it was kicking-out time it was back to his, where the fridge was always stocked with champagne.

Years passed. As Tony got older, the types at the pub stayed the same – a rotating band of eighteen-to-twenty-five-year-olds, grateful for him subsidizing their drinks. Young people with their energy and life, like some embodiment of Dorian Gray, passed through and revelled in the joys of youth and hedonism, leaving Tony in their wake, stained and aged with sins. In a cycle of just four summers, Tony had burnt through the money from the holiday site sale. His hair started to pepper with greys, the lines under his dark eyes grew deeper. He traded in the neat shave and pleasing cologne for a scruffy beard. He'd forget to wash.

Drunk most days, he neglected basic responsibilities, like paying his mortgage or council tax. The tenant in his rented-out house stopped paying the bills but Tony could never find enough energy to get her to move out. The bills on both properties mounted up: tens of thousands of pounds once the late mortgage payment fees and bailiffs' bills were added on. Letters arrived one after another in the post, angry red ink heralding their urgency. The bank was threatening to evict him. Tony glanced over them, then left the papers on the side, gathering dust. By September 2016 he had been officially declared bankrupt. A year later, in September 2017, he was evicted from his home; police records show they were there to see him out. The two properties were sold off to pay back his debts.

At fifty-seven years old, Tony found himself homeless, sleeping in an armchair at his elderly mother's house and desperately addicted to alcohol.

Even now, Jeremy was bubbling with frustration at the way his brother's story had gone. The family had fought hard to support Tony, he told me, sinking tens of thousands of their own money to cover the debts and fines he had accrued. They had tried, too, to get him to Alcoholics Anonymous, and Jeremy had succeeded once, but Tony had been against it from the start. As the brothers had sat in the church hall waiting area, he had complained to Jeremy: 'Look at all these bloody piss-heads . . . Scum.' Jeremy tightened his jaw. *You're worse than them*, he thought to himself. *At least they realize they have a problem.* They never got him to a second meeting. I later checked with the council's substance support teams. They didn't have any record of dealings with Tony. He was off their radar.

Instead, it had been left to the family to try and support him in his addiction. Too often Jeremy had found himself jumping into his Land Rover (which I'd spotted parked outside, with its personalized 'JEZ' number plate) to make the short, five-minute drive from his home to check on his brother.

I could feel the frustration radiating off Jeremy. Even now, after Tony's death, he was angry at him, angry that he hadn't managed to pull himself together, so deep was he in his own selfish addictions; angry that, due to his elderly mother's Alzheimer's, he had been stuck for months in a Sisyphean cycle, where every morning she would ask her middle boy where her eldest was, and he'd have to break the news to her, over and over – sometimes ten times a day – that Tony was dead.

Jeremy pulled himself up from the leather sofa, scratching at his short, grey hair as he disappeared off into the kitchen, returning with a bundle of papers, some still in tattered envelopes. 'Here, you can have these if you like,' he said, dropping the pile onto the coffee table in front of me. 'I don't need 'em anymore.'

Inside the envelopes were reports and documents, jigsaw pieces of the story, of how Tony had come to die the way he did. There were logs from the police's call records, interviews with neighbours. Later, trawling through those sad pages, I was able to put together the pieces of those twenty-four hours between Tony leaving his mother's house and the moment he was found dead the next day. The documentation of a death that now, looking back, was tragically inevitable.

But while the papers answered most of the 'how', Jeremy was still no closer to working out the 'why'. That had been troubling him. The coroner's office had been in touch regularly, irking him by constantly referring to his brother as 'the body'. 'I said, "Hang on, love, he had a name,"' he told me.

They had called to tell him the Independent Office for Police Conduct, the police complaints office, was going to be looking into how the call was handled. The call handler had quit her job soon after, and guidance was distributed on how to deal with calls about vulnerable people. But that was all the complaints office had found. When the report detailing as much had arrived, thin and light in a brown paper envelope, it was disappointing.

Jeremy sighed. 'They couldn't even tell me the time of death,' he said. 'Surely the idea of the autopsy was to find the time of death. If nothing else, because obviously if he died two hours after he lay down, well, that's not as bad as seventeen hours after – you know? I just want to know if my brother went quickly – did he pass out, did he freeze to death slowly, was it painful, did he know he was dying . . . ?'

After saying goodbye, I headed out into the light rain and made the one-mile walk down the road to Tony's old house. Following the footsteps of a ghost, my mind wandered. Evictions could happen quickly, I knew that. As a journalist, I'd spent time sitting quietly in possession courts and had seen first-hand the speed at which cases would whip through the hearings, in and out, while an endless stream of people waited their turn in the corridors. Tony had a mortgage and the bank got sick of the missed payments, but those renting were in even more precarious positions: landlords could pull tenancy agreements out from under them like some cruel magic trick.

In the context of zero-hour contracts and spiralling living costs, making the rent could be a monthly struggle. A survey of more than 8,000 working adults found that more than a third of respondents would not be able to pay their rent or mortgage if they or their partner lost their jobs, and would be at risk of losing their homes. Across the UK there were more than 16.5 million working-age adults who did not have enough in their savings to cover the month's rent or mortgage.[1]

For Tony, losing his home had been a downwards slide, ineluctable in its trajectory. First came the bills, then the letters from the bank, replaced by letters from the bailiffs – and then came the bailiffs themselves. He was kicked out. The locks were changed. His home, his castle, was gone, the drawbridge pulled up behind him.

Yet this was not the story I had expected of a homeless man. Far from being the socially isolated pariah, cut off from society, ignored by all, Tony had had everything going for him: charm, wealth, opportunities. He had a family that loved him, who lived minutes away and fought desperately hard for years to save him. How had he come to choose this life? Why couldn't he snap himself out of it? What's more, in the few hours before his death his situation had been brought to the attention of social services, his neighbours, the police and the ambulance service. People knew he was there, knew he was in trouble. But still he died.

As I walked along Priors Close and stood before the empty house that Tony had once called home, I was filled with questions. This was twenty-first-century Britain, we were the fifth largest economy in the world. Something had gone wrong, seriously wrong with the system if people were dying like that on the streets. I thought of the people I walked by every day on my way to work or home again, the people who I tried, as politely as I could, to ignore. I couldn't do it anymore.

I wanted to know how many other people had suffered similar fates: how many had died while homeless? How had they come to live in a kind of parallel reality, a substrata of existence where someone could be drinking themselves to death and drenched to the skin mere metres away from people tucking into Christmas mince pies? How have we got here, to a place where sidestepping tents and dirty pillows has become just a standard part of our daily routine?

How many other Tonys were out there? How many people were dying homeless, like him?

I am a journalist. It is not my job just to wonder about things. It is my job to find out. I pull together the figures, piece together the evidence and come to a reasoned conclusion. This question was just like any other, I thought; I just needed the data. So, later, back in the warmth of my home, I set myself a macabre little task. I started to collect names. First Tony's and then others. I'd type my sad request into Google: 'Died homeless'. And with each result I'd add a line in a spreadsheet. An hour passed, then two. The list grew. My journey had begun.

CHAPTER 2

Search for shelter

Weeks passed and, while my list was getting longer, I wasn't getting anywhere with finding any real data on the issue. It was late January and the grey, long evenings showed no sign of abating. Storm Eleanor had battered the country, bringing with it flash flooding and power outages. In London, the thick snow that cloaked the city had quickly lost its magical appeal, and now was nothing more than a daily frustration as commuters shivered and slipped their way across the city. Meanwhile, I hadn't been able to get Tony's death off my mind.

I had spent the last month reading up on homelessness, scouring reports and government spreadsheets wherever I could find them. I had been shocked to read that by the mid-2000s, rough-sleeping had all but disappeared. In 2010 there were just 1,768 people counted as sleeping rough across all of England – the government called it an eleven-year low. Just seven years later, that figure had risen to 4,751, a jump of 169 per cent. Even that was likely an underestimate – the national homelessness charity Crisis put the figure closer to 12,000.

Twelve thousand people out on the streets, and many thousands more like Tony – those without a home of their own, sofa-surfing and relying on the kindness of friends, or else bedding down in hostels or squats.

But there was a figure I couldn't find in all my research.

A figure I thought should have been easy to come by: the number of people dying while homeless. If we knew how many people were experiencing homelessness, I reasoned, then surely someone was counting how and when people were dying. The niggling need to know whether Tony's death was an aberration, or part of a larger pattern, was eating away at me.

My own list of deaths, gathered from sorry internet searches, was growing.

There was Neil Martin, found dead in his tent on 2 January. The forty-nine-year-old man had suffered a stroke previously and used a walking stick to get around.

Eighty-one-year-old Alan Higginson: he died in hospital but was often seen sleeping rough outside a shopping centre in Norwich. I double-checked the details in disbelief that an eighty-one-year-old man could be sleeping on the streets.

Then there was former soldier Darren Greenfield. He was forty-eight when he died in hospital. He'd been sleeping rough after leaving the army.

Fifty-six-year-old Fiona Watson had been sleeping on the streets before she died under a bridge by the Dark Arches, a series of cavernous brick tunnels under Leeds' main railway station. I studied the photograph of her weather-worn face carefully, taking in the deep lines on her brow, and her grey hair shorn so short she looked almost bald. It was clear from the scant details of that news story that life on the streets had not been easy for her. Her right leg had been amputated above the knee and she regularly used drugs and drink.

She had been found on the morning of 8 January, just eleven days after Tony, lost in a jumble of blankets and sleeping bags under the bridge. Three other people were sleeping rough alongside her. When paramedics arrived, alerted by a call from a passer-by, they found the huddle of people using her body like a pillow. She hadn't moved for an hour. Her body was still warm but there was no sign of life. One of the paramedics would later recall how 'members of the public were passing by with what appeared to be no concern'.

She was the fourth person to die in Leeds in four months, according to my spreadsheet. Surely all of these people couldn't be dying without anyone taking note? I sat at my desk and thought of all the places that might have data on how many people were dying. Then I hit the phones.

Days later, and I was getting nowhere. The hospital press officer wasn't able to help. 'I'm sorry,' she said. 'Try the coroner's office. They're bound to have the numbers.' Another dead end. I stared at the list of crossed-out contacts on my notepad. The suggestion to ring the coroner's office wasn't a bad one. The thing was, I had already asked the coroner's office. And the police. And the Office for National Statistics. And the government. Nobody knew.

They didn't know, I realized, because no one had counted. There was no centralized body tasked with logging how and when people were dying homeless. I felt dazed. When I tentatively told my colleagues at the Bureau of Investigative Journalism, their disbelief was palpable. 'Really?' spluttered the usually calm editor, Rachel Oldroyd. 'How can that be?'

This was going to be harder than I thought. In order to find anyone who was taking note, I was going to have to go deeper and collate the information myself. I emailed scores upon scores of shelters and day centres, phoned homeless charities and shouted about my plans on Twitter. And then, weeks later, I found myself with a new ally, a man who would become something of a spirit-guide on this strange journey I had set out on: Jon.

*

Jon Glackin, an ebullient Northern Irishman, ran an organization called Streets Kitchen, a totally grassroots affair which sourced and served hot meals to homeless people across London every night of the week. A journalist called Bob Trafford had seen a story I'd put out a few days earlier about my research for my log of homeless deaths, and sent it Jon's way on Twitter: 'Amazing work and so needed. @streetskitchen you following this?'

A notification pinged on my phone. Jon's response was terse: 'You do realize how dark & headwrecky for frontline outreach people your request is . . . we've been shouting for too many years unheard.'

I sighed. I knew all too well how sensitive a topic this was. Before I'd published anything on the Bureau of Investigative Journalism's website, I'd talked to dozens of charities and outreach groups, but all were nervous about how the project could go, scared that the lives of the people they were trying to help would be blown up and picked over, tabloid fashion.

As my fingers hovered over the keyboard, trying to find the right response, my phone pinged again: 'Come on Jon,' wrote Bob in another tweet. 'These are exactly the kind of guys you should be working with.' I waited nervously, unsure what would come next, until hours later I spotted a private-message notification flashing on my screen. It was Jon.

'Hey . . . perhaps it would be better if we could speak directly regarding gathering stats . . . this is something i have been banging my head against for years . . . i coined and ignited the #NoMoreDeathsOnOurStreets campaign too many years ago . . .'

I called the next day. Jon answered in a thick County Tyrone drawl that spluttered out thoughts a mile a minute. 'I'm always getting journalists just wanting to hear the sob stories and then piss off,' he told me. 'I'm not into that. You want to come out here and see what we're seeing every night. I have people dropping dead left, right and centre, and does anyone give a fuck?'

I tried to explain that this wasn't what I was doing – that my project was long-term, not sensationalist; a proper picture of what was going on. Eventually he relented, and agreed to meet me. 'Come out here, see what we're facing, and then we'll talk,' he said, before hanging up and leaving me, phone in hand, shell-shocked with the force of the call.

Not long after, I found myself wandering through the streets of Hackney, trying to make eye contact with any man I walked past, in case it was Jon. I was nervous. I knew I wanted to do this project, but I was out of my comfort zone. I was used to smiling politely at those on the streets, or else studiously looking away. Now, as I headed to meet Jon and the people he was trying to help, I realized I had never had a real conversation with someone who slept rough. How would that go? What do you ask someone whose life is so very different from your own? I felt as alien as I did on foreign reporting trips, but there I'd have a translator or fixer to stretch across the divide. Here I was on the very streets I would come to for the bars or theatre, but I felt like I'd touched down in some far-flung country.

I was following the map on my phone to a small square outside Hackney Town Hall. I knew when I'd got there. There they were, dotted around the square in groups of two or three, and they were older than I'd expected. One man sat on a low brick wall, his chin resting on his fist. Another sat slouched with his back to the library, reading a free newspaper. Another lurched around the corner with darting eyes, beads of sweat running down his neck into the collar of his dark-blue suit. Spotting me lurking at the side of the square, he made in my direction. 'Where's the banquet?' he asked eagerly. 'I was told there would be a banquet.'

I recoiled slightly, panicked by the feeling of being ill-prepared and out of my depth. I was just about to explain that I had no idea, when out of nowhere a silver rental van pulled up to the kerb beside us. As if in a well-choreographed dance, people jumped out and began setting up trestle tables and pots in earnest.

Behind the van a black saloon car pulled up and out hopped a wiry man in boardshorts, a short-sleeved checked shirt and a flat cap. His blue eyes darted across the scene and in a thick brogue he began to hustle the small band of volunteers that had spilled from the van. This must be Jon.

'Right, tables up over there, let's get this show on the road,' he told the group as a thin blonde woman lugged a huge plastic bucket full of lentil dahl over to where two other women were struggling to secure the legs of a fold-out table. Within minutes the team had laid out trays of beetroot salad, sliced crusty bread, rice and new potatoes as well as a decadent-looking tray of croissants and doughnuts. The air grew fragrant with spices, and the men gravitating towards the spread began to salivate.

I was scribbling down notes on my pad when Jon bounded towards me and stopped uncomfortably close to my face.

'You're Maeve, are you? Here you are – you can help with this,' he boomed, ushering me over to two large thermos flasks for tea and coffee.

'Er, no . . . I was just hoping to ask you . . .' My voice

trailed off. Jon had stopped listening and was barking orders at some other sap. He didn't trust journalists, he explained later, and if I was looking for someone to hold my hand I'd come to the wrong place.

I looked around helplessly; this wasn't part of the plan. I really just wanted to find out if Jon had been keeping count of when people had died. But there was little point in protesting. Besides, busying myself with the hot drinks gave me a nice, safe interaction point; I could pour someone a tea without accidently opening up the emotional floodgates on their complex past, surely. I gave up my note-taking, laying my pen and pad on the ground, and got myself ready for the snaking queue of people eagerly scanning the table for what was on offer.

A tall, lanky man with fluffy white hair and a wide, toothless smile eyed up the offerings appreciatively. I later discovered this was Stephen.* He was at the square most Thursdays; other days he'd rotate around the city, hopping from one soup kitchen meal to the next. He'd been rough-sleeping for years and was currently bedding down about a mile and a half away in the Stoke Newington area. Not that he slept much anymore. He had nightmares – or rather, one recurring nightmare, over and over again. A memory: a dark house, morning, too quiet, wandering through the darkness, a body, his father dead on the floor. He tried his best to shake it off, and the smiling, cheery man in the queue looked far from haunted, but it was there, deep down: something pulling him back.

That day Stephen filled up his plate and asked for his tea to be made as strong as possible. 'I love a cuppa, me,' he told me, his eyes twinkling. I started to relax a little. Stephen was cheery and coherent, as were many of the other men who held out their plastic cups. I kept the tea and coffee coming, and gradually warmed up, stopping for chats when I could.

I met Andy and his staffie Bailey, who would stand patiently glued to his loving owner, no need for a lead. Andy had bought his best friend from a street beggar, who took the £12 offered and used it to buy Irish-whisky cream, giving Andy inspiration for the pup's name. At the same time as breaking his heroin habit, Andy had also nursed his new pet off the Valium the beggar had been using to keep him subdued. They were bonded together now. It had been the sight of Bailey, vulnerable in his dependence, that had stopped Andy from throwing himself into the dark, violet waters of the Thames one night.

After getting his own plate of food, Andy gratefully took a bag of dog food too.

I still found myself looking around for help at times, unsettled by a simple question about what drinks were on offer and unnerved by the intense stare of one of the more dishevelled men in the group. And I wasn't really getting anywhere with my investigation.

Beside the trestle tables, Jon was still choreographing the dance. While trays of food were cleared and new ones were laid out, he pulled out a small speaker, attaching the jack to his mobile phone and hitting play. 'Pure Shores' by All Saints came blasting out, taking a few people nearby by surprise.

As the minutes passed by and the food started to disappear, grocery runs were made to pick up more sugar or bottles of water. More than 30 people were fed that day.

By the time we came to wipe down the tables and drag them back to the local pub where they were stored, I was exhausted. My notepad was more or less empty, save a couple of tea stains and some scribbled names.

Jon was still buzzing. 'This is pretty much standard,' he said, 'about this many people. But you know we see more and more all the time. It's not getting any better.'

He'd been doing this for five years. Today, Streets Kitchen serves nearly 1,000 people a week in nine areas across London, but back in 2013 it was just a crazy idea of Jon's. He'd been living in squats around Camden at the time, and after decades working with homeless people in Northern Ireland and the north of England, all the while homeless himself, he'd grown frustrated by the lack of provision for homeless people in England's capital. Sure, there were soup kitchens on the Strand or the more central parts of the city, but at the edges, in the neighbourhoods that most needed them, places like Camden, there was nothing. 'Plus, I fucking hate that term "soup kitchen",' Jon told me. 'We can do better than that.'

So he had started: skip-diving for still-good sandwiches thrown out prematurely from overcautious supermarkets, scavenging donations where he could get them. He roped in friends from the city's squatting community who gathered together tables and trays and Streets Kitchen was formed, born under the banner 'Solidarity Not Charity'.

I started to go along to Streets Kitchen events every now and then, and little by little came to understand Jon more. He wasn't content with just making sure people had a daily meal. Pitching up trestle tables of food across the city centre was all the more galling to him when he scanned the buildings around him, he told me brusquely. Almost every time we met, while I tried to bring him back to names and details of those who had died, Jon spiralled off on a monologue about the fact that there were so many empty buildings around. And he was right. I had read that there were around 24,000 commercial buildings sitting empty all over London. I did the calculations: that's six buildings for every person sleeping rough. You can see it wherever you go in London, if you care to look – whole neighbourhoods of the capital where, after dark, the buildings sit cold and empty, the windows blank and dull.

Jon had had a winter full of dark windows calling to him, teasing him as they hummed with the pummelling of wind.

We're waiting, they sang. *We're here. A taste of what the future could look like.*

'That's why we took Sofia House,' Jon explained one day. 'Ah, you should have seen it.'

In early March 2018, the country was brought to a standstill, first by Storm Emma and then the 'Beast from the East'. For days the freezing winds from a polar vortex had dumped layer upon layer of snow onto the already paralyzed country. Schools were closed, cars spun off roads, and everything slowed down.

Flicking through his phone, Jon found his Facebook profile alight with notifications. He was part of various forums about homelessness and grassroots action, and the pages were blowing up. People were frustrated that councils were being slow or at least unforthcoming about activating their provisions under the Severe Weather Emergency Protocol, a responsibility to house those sleeping rough if the weather reaches its worst.

Some councils had opened community halls here and there, but on the streets it was chaos. People didn't know where to go, where was safe. And even among those that had heard that their local area was offering a bed, many didn't want to accept, either because of the strict rules around alcohol or pets or, in some cases, due to a deep-seated distrust of authority. It's those people, the hardest to reach, who're the ones that'll die, Jon had reasoned.

Jon, too, had a deep distrust of councils. Every week at Streets Kitchen meals he'd talk to people who felt the official services had let them down. Worse still, he'd see council enforcement officers fining people for begging, or removing tents. He didn't trust those same people to appear now, to magically save folks from the storm. No, this was going to be a grassroots thing, Jon decided.

And then the solution appeared. 'I have a place,' one of Jon's old squatter friends posted, 'and it's perfect.'

Jon craned his neck and took a step back. He needed to take it in, in all its glory: Sofia House – a red-brick, four-storey, £17.5 million commercial building in central London, just off Great Portland Street, surrounded by the upmarket shops of Fitzrovia. This was it.

The building was just waiting for them, or so it had felt. It had sat empty for at least five years (in 2013 the local council had received a planning application to turn it into luxury flats, though building work had not yet started). Now there was just a solitary security guard keeping watch. Apparently, getting in was easy, though to this day everyone I've asked is cagey on the details. The rumour goes that the guard simply let them through, moved by their request and the horrendous weather around them. However it happened, by 2 March they were in – just Jon and a handful of others at first, but soon they came, one by one, out of the cold.

Photographs from the squat give a sense of the world they built there. Tarpaulin dividers were strung between concrete pillars. Strings of lights garlanded the walls. Tents, mattresses and camp beds were spread out across the floor from one side of the room to the other and over three floors of the reclaimed building.

In one corner Jon had set up a kitchen, with shelves that soon filled with pots, plates and food. They cooked stews and soups – and there was no shortage of donations, said those I spoke to. Sofas were brought in, and a TV. Someone painted a colourful butterfly mural on one of the walls; on others there were black rectangular stickers with white writing announcing: 'The homeless are revolting. Join them.'

Word spread. A hundred people turned up in the first week. And they kept coming.

Gap-toothed Stephen was there, making jokes and telling stories to anyone who would listen. 'Irish Willie' volunteered to work as security, donning a neon vest and making himself useful where he could ('though what kind of security you can have at a squat, I don't know,' he later joked). Still, he'd welcome people in at all hours – drunk, high, it didn't matter. 'I'd say, "Set yourself down there and have a cup of tea",' he told me.

Jon's friend and fellow Streets Kitchen organizer Tom took charge of the donations that rolled in from concerned members of the public. Piles of clothing and bedding were sorted through and set up in a 'free shop'. The guests coming in from the streets would sift through the items there, picking out the best they could find.

One day a lady phoned up, sounding frantic. 'Err, there's a problem,' she spluttered. 'I sent along a pile of duvets and things . . . It turns out I gave you a patchwork quilt that's a family heirloom – my mother's been in tears all day.' Tom blanched. 'Ah,' he managed. 'See, the thing is, the stuff's been handed out, people have taken it and moved on . . . Sorry.' Months later that story still made Tom chuckle. 'I was like, "You can come and ask for it back if you like love, but rather you than me!"'

The aim was that the place would run on collective organization, which it more or less did. There were hiccups, of course. Bundling crack addicts, entrenched rough-sleepers and those with mental health issues into one space was never going to be easy. Jon remembered arriving one day to a putrid smell wafting down the halls. A beleaguered volunteer rushed towards him, breathlessly: 'Someone has shat in the sink.'

But mostly, the 200-or-so people staying there got along. As one journalist who stayed and slept at the squat wrote at the time: 'Irish republicans with militant leanings worked and slept alongside ex-squaddies with six tours of Northern Ireland under their belt'; elsewhere a grown man wept 'over a styrofoam tray of lasagne following six weeks spent sleeping in a bin chute'.[2]

Just when he thought he'd got a handle on what to expect, Jon would be faced with some new drama to sort out – once, in the shape of Hollywood star Susan Sarandon, who swept through the doors one day, glamorous in a white coat and immaculate make-up. She'd brought a bulging red plastic bag, full of bedding.

About a week after opening the doors of Sofia House to the cold and downtrodden, an elderly, saturnine, round-bellied man had come wheezing in from the cold. Leaning heavily on a wooden walking stick, he'd paused at the door, his breath rattling in his chest. The sixty-seven-year-old had a serious lung condition called chronic obstructive pulmonary disorder, or COPD, and a host of other ailments. This was Richard. He'd been homeless for years and most recently had chosen the night bus as his bed, though it had been far from ideal: the juddering of the stop-start engine would tug on his catheter bag, sending jolts of electric pain through him. Then there were the young folk, drunk or high, pickled in bravado, spoiling for a fight. Sleep on the night bus had only ever lasted minutes, not hours. Now, with the snow blocking the roads, the bus services had become less frequent. He'd been shivering at the bus stop one day when a text had come through from a friend of his, a volunteer at Sofia House: 'You should come along here,' she'd written. 'All are welcome.'

Richard had cast his eyes around and taken everything in. It was hectic, he'd later tell me. With no single person in charge, people were making up the rules as they went along. Still, it was dry, if a bit cold. And among the clutter there were welcome sights: the tea urn gurgling in the corner, a bunch of daffodils exuberant among the mess. He'd found himself a spot and settled down to sleep.

Three weeks after they'd opened, Jon arrived to find an eviction notice stuck to the door. The squat was being closed down by a court order. The day after a judge ordered them out, workmen appeared and boarded up the ground-floor windows with slabs of MDF. As the residents inside resignedly packed up their things, graffiti artist Dotmasters adorned the wooden boards with the words 'You can't hide the homeless' sprayed in angry red letters and accompanied by a neat black and white stencil image of a young girl apparently just finishing her work with the spray can.

Up the road someone had already set up a tent. Nearby, in rough white letters, someone had sprayed the words 'Tents in the streets . . . £1,000,000 apartments left empty'.

But Sofia House had given Jon the idea: a shelter run for and by homeless people, a creative use of wasted space. This was it – a blueprint, rough around the edges, sure, but solid in its principles, a way forward. All Jon needed was space – a roof – and they could build the rest. And I'd soon come to realize that Jon Glackin was not a man to give up on a dream.

CHAPTER 3

I left Jon at the Streets Kitchen event slightly despondent. He had been shouting about homeless deaths for years yet no one had really taken any notice, so why would it be different for me?

I went back over my list of places I'd hoped collected data. I could understand why councils might not be keeping track of those that died, but I'd assumed hospitals would have a clearer idea. Yet the hospital trusts said they wouldn't note on the central death records whether someone had been homeless or not. While they might record something like hypothermia as a cause of death, there was no way to deduce from this that the person died while homeless. I was shocked that hospitals weren't routinely recording when someone had had nowhere to live. I would come to understand the consequences of that when I first met Richard.

Richard wasn't shy about railing against the injustices he faced. He tweeted regularly, angry at the appalling conditions faced by many who found themselves homeless. It was an issue close to his heart; he had now been homeless for more than thirty years and for much of that time he had been in and out of hospital. He knew better than anyone how they never logged whether or not he had a safe place to go to.

I first met up with Richard outside Holborn tube station. In the chaotic melee of stony-faced commuters, I spotted him right away. With his bristly white beard, mottled skin and flat cap, he stood out starkly from the slickly dressed shoppers and office workers. A portly, roughly hewn man, he leant on a stick, his tattooed fingers wrapped around the handle.

After a stilted hello and awkward handshake, we made our way to a nearby McDonald's. I consciously slowed my pace as he hobbled beside me, his breath a ragged pulse at my side. 'I'm a regular here,' Richard joked as I struggled with the touchscreen ordering system. 'They've got a good disabled toilet, you see, so I can just sit here most of the day.' I smiled politely. I still wasn't quite sure what to say to someone in Richard's position; where to start.

Luckily for me, he needed little prompting. Richard's voice wheezed out of him, thin and high-pitched, as he launched into the story of his life, and I found myself leaning forward to make him out over the piped-in pop music playing in the restaurant. As it turned out, Richard had known Jon for years. 'Oh yeah, we go way back,' he harrumphed. It seemed life on London's streets could be a small world.

After Sofia House shut down, Richard had followed Jon back to a day centre he'd set up in Holloway Road. Jon was pleased to see Richard warm and dry – he'd affectionately bestowed Richard with the nickname 'Grumpy Git', though Jon later confessed to me that he had a ruder version of it he'd use in private.

The winter had been taking its toll. The cold weather was causing Richard real problems with his lungs. He'd wheezed and panted through the night. 'It was like breathing soup,' he recalled.

The space in Holloway Road, another old commercial premises, was supposed to be for daytime use only, but Jon wasn't one for playing by the rules – he told Richard he could stay on the centre's sofa for a couple of nights. But just like Sofia

House, the space was only temporary. When the time came to close it down, Jon told Richard he'd have to leave; perturbed, Richard declared that there were only two ways he was leaving: 'in a body bag or in an ambulance.' Jon dialled 999 and had Richard describe his symptoms to the operator. 'You should have come in days ago,' the operator said, and an ambulance swiftly took Richard to Whittington Hospital.

Richard knew the hospital well. He found it easy to explain his list of symptoms, he told me – he'd done it so many times before: COPD that gets worse with the cold, cataracts, ulcers on the legs caused by cellulitis, incontinence, heart disease. Coming and going from his bedside, the doctors ordered blood tests, prescribed new inhalers and medications, while Richard sat benignly watching the ward. Sometimes he'd see others he knew from the streets, also being treated. It was hardly surprising; people who are homeless go to A & E five times more often than the general population do, and when they're admitted to hospital they stay three times as long.[3]

Richard was a connoisseur of all the hospitals in London. 'They're all the same, really,' he wheezed to me, and described the restless boredom of the patients, the constant slamming of doors. 'If you ask nicely, you can get a nurse to drape a towel over the top of the door to muffle the bangs.'

Still, there were moments that stood out in his memory. The healthcare assistants who worked the wards of UCL on rotation, washing patients down, changing the sheets. A friendly chaplain at Homerton Hospital who had looked out for him, chivvying along the doctors in their work looking after Richard. The sight of a nurse keeping watch at 3 a.m. on a darkened ward, her face lit by the warm glow of a computer screen as she tap-tapped patients' updates into their files – 'A modern-day Lady with the Lamp,' Richard smiled.

He had been in a hospital on New Year's Eve, watching

the theatrics play out like an action movie. The televisions in most hospitals' wards were run on a pay-to-view basis but he wasn't going to spend the little he had on daytime soaps, not when there were so many dramas to observe right in front of him. Every time the doors of the ward swung open it was 'like nuclear war coming on two legs'. By the time he left the next morning, he felt like he'd seen the very soul of the place.

In the four months after he left the hospital that New Year's Day, he was admitted a further eleven times. Each time, they'd patch him up, get his breathing smooth again, then send him out into the world, back to whiling away the days in a McDonald's, one eye on the disabled toilets for when his failing bladder called; to nights on the buses, bumping through the dark, uncaring streets.

And each time he was sent on his way he would collect the discharge sheets, where the cold text would impassively note the day he'd arrived and the day he would leave. Sometimes they would note on the discharge form that he was of 'No fixed abode', but they still sent him back out onto the streets. 'I have them all collected. You should come and see them,' he smiled at me. Richard remembered that one discharge sheet had noted he was 'Homeless by choice', he recalled angrily. It was not a description he recognized.

Born in 1951, Richard had spent his childhood moving around from one bed and breakfast to another, changing schools regularly. 'That's where I think I learnt not to be too materialistic,' he explained. 'You move on. You leave it.'

He was fifteen in 1966, when the film *Cathy Come Home* had woken the country up to the plight of those experiencing homelessness. Despite the public outcry, the numbers of those sleeping rough continued to rise.

The decades rolled on. The erasure of slums post-Second World War was followed by a flurry of building, leading to unprecedented levels of social housing, but by the mid-1980s Margaret Thatcher's 'Right to Buy' policy had seen much of the new housing sold to tenants and no longer available to councils. Instead, more than 20,000 people had been put in hostels and other temporary accommodation, and thousands more had been forced to sleep rough.[4]

In the late 1980s, rough-sleeping was at near-epidemic levels. A global recession that was buffeting UK life led to spiralling inflation and drastically rising unemployment, exacerbated by the closure of shipyards, factories and coal mines. As a young man searching for work, Richard had come to London, but a job at the dockyards had fallen through along with the attached accommodation, and he found himself walking the streets, jobless and homeless.

The very first night on the streets, he walked from the East End to Paddington, over in the west of the city. He wasn't walking with any purpose; it was the only thing he could think of to do to avoid having to lay down on the cold ground to sleep. Eventually he ended up walking all the way to west London and through the doors of St Mary's hospital, his feet blistered and aching. The nurses told him just to go home and soak his feet. He didn't know how to explain that he had no home to go to anymore.

Quickly, Richard learnt the ways of the streets: where to get the best food, where to bed down, who you could trust. He'd stay in hostels or sleep in popular rough-sleeping sites. 'I stayed at the Savoy for quite a while,' he told me – meaning, of course, in the alleyways around the back of the five-star hotel. Much of the day was spent in a state of survival mode: being warm, dry, fed. But there were some aspects he got to like. Sleeping rough was a great equalizer. 'It doesn't matter what race, colour, creed you are,' he said. 'If you're sleeping on the streets, you're all in the same boat.'[*]

Then there was a sense of being at one with your surroundings, a deep connection to the world. His brain learnt to constantly observe what was going on around him. He'd clock faces, remembering people he had seen weeks or months before. He learnt to read body language, quickly assessing if people were a threat or not. When there is nothing else to do, watching the world go by becomes an art form – and a deeply ingrained survival skill.

Richard had already been living on the streets for some time when he first came upon 'Cardboard City'. The sky-rocketing homelessness in the capital had resulted in the colonization of an area of the criss-cross pedestrian underpass beneath the Bullring roundabout near Waterloo station; a sprawling camp of wooden MDF structures, blankets and repurposed cardboard boxes that spread through the concrete underpasses. I had read a good deal about the neighbourhood; to this day it is etched in the memories of older London natives, who remember the trepidation and horror it had evoked. 'You knew not to go near there,' a Londoner friend told me.

Richard had made himself a 'bash' there, a lean-to made from bashed-together bits of packaging and wood he had

---

[*] This was something I heard repeated in Northern Ireland, perhaps the most segregated place in the UK. Indeed, my mother, a Catholic and a teacher's daughter, met my father, a working-class Protestant who left school at fifteen, when she volunteered at the homeless shelter he worked at, on the Antrim Road in Belfast (the first time she had ever met a Protestant, she later recalled). At that time, in the 1970s, the homeless community was one of the few places where the sectarian divide, which was cleaving the country in the most bloody way possible, was forgotten and both Protestants and Catholics came together, unified in a shared exclusion from the rest of the world.

found. While most well-to-do commuters would fear passing through the area, Richard remembered there was a real sense of community in that purpose-built village. Around 200 people lived there at one point. Under some parts of the underpass, people would lie down, side by side, six or seven in a row, stretched out under blankets on cardboard mattresses, some with boxes shielding their feet and heads, like strange, angular tombs. Others bedded down in and around Waterloo Underground station.

One balmy June evening in 1994, Richard had been playing with his dog, getting ready to feed it dinner, when he'd heard a commotion. People were jogging by, whispering in excited voices. 'What's going on, eh?' he grumbled to his pet.

'Diana! It's Princess Diana,' a neighbour squealed.

'Hang on, hang on, I've got to feed the bloody dog first,' he grumbled.

A laugh ran out like bells, jangling through the echo chamber of the tunnels. Richard wheeled around. There was Princess Diana, looking relaxed in slim trousers and a black blazer. No security guards that he could see, just a couple of the staff from the Centrepoint homeless charity showing her round. She had overheard Richard's coarse rebuff and was laughing at the slight, he remembered fondly.

For some time, Diana made her way round the cardboard village, talking to people and asking about their lives there. A TV crew followed her, recording the shocked faces left in her wake. 'I see you've dressed up for the occasion,' she joked to one man, dressed only in a pair of shorts. 'Well, me Savile Row suit's in the cleaners,' he quipped back.

Days earlier, Prince Philip had declared the end of poverty in Britain and Prime Minister John Major had called for the streets to be cleared of beggars. That quiet evening spent with Richard and his neighbours sent a powerful message in response.

In the years that followed, Richard had seen drastic changes in the number of homeless people on the streets. In 1997, the government established its Rough Sleepers Unit to oversee the work of various departments. Funding was pumped into prevention initiatives and given to councils to pay for local support services. Rough-sleeping numbers dropped dramatically. The residents of Cardboard City were all evicted by 1998, and now the shiny circular BFI IMAX cinema sits in the spot, a poetic shift from a reality, that could be deconstructed box-flat, to a 3D fantasy. By the turn of the millennium, rough-sleeping was almost a rarity.

But Richard had stuck around, and more than a decade later the cardboard camps were springing up again. They were everywhere – in underpasses turned into campsites, park hedgerows full of the detritus of lives hidden away in the bushes. The pendulum had swung back.

In the days after leaving Sofia House and being admitted to a quiet ward at the Whittington, Richard was in no mood to contemplate the government policies of the past. The doctors had reviewed his chart and were talking about discharging him. Tired of constantly being bounced out of one hospital after another, fearful of the night buses that would soon be his bed, Richard spoke up, arguing that sending him straight out onto the streets would be unsafe. The hospital staff agreed and a taxi was arranged to take him to the local council housing team. The housing officer looked him up and down. Richard showed him several letters from his GP, recommending he was housed urgently. 'He has severe chronic medical conditions, made worse by sleeping on the street,' the letters said.

'Right,' said the council officer, 'we'll find you a place to stay.'

A taxi dropped him off at his new home at 7.30 p.m. on

the evening he'd been discharged from the Whittington. The spring night was already dark; from the outside, the four storeys of the brown-brick hotel gave nothing away of the life inside.

The deputy manager gave Richard the 'grand tour', pointing out the reception desk, where visitors had to sign in and out, and the small break room, bare except for a perimeter of chairs around the edge and a TV mounted on a wall. (Richard soon found that not all the guests used the room – you had to know your place here. Look at someone the wrong way and it'd be quite clear you weren't welcome.)

The building had somehow been dissected into 110 rooms, many of them only a little wider than a single bed and about twice as long. There were bedbugs and rats. Police were called out to the premises every couple of days. Residents here had been arrested for rapes, murders, beatings. These were to be Richard's neighbours. The building had a somewhat notorious reputation for warehousing vulnerable people. Many had died while staying there.*

Of course, the deputy manager didn't go into all this when

---

* A spokesperson from the hostel told me: 'All rooms meet the national space standards and are regularly inspected by local authority teams.' They continued, 'We do occasionally have pest issues, which are dealt with by our independent specialist contractor who visits the hostel twice a week to deal with reported issues within strict timescales and additionally carries out preventative treatments. We have no rats inside the building.' They also explained: 'We have rigorous safeguarding procedures where we have serious concerns for the residents' welfare, however as we are an unsupported accommodation, we would always liaise with the local authority in the first instance, and the residents' support professionals, to decide on the most appropriate safeguarding action, as we are not able alone to meet the residents' needs. We are an accommodation-based service and are not required to provide any support directly outside of our housing management service, however in order to better serve our residents' needs, we regularly liaise with their support professionals on their behalf. In addition to this, we provide additional services such as free computers for them to use, a service-providers' information area, assistance with form-filling and signposting to the appropriate services, collecting food.'

Richard first arrived. He stuck to the script of breakfast times, communal areas and pointing to the small toilet cubicles at the end of the hall that doubled as shower rooms.

Richard could only take some of it in. He was finding breathing even more difficult than usual; the short walk upstairs to the first floor had exhausted him. Inside his new room, he sunk onto the narrow bed and rested his hand on the small sink nearby. When he got his breath back he assessed the room. 'It was tiny,' he told me. 'Like a bathroom they'd just turned into a room.' But it was his home, and he was happy to be there.

After so long sleeping on night buses or in doorways, lying down on a mattress felt like sinking, he explained. He'd later come to notice the hard, plastic cover on the mattress, but right then the bed felt so soft it was like he was descending into the pits of the earth. At night, voices echoed down the white-tiled halls and the paper-thin walls carried the muted conversations of his neighbours into his room like bedtime stories. When the toilets flushed, the pipes by his head rattled a strange lullaby. He hadn't seen it that first night, but the large, single-glazed window at the end of his room looked out onto the hotel's smokers' hut, and beyond that a supermarket car park. Opening the window just a crack brought toxic air spewing into the box room. But this was home – for now.

CHAPTER 4

You are homeless. Do not pass go.

After I left Richard idling contently in the glow of McDonald's strip lights, I found myself wandering the streets bewildered. I had been struck by his description of his first night without a place to stay, how he had walked for miles without purpose, simply to avoid having to sit down and accept defeat. How he had run out of options other than sleeping rough. I found myself scanning doorways and side alleys, squinting for clues that the spot had been someone's bed for the night: the body-flattened cardboard, the cigarette-butt borders. 'You never forget your first night out,' Richard had told me.

But what I still didn't understand was what came before that night. How did people wind up with no other option in the first place?

The support system had changed many times in the decades that Richard had been experiencing homelessness, but these days it was supposedly better than ever. Local councils had legal duties laid out in legislation, duties to help and support those in need. And yet, the more I talked with Jon and Richard, the more I read about the reality, I came to realize that people were still being turned away every single day. Back at the office, and during my digging around, I had come across figures from councils that showed that the number of people approaching them for help was on the rise, but many were accepting fewer and fewer people as genuinely homeless.

I was in the middle of wondering why that could be when the phone rang. On the other end was a woman, calling because she was angry. She was working for an organization that supported people who were facing homelessness and one man she knew had been turned down by the council because he wasn't deemed at risk enough. He had epilepsy and suffered from inflammation of the oesophagus, depression and alcohol addiction. The council had sent off his records to a medical assessment company who, without ever meeting the man, had given their opinion on his case – that he was not that vulnerable – and the council turned him down. When the man started to rapidly lose weight and suffer vomiting and diarrhoea, the woman tried to get the council to review their decision but they stuck to it, noting that the new symptoms 'could be a side effect of his alcoholism'. It turned out that the man had terminal cancer. He ended up sleeping in a shed until a few days before he died. 'Years ago somebody with [his] conditions would have been accepted as "priority need",' the woman told me. 'The shortage of accommodation means local authorities just waffle their way round how somebody with those disabilities can cope just fine living on the streets.'

I put down the phone, shell-shocked. It was incredible that councils could refuse to help people so ill and, indeed, that they were outsourcing advice on such decisions to an arms-length organization which would rarely meet the person in question.[5]

But I soon learnt I shouldn't have been surprised. I was about to meet another man who had suffered rejection by the system, a man who on paper really had no right to still be alive. David.

*

David had barely heard the housing officer as she declared his fate; he was trying to focus through the hunger pangs. They were closeted away in a small office and it felt as though the world was closing in. The woman sitting across from him was explaining that, because he was an able-bodied, single man, he wasn't considered 'priority need': vulnerable enough for emergency housing. 'I'm sorry, there isn't much more I can do. My hands are tied,' she'd said to him.

Not priority need. It was almost laughable.

I met David in a park less than a mile from the council office where this conversation had taken place. He jumped up to greet me warmly, his gangly limbs reaching out to pull me into a hug, trapping my hand – out-reached in an abortive handshake – between us.

Over the course of a little less than two years, his life had blown up. A tall, lean man with dirty blond hair and twinkling, pale-blue eyes, David had worked for most of the 1990s as a chef in the army. He'd travelled the world, cooked for the Queen and, after leaving the army in 1997 and moving to London, he worked first as head chef at the British Film Institute Southbank, then set up his own pub restaurant. The hours were long, the stress intense and David drank heavily. On Easter Sunday 2011, as families buzzed into the restaurant and the food orders piled in, David started to lose feeling down the left-hand side of his body. His speech became slurred. He was having a stroke.

After being raced to the hospital, he made a fast recovery, so much so that he was soon back at work. But the exhausting pace of a professional kitchen was too much for his weakened state and he quit soon after.

The following months brought body blow after body blow of misfortune. In the space of two years his boyfriend left him, he was diagnosed with colon cancer, then neurosyphilis and HIV. It was almost too much to process. One day, he was waiting at the council office with a friend when a doctor called with yet more bad news: he had been diagnosed with hepatitis C. David's response had been blasé. 'OK,' he'd said as he hung up the phone. His friend stared at him askance, shocked at the news, but David had barely flinched; he had become numb to it all.

Ill and bewildered, he knew he couldn't go back to the intensity of working as a chef so he enrolled on a university art course. For a time, art became his therapy. But, unable to work and, being a student, not entitled to any housing bene-fits, David was struggling to pay both the £6,500 tuition fee and the £480 a month in rent for the flat he shared with a friend out of the meagre savings he had.

He missed several months' rent and he knew the land-lord and his flatmate were becoming increasingly irate. Ashamed and fearful of the anger that might be unleashed if he showed his face, David found any excuse not to go home. He stayed on friends' sofas or rotated between a house party one night, to a sex party the next – anywhere just to have a bed for the night. He got used to turning up at the flats of friends' friends, strangers who he'd ask if he could use the shower, with some excuse for why he needed it. Anything to avoid facing up to the unpaid bills at home.

When he went to the council for help they said there was nothing they could do until he had actually been evicted. 'Bring us the Section 21 notice,' they said. But there was never any official letter. Instead he ventured home one day to find the landlord had changed the locks.

Which is how he found himself at the council housing team, presenting as homeless.

'But surely you . . . surely you would be classed as vulnerable?' I spluttered.

No. As David was an army veteran, the council worker explained she would put him on the waiting list for a specialist Veteran Housing organization, but the wait could be years. I later looked into that and it turned out that, as an army veteran, David should have been offered extra support. It is well known those leaving the army suffer all kinds of mental health issues, and it is generally acknowledged that by serving one's country in the armed services you are owed an extra level of protection on return.[6] Yet in 2014 the Ministry of Defence estimated (probably conservatively) that about 3 per cent of London's rough-sleepers – more than 200 people – were former military personnel.[7] The council David went to was later criticized in an academic report for its online assessment tool, which incorrectly informed veterans that they would be ineligible to join the housing register.[8] But he hadn't known that at the time, so he'd just accepted it.

More than thirty people become homeless every single day across Britain; now David was one of them.[9] Eventually, he ended up living in his car, a cramped Peugeot 206. A tall man, six foot three inches, David had to stretch his body across both front seats, a pillow over the gearstick, his legs in the front-passenger footwell, to try and get any sleep. When he couldn't afford fuel, he wasn't even able to put on the heater. He'd shiver through the night, trying to ignore the cold by scribbling sketches in a small notepad.

'I thought, *I should be able to make this work*,' David explained sadly. After all, he had been in the army, he was a man who knew how to survive. In the mornings he would furtively find a hidden spot on the residential road he had parked in to go to the toilet. He ate fruit off the trees in nearby parks and scouted out the best cafes and delicatessens, loitering outside and waiting for the staff to throw away the uneaten food at the end of the day, then picking it out of the bin to eat. His weight dropped to a precarious 65 kilograms.

That is how David lived. Sick. Alone. Afraid. He had done what he was supposed to – he went to the council for help – but there was none to be had.

It was easy to hear David's story and hope it was an aberration, a glitch. Or maybe to cling to the idea that there was something about him, about his case, that made him genuinely unsuitable for support. But the truth was, I was talking to more and more people who had faced the same obstacles. People who had done everything properly, approached the right authorities, and had still been turned away.

It's hard to imagine how that would feel, how one could slide, so smoothly, into homelessness, but I found myself lying awake at night playing over thought-experiments in my head. So now I challenge you, dear reader, to play along with me.

Ready? Here it goes.

You are feeling queasy with nerves. It has been a week since you walked out of the door of the place that you called home. Perhaps your landlord had sent a letter stating this was a 'Section 21 eviction' (a clause in the Housing Act that allows landlords to kick tenants out for no specific reason) and, after looking up what that meant online, you realized there was no comeback: you were out.

Or perhaps the violent blows from your partner, the person who says they love you, became unbearable, and you had to run or die.

Maybe you lost your job, the one you had for ten years, because a thick cloud of depression had fallen and you physically couldn't get yourself out of bed on some days.

Whatever has brought you to this council building, with its magnolia-painted walls and stiff plastic chairs, is now secondary to the question of 'What comes next?'

You've spent the last week in the cheapest local hotel you could find. You check your bank balance: the figures are diminishing alarmingly quickly. You've spent a few hours working through the Universal Credit sign-in online in the hope of getting access to benefit payments, but you're worried you misunderstood the questions – and they said it would take five weeks before you could expect anything in your account. Already you miss having a place to cook or wash your clothes. You're aware that your small suitcase-worth of possessions is beginning to smell. You've lived off sandwiches and Pot Noodles for a week.

The ticket in your hand seems to seal your fate. You're waiting in turn at the council housing department, waiting for your number to be called as if this is nothing more serious than standing in line at the deli counter of the local supermarket. No. Stop that. Try not to think of food – you'll need a clear head for this. You've been here since 10. a.m., and it's now 3 p.m.

Your number's up.

Inside a side office, a council officer looks your application over. It doesn't matter whether this council is in the hands of Labour or the Conservatives; all of them are suffering cuts, all of them are turning people away.

The council officer seems a little harried and tired. The drip, drip of the hopeless into her office has been relentless all day. She starts to speak. Your application has been reviewed. Luckily you have been able to prove you have lived in the area for the last three years – if you hadn't then the conversation would have stopped there.

Your medical complaint – the depression which has kept you chained to your bed for weeks, or the nebulizer you need to keep your airways working – has been taken into account. They even sent off the details to medical experts for their opinion. (The council officer doesn't mention that those experts may have done nothing more than read over your GP notes, the ones that suggested you should be supported, and then come to a different conclusion.)

They've taken this all in, the officer is telling you, and, all things considered, have decided you are not priority need. You're a single, healthy (or so the experts say) adult. So, sorry, the council has no legal responsibility to house you right now.

The illness doesn't matter.

The fact you're fleeing domestic violence doesn't matter.[10]

You'll go on the waiting list for social housing, but it's best not to hold your breath, the wait is long. For now, she hands you a list of private landlords to try; you'd be better off renting anyway.

You spend the next week calling or emailing all the land-lords on the list the council has given you. Many say they won't rent to anyone claiming benefits. Others explain that since the 'Right to Rent' scheme came in as part of Theresa May's hostile environment policies, landlords are legally responsible for checking the immigration status of their tenants and so simply won't risk renting to anyone without a British passport. They get in trouble if you turn out to be here illegally. It's more hassle than it is worth.

You've asked around about hostels, but they require you to already be receiving your housing benefit. That's how you pay for the rooms. Besides, they say they can't take someone with your needs – they're too complex.[11] Your case isn't serious enough for the council to help, and it's too complex to get into a hostel, even if you had the funds.

Where do you go now? What do you do?

David was popular and had some family. He stayed on friends' and family members' sofas and floors for as long as he could. Eventually his options ran out. Sleeping in his car was the only choice he had left.

Talking to David I felt a deep sense of despair. Councils, pushed to their limits by funding cuts, were unable to support those coming to them for help. I knew council-housing stock had dwindled. There were 1.1 million people on the social housing waiting list, but little more than 6,400 social homes had been built the year earlier.[12] The private sector was struggling too. The stark fact was that in many parts of the country there just weren't enough affordable houses to go around, leaving many shut out of the option of ever buying their own place. Property developers were being awarded permission to put up luxury flats, promising a certain quota would be affordable, only to go back on that agreement later.[13] In other parts of the UK, where there were affordable properties, people were turned down for mortgages because benefits or payday loans had left them with unattractive credit ratings. Meanwhile, costs in the private rental sector had sky-rocketed way out of step with income.

People were ending up on long waiting lists for the few social homes available. And even if they succeeded, I'd heard tales of people in England being offered dingy flats hundreds of miles from the place they called home and their friends and family there. If they turned down the offer of being deposited somewhere far from their work or children's school, they might be declared intentionally homeless and would never be offered anything else.

I'd heard that in Northern Ireland, where the common perception was that it was easy enough to get a council home, the post-conflict hangover of sectarian divides in the country resulted in complications in where to place people. Those raised in West Belfast were unlikely to move to the other side of the 'peace walls' which dissect the city like a scar. In Derry the city was neatly split into two sides; people simply didn't move across the lines, even now. All this came into play when the officials were offering a property. 'West Belfast is almost like a city within a city, so if people have grown up there and are then offered somewhere elsewhere, you know, moving to the other side of the city can be incredibly difficult,' Jim Dennison, CEO of Simon Community Northern Ireland, told me. 'We can't ignore our past.' Housing expert Nicola McCrudden said, 'We are living in a post-conflict society, in a divided community, and that does affect people's housing choices.'

Elsewhere, many councils just didn't have the places to put people who were finding themselves in need, so people were put in temporary accommodation like B & Bs or hotels for months or even years (in 2018 there were more than 200,000 people in temporary accommodation in England.[14] An estimated 9,100 were sleeping in tents, cars or on public transport, while another 67,000 were sofa-surfing, relying on the kindness of family and friends).[15]

Thousands of people off the radar, struggling in the darkness, unrecorded.

Suddenly, my quest to try and find out how many people were dying seemed ill-fated. I hadn't wanted to believe it could

be so hard. Weeks earlier I had sent off information requests
to hundreds of councils all across the UK, in the vague hope
that maybe Freedom of Information officers would wheedle
out data that the press officers had insisted didn't exist. But
as one reply after another came back, it was the same old
story: 'The data is not held.'

I was stuck. I had no idea what to do next. The hospitals
had no data. The councils had no data. When I went to central
government for the same information I was told it wasn't their
responsibility, it was a council-level thing. The coroner's office
had explained there was no requirement to record someone's
homelessness status on the death certificate. I was running
out of places to try. I was ready to give up. Maybe this was a
fool's errand? If the data wasn't collected, how could I, from
my desk in London, rectify that? If councils didn't have the
figures, who would?

I looked down at my list. It had grown, thanks to Jon;
every time he heard of someone dying while homeless, he
would tag me on Facebook, tweet me or, more often than not,
call at some mad hour of the evening. 'You'll be sick of hearing
from me, I'm like the fucking grim reaper,' he joked. Name
by name, the list had got longer. I read over the sad details
I had gathered.

Journalistic pursuits often fall by the wayside. You start
with a hypothesis, and then, if the evidence isn't out there,
you might leave it be and move on. But these names, these
stories, were calling to me. Maybe this was the answer . . .
If no one was collecting this data, then maybe I had to. If
there were no official figures, I would make my own.

I realized then that I had found my mission. For one year
I would log every case I could find.

*

But where to start? There had to be more people than just Jon keeping track of these deaths. And then I thought of David and his many terrible medical diagnoses, and of Richard, wheezing away with his many ailments. And that gave me an idea.

CHAPTER 5

Doctors on the borders

Winter gave way reluctantly to spring, the extreme blasts of ice and snow melting into longer days and brief periods of warmth. There were around eighty people in my database by now and I'd got into a rhythm, spending most days on the phone trying to get shelter workers to talk to me, or else trying increasingly obscure combinations of search terms on Google to try and weed out stories I hadn't seen yet.

That's how I came across Tim.

A few months earlier, GP Dr Tim Worthley, dressed in a sombre dark jumper, had taken a pen and written all the names he knew on slips of paper, placing each one by a glowing tea-light candle while around him people stood or sat in quiet contemplation. He had helped organize a memorial service for all those who had died while homeless in Brighton that year. A local paper had covered the small ceremony, and as soon as I had read that article I knew I wanted to talk to Tim.

The sun bounced off the concrete in the small side street, the faint scent of salt blown in from the nearby sea. A few streets over, the grand, domed ice-cream cone of the Royal Pavilion peeped above the rooftops.

Hidden inside an unassuming, squat, red-brick building,

a jumble of people sat anxiously twitching their legs or fiddling with their plastic seat covers, waiting to see Dr Worthley. I sat quietly among them, watching as a grey-haired man hobbled towards the reception window, impatient, like many of the others there, for his methadone prescription to be renewed.

'Any update?'

'Sorry, love,' smiled the curly haired receptionist. 'We're backed up here. There's a bit of a wait yet.'

It was May, and the newspapers in the waiting room were filled with news of the wedding of Prince Harry and Meghan Markle, though I had become so fixated on the issue of homelessness that when I read stories about their big day I'd think only of the rough-sleepers being shipped out of Windsor, or shuttered temporarily away in hostels, so as not to blight the fairy-tale scene. I shuffled the newspapers aside and started mentally preparing the questions I wanted to ask Tim.

I was there because Brighton was on the frontline of the UK's homelessness scene. There were 178 people registered as sleeping rough in the city, many attracted by the relatively mild weather and the potential for drunken generosity from the hen parties and stag dos that so frequently caroused through the city streets.

Upstairs, above the waiting room, Dr Tim had seen patients back-to-back all morning. Over 1,400 people were signed up to this small clinic, which wasn't just any doctor's surgery – it specifically treated Brighton's homeless community. A steady stream of complex issues came through Tim's door each day: patients with potent combinations of mental illness, drug addiction and medical complaints (the technical term is 'tri-morbidity'). Often it was all Tim could do to patch them up and get them through the immediate future, until the next time he'd see them.

He was only now managing to find time to sit down with a cup of tea. Sighing as he slumped into a hard plastic chair, Tim ran a hand through his bristly russet hair and rubbed his tired-looking eyes. Working in this practice, he had seen more than most GPs would see in their whole career, and he had quickly learnt the limits of what he and his small team could offer. Services in the city were stretched. Cuts in funding for the Substance Misuse Service had meant the loss of two of its three psychiatrists over the last two years. Then there was the fact that there were no longer any NHS detox facilities in the city, so every time a patient would come in telling Tim that they were ready to kick their addictions, he'd have to advise them to head to London to access facilities there.

Drug use and alcoholism was a major issue in the Brighton homeless community. 'They play a huge role in the deaths we've seen,' Tim explained, pulling a folded print-out from his pocket. Tim had been keeping his own list of homeless deaths since 2011, and each year it felt as if it got longer and longer. There in cold black type were seven names, all collected in the last five months alone. He smiled sadly, and for a minute it felt like we were members of some strange little club: the death-counters of the homeless world. I was so bowled over by the fact I'd found another member of this strange party that I could barely formulate my questions. 'So you've been counting cases too . . . But . . . why?' I asked.

Tim stared down at the list for a moment. 'I guess I felt that I was seeing people that maybe nobody else was seeing, then they were dying, and it felt like there was no marking of their life or their death,' he offered eventually. 'At least if I wrote their names down, that gave them some sort of posterity – it marked them in some small way.'

I nodded slowly. That was it, that was the strange compulsion I had found growing inside me each day. A few months ago, this had been about the numbers, about trying to solve a simple factual equation. But as the days passed and I read story after story about people dying, it had morphed into something more. And now Tim had expressed what I hadn't been able to myself. It was about seeing people, making sure they were being counted. I didn't understand what was happening or why, or who these people were, but I wanted to make sure that, somewhere, at least their names were written down, their deaths remembered.

So it was with a strange sense of hope that I left Tim in his surgery that day. This was the way forward. People like Tim, who were treating people who were homeless, were the ones at the front line, and they were going to be the key to getting the real picture of what was happening.

As I headed back on the train up to London, following the route of all those who Tim had been forced to send to detox miles away from home, I thought about the sad stories from Tim's list of names. How were people dying at the age of nineteen, twenty, twenty-three? How could the average age of death in the names I'd collected so far be thirty years younger than the standard life expectancy? Something was stopping homeless people accessing the healthcare they needed. I wanted to find out what that was.

In a small, beige, windowless office in Soho, Dr Dana Beale was leaning forward in her chair and waving her arms around as if in a bizarre game of charades where the aim was to guess the phrase: 'The blood test results have come in and they show there is no infection.'

Opposite her, sitting on a low chair squeezed in between

the desk and the wall, a dull-eyed African woman watched her warily. At her feet was a black rucksack.

I had first come across this patient, Maha,* when I'd arrived at the surgery earlier that morning. Having made my way past the Soho bustle and down the dark steps into the doctor's office, I found her waiting at the locked door. She pushed through with me when I was buzzed in, not understanding that the clinic was not yet open to patients. Now, what I had taken as rudeness, was explained. She spoke Arabic and had only a few words of English, but despite having a translator on speaker phone, this lady performed her own mime act, rubbing her elbow and wincing in pain.*

'Do you remember if you ever had an X-ray on your arm?' Dana asked, her charades going into overdrive. The lady paused as the male voice on the other end of the phone translated the question.

'No,' she replied.

'OK, we can get one sorted. Now, is there any chance you are pregnant?' Dana asked.

'Sister, doctor!' Maha cried indignantly. 'I am no husband, why am I pregnant?'

Dana smiled patiently, trying her best to explain that she had to ask that of every woman she sent for an X-ray. Reaching into a drawer, she pulled out a map and started to attempt an explanation of how to get to the local hospital. The lady looked at the doctor, who was all primary-school-teacher-energy, bemused.

Dana had been part of a team running Great Chapel Street Medical Centre, a specialist doctor's surgery for the homeless, for just over a year, though she had helped out there previously.

---

* The names and identifying details of Dr Beale's clients, as well as the exact nature of their ailments, have been changed to protect their privacy.

Pinned to the wall of the clinic staff room was a faded press release branded with the stamp of the 'Department of Health and Social Security'. The paper was dated 6 January 1976 and announced: 'The Department of Health and Social Security today announced the opening of an experimental centre in London's Soho area to provide primary health care for home-less young people.' The clinic had been a game changer, providing first-of-its-kind, specialist medical services for home-less people. It had remained something of a rarity: of the 7,000 GP practices across England in 2018, just 123 were specialist services for the homeless.[16]

Back when the practice first opened, there had been a homeless shelter occupying the floors above the basement level. That had since been closed down and now that part of the building was a fashionable backpackers' hostel offering a prime Soho location, with a rooftop bar and a games room, where dorm beds went for £25 a night. The clinic had almost gone the same way; the year before, the GP contract with the local NHS Trust had run out and the medical centre was put up to tender. After initial reservations, Dana decided that she and a colleague needed to step up, and together they formed a company and bid for the contract. It came through and, Dana recalls, 'almost accidentally' she found herself heading up the centre.

Now, they had 500 patients on their books and Dana worked four days a week treating some of the most vulnerable people in the area. The need was intense. The London borough of Westminster, where the centre was located, had the highest number of rough-sleepers in the UK. Dana and her colleagues treated as many as they could, but many of those on the streets mistakenly believed they couldn't register with a GP without official ID and proof of address.[17] It's an understandable concern, and something most of us will have faced at one point or another; the frantic scramble around the house looking for enough official pieces of paper to prove you live in the catchment area is a tricky enough task in an increasingly paperless system. How would that work if you were living in a tent or a hostel? In fact, you don't technically need this proof to register: no proof of fixed address, no formal identification. But try explaining that to the receptionist behind the desk. Faced with inevitable refusal, many homeless patients waited until things became critical, then took their ailment to A & E instead.

Dana was working hard to ensure that those that came to her didn't get to that critical point. This African lady with the aching elbow was her first patient of the morning, though the lack of windows in these basement offices made it easy to lose track of time.*

Behind her on the off-white walls were pasted reminders about sepsis screening and a poster about the psychotropic properties of the herbal drug kratom. But the poster that often caught Dana's attention was one about 'Recognising urgent and immediate necessary care for chargeable patients'.

The term 'chargeable patients' was at the forefront of everyone's minds at the centre. New rules brought in in 2017 meant that, while access to primary health care remained free for everyone in the country, those without the legal right to be in the UK could no longer access follow-up care – anything more than GP services or A & E – without paying for it.

---

* Many of the country's homeless-specialist GPs are housed in suboptimal buildings, often closeted away in basement properties with no natural light. In Edinburgh, I visited an amazing service hidden away down a narrow, grey alley; the steps down made access tricky for some. Inside, false windows had been put on walls to give the impression of openness. 'It's far from ideal,' GP John Budd told me. 'Conditions like this can be retraumatizing for our patients.'

Glancing again at the poster, Dana couldn't help but think about an East Asian man she had been treating. He had lived in the UK for a decade when his 'Right to Remain' ran out. When Dana saw him he had seemingly operable cancer. When he went to hospital he was told he would have to pay up front or face a black mark on his immigration record. It was about £300 for an outpatient meeting and £240 a time for an MRI. The man couldn't afford that. He had then gone missing and hadn't been seen for the last four months. Every day that passed, the chances of him surviving the cancer lessened.

'Doctor, what do I do now?' Maha pleaded, snapping Dana back to the moment. By the time the appointment was over, Dana had spent thirty-five minutes with the woman, much longer than the twelve minutes most GPs are recommended to give to each patient.

'You're a good doctor. You take care of your patients,' the lady told Dana through the disembodied voice of the translator on the phone.

'Thank you. You're a good patient,' Dana replied.

Dana saw another three patients that morning. There was an elderly Eastern European man who had been sleeping rough for several years. He dragged a wheelie trolley, lashed with bags and assortments, into the small room. He had found blood in his urine and Dana was concerned. She packed him off to hospital for tests, nervous it could be a sign of cancer.

Next was a handsome British man in his mid-twenties who had been sleeping rough for years after starting to use hard drugs. These days he was clean but he was still having chest pains, possibly a hangover from smoking crystal meth and heroin. 'Some days I'm all day like this,' he explained, huddling down in his chair, his sore chest collapsing in towards his spine.

'Do you have a plan?' Dana asked with a sympathetic smile.

'You know, I work Deliveroo, go to the gym, study. I'm just waiting to get my Universal Credit now. I try not even to talk to homeless people because they say take drink, drugs, you know.'

By the time he had left, Dana was tired out. It had been a relatively quiet morning but that still meant she had seen one person after another.

I left Dana and made my way back through the bustling streets of Soho. Dana was there at the coalface of homelessness in the UK, and despite her and her colleagues' best efforts, people were continuing to die tragically young. I thought of Richard, with his chronic lung condition, coughing and wheezing on the cold night buses, or David, whose body had been pummelled by a stroke, HIV, colon cancer and neurosyphilis, who had tossed and turned at night, trying to sleep squashed up in his car. How was their health supposed to improve when they could barely get a night's sleep? I was worried about their prognoses.

My database of names was filling up with young men and women dying of illnesses including tuberculosis and pneumonia. I was shocked by many of those cases; I had thought tuberculosis was a thing of dark centuries past, and yet people were dying in twenty-first century Britain of something that could be treated with a simple course of antibiotics. Research later found that a third of homeless deaths studied were from illnesses that could, and should, have been treatable, and that those without a home had a higher chance of dying than even the most economically deprived housed person.[18] It seemed that homelessness itself killed.

It was becoming clear that those who were dying homeless were battling against myriad complex issues. This was no simple problem. I began to feel a creeping sense of disorientation.

How would I ever make sense of all of this? Where could I possibly begin?

If I was going to complete this project I was going to have to go deeper, to try and really understand which people were dying, and how.

PART TWO

Who Will Catch You When You Fall?

Hamid pulled a creased piece of paper from his bag and handed it to his friend Adam: proof.

The letterhead stood out – bold print that read: 'The Department of Applied Mathematics and Theoretical Physics, Silver Street, Cambridge.' The letter was short and to the point. It informed Hamid that his application had arrived for a graduate assistant position with Professor Stephen Hawking, and that the esteemed physicist would soon be choosing who to interview.

Adam looked up from the page at the wild-haired, bedraggled man standing before him, the pride still shining in his wrinkle-framed eyes. Hamid had come a long way to end up like this.

Adam hadn't been sure whether to talk about his friend. I'd tracked him down despite the pseudonym he had used in a local newspaper interview. When I'd had no luck finding anyone of that name I noticed that there was an online fundraising appeal to support Hamid. I managed to find the Facebook profile of the person who had set the page up: Adam. I had come across Hamid's name on one of my many searches online, and sadly added his details to my list, but something about his story kept playing on my mind. I kept returning to the short, local newspaper article I had found him in. His story was extraordinary and I wanted to know more.

So I explained to Adam that I wanted to understand who Hamid was, what had happened to him. I wanted to know if there had been missed opportunities to help him. After a couple of wary messages, he had opened up and filled me in on the remarkable story of their unusual friendship.

They had met during one of Adam's frequent trips to the local supermarket; he was always running some chore or other for his wife and kids. At first he'd barely noticed the odd man who was always sat in his car by the supermarket car park, door open while the rest of the shoppers buzzed to and fro like insects. But after a few trips, Adam finally plucked up the nerve to walk over and introduce himself. They'd been talking ever since – funny little chats about far-off adventures and scientific marvels.

A softly spoken refugee from Iran, Hamid seemed kind and reserved, but lucid and quick-witted when he wanted to be. Adam had always half-suspected Hamid was a fantasist, talking the way he did about the time he almost worked with Steven Hawking, but then he'd presented the letter proving he had indeed applied for the job. And then there was the way he talked about physics and cosmology. *There's no doubt he's really intelligent*, Adam thought.

Little by little I put together the details of what had happened. Born the second of four siblings to a middle-class family in Tehran, Hamid was clearly bright from a very young age, 'Academically brilliant,' his big brother called him. In 1981, at just nineteen years old, Hamid had been conscripted to fight in the Iran–Iraq war. His academic record meant he was given the role of lieutenant, responsible for a platoon of men bundled in from villages around the country. A photograph from the time shows Hamid standing seemingly ill-at-ease in his army fatigues.

It was a long and brutal battle often involving large-scale

trench warfare: barbed wire, machine gun posts. It was like the worst of the First World War with the addition of Iraq's employment of chemical weapons and Iran's use of human wave attacks, where lines of men would be sent running across open ground in an attempt to shock the other side into falling back. Many of Hamid's platoon never made it back alive.

Decades later, the memories of those days were dug deep into Hamid's soul, like blood-sucking ticks. I had heard how post-traumatic stress disorder (PTSD) could bring the brain spiralling back to the same emotions and fear experienced in the moment of the trauma itself: the sounds of shells whizzing overhead, the iron-hot smell of blood, all as real in that moment as it had been then. Hamid was haunted by a nightmare: the war-weary faces of Iraqi soldiers trudging defeated towards him, their hands raised helpless in the air. In the dream Hamid found himself raising his gun and shooting them down, the guilt waking him from his sleep with a start.

After the war Hamid fled to India, where he studied theoretical physics and neurology at the University of Pune, seeking solace in the grand arched corridors of the grey-stone university building. But some things you cannot run from. Already the flashbacks were starting. The death of a girlfriend was the tipping point. Hamid started drinking.

He ended up in the UK, where he had applied for asylum, explaining that his opposition to Iran's post-war leadership had made it too dangerous for him to live there. It was time for a fresh start. His plan was to keep his demons at bay by diving into his work, testing his impressive intellect. In 1997, when he saw an advert in the newspaper for a research assistant to Professor Stephen Hawking, his heart soared. He carefully cut the advert out of the paper and got to work on his application, daring to dream of what it could lead to:

afternoons battling wits with one of the sharpest minds on the planet, evenings spent strolling among the imposing architecture of Cambridge University.

Weeks later a letter arrived in the post from Professor Hawking's office, acknowledging his application. But the hope was short-lived. Hamid told friends he was one of the final two candidates, but had been pipped to the post. When I later tried to verify this I got nowhere – decades had passed and this was in the days before computer records. But his friends through the years certainly had heard the same story.

It was a crushing defeat, but he picked himself up. He went to Bristol and studied avionics, later getting a job as an aeronautical engineer at Filton Airport. But he was drinking again. Periodically he'd take antidepressants, but he would stop taking them and would soon be back on the alcohol. He lost his job and struggled to hold down another. A relationship he was in turned sour. His neighbours complained regularly about the state of his front garden, the damage he had done to their car. Eventually he was evicted.

He headed to Harlow, a town in west Essex, a short train ride from London. That's where his story ended.

It was spring when I found Hamid's last home. The sun was hot and high in the sky, a marked difference from the freezing weather that had buffeted the country just a month ago. I'd followed the instructions passed on to me by Adam: 'Head to the big Tesco on the edge of town, in a place called Church Langley. Behind the car-wash place there's a side road. You'll find it there.'

It was the flowers that gave it away. Sun-dried and bleached, several bouquets lay across the bonnet of a dusty silver Peugeot 206 convertible. The ink had faded on the attached cards, but I could still make out the words of many: 'We'll miss you.'

The car had been given to Hamid by a kindly town resident, perturbed by how he was struggling. He had made a little life there, behind the supermarket car park.

Through the window I could make out the crammed bags, blankets, books and bric-a-brac that Hamid had collected; chocolates and coconut-covered sweets in a plastic bag on the dashboard, a *New Physique Look* coursebook yellowing in the back window.

Chrissy, a woman from the car rental hut a few metres away, tottered over to me, her black beehive hairdo wobbling on her head. 'He was such a character,' she smiled. 'He had so many stories about the war. I think he really missed his friends from that.' She had tried her best to help Hamid, buying him a hot drink now and then, helping him store his many books on engineering and maths in her daughter's shed. 'He was just left here. I thought that was really wrong,' Chrissy sighed. 'It's not right, is it? I mean, if Jeremy Kyle can do it – get people back on their feet – then why can't the council?'

Harlow had various homeless outreach services, but Hamid rarely engaged with any of them. The council told me, 'Despite several attempts, our Housing Team were never able to complete a housing assessment with Hamid so that we could offer him housing support.' It seemed this situation wasn't uncommon. 'Frustratingly, failure to complete a housing assessment is often the case with people living on the streets,' the council's email continued. 'Each case can have many different complex circumstances behind it and there can be a variety of reasons why someone just doesn't want to engage or take up the offer of support.'

Travelling across the country, I had heard too often a

worrying conclusion sometimes vocalized as 'Some people are beyond help' or 'Some people just don't want to change.' Could that be true? Were there just lost souls out there, was Hamid one of them? He didn't engage with the official support. Neither did he mix much with the seventy-or-so other rough-sleepers in the town, many of whom pitched their tents in the local woods or in the small garden of a church down the road, where clothes dried on a line stretched from tent to tent, like some sort of strange bunting. As it turned out, the council was already struggling to house even those that were engaging with them. Despite the glut of social housing built in Harlow to house families ejected from London by the Blitz of the Second World War, the sell-off for Right to Buy homes had left the council with few options. There were now around 750 people in temporary accommodation in the town. The council had even started to give permission to change office blocks into residential accommodation, but warehousing a mix of the most vulnerable people in buildings far from the rest of society took its toll. In one fourteen-storey block, skirmishes and crime were rife, and residents found themselves forced to keep their young children in the small rooms they shared, nervous about letting them mix with drug-using neighbours.[19]

It is hard to imagine someone like Hamid doing well in a place like that converted office block. Instead, he stayed holed up in his car. But saying he 'wasn't engaging' was too easy a cop out by the council. I appreciated that it was hard, and you generally can't force people to accept help (unless you resort to sectioning people under the Mental Health Act), but leaving someone to live in their car was just giving up on them.

I had been trying to understand why some people were so hard to reach and had heard that many people who were sleeping rough long-term might be diagnosable with 'person-ality disorders', a broad-brush term that can encompass disturbed ways of thinking, problems controlling emotions, antisocial behaviour and a deep distrust of others. Alex Bax, CEO of Pathway, a hospital-based homelessness team, told me: 'Sometimes there is so much pain and grief inside a person they will try and get their caregivers to feel their pain. Challenging patients will do things to exert power and control. That might be sabotaging the care you offer them or pushing people, testing their limits.' It was true; some rough-sleepers had told me that to survive on the streets you have to learn to manipulate people, to tell them what they need to hear to get the reaction you want.

Finding long-term, supportive systems for these people was tricky, it required patience and long-term thinking. 'The clinical advice is try and be as consistent as you can in what you're offering, and keep coming back. No matter how many times someone refuses your help there is the possibility that the next time is when they will open up to you,' Alex explained. Too often, these were the people deemed hopeless cases. A local homelessness charity had told me they, too, had tried to help Hamid but he had refused all offers.

Of course, if Hamid had been housed in a place with support services, people might have had a better idea of what help he needed. They might have built up the trust to get him to engage with help for his PTSD. The trouble was that mental health services across the country have been decimated.[20] (Nationally, 86 per cent of homeless outreach teams told homeless charity St Mungo's that there isn't enough specialist mental-health-supported accommodation available for their clients.)[21]

All too easily, people like Hamid could become long-term, entrenched rough-sleepers. Those sleeping rough with mental health issues are 50 per cent more likely to still be rough-sleeping a year later, compared to those without mental health issues. Lost in his trauma and left to his own devices, Hamid had numbed the pain with alcohol and spiralled to the point where he was living in the cramped chaos of a permanently parked car.

And then the weather turned bad – the spring snowstorms had come. Hamid's car became camouflaged under a layer of snow, blurring into the road and pavement around it.

Worried about him in the cold weather, a local homeless charity had convinced Hamid to take up a place in a local hotel, paid for by the council. Rated just one and a half stars on Trip Advisor, the hotel was a no-frills affair just under 2.5 miles from where Hamid's car was parked. He was in there for six or seven nights but wasn't answering Adam's calls. His friend was getting worried. 'He was on so much medication, you know. He'd talked about suicide before but I'd always managed to talk him out of it,' remembered Adam. Concerned, he called the hotel's booking line, and spoke to the manager, Nav Hussain.

Nav, a bespeckled bald-headed man, made his way along the corridor to the room Hamid was staying in. He knocked, quietly at first and then louder. Taking out his keys, he unlocked the door. At once he spotted Hamid's shoes in the corner of the room. He called out to Hamid a couple of times, trying to get his attention. No answer. Edging forward into the room, he found him on the edge of the bed, a half-full bottle of alcohol beside him. Strange . . . Then he spotted Hamid's hands – pale, almost blue. He realized then that Hamid was dead. Later, an autopsy showed the cause of death as organ failure.

Around a week after Hamid passed away, his hero Stephen Hawking also died. Hawking was buried with pomp and ceremony on 31 March 2018. Hamid's funeral was a much smaller affair, paid for by the council, and didn't take place until May.

Hamid's coffin was moved into the crematorium to a song called 'Return To Innocence' by the band Enigma. It was only at the very end of his life that Hamid managed to escape the trauma of the war he had been forced into, and the guilt that had clung to him since.

As I travelled back from Harlow, the train rushing through the green belt and back into London, I was racking my brains, struggling to form an idea that was lurking in the back of my mind. It turned out that more and more people who were dying homeless had a mental health issue – up from 29 per cent to 80 per cent between 2010 and 2017.[22] It wasn't always the mental health issue killing them, but it was worryingly prevalent in those who were dying. It all was too bleak. If people were dropping into homelessness because of untreated mental health issues and then stuck there because they 'weren't engaging', then what was the way out?

I flicked back through my notepad, now full of stories and names, and then I found it: a ray of hope from the Great Chapel Street Medical Centre in London's Soho.

Dr Sara Ketterley, the consultant psychiatrist at the clinic, told me how, each day, in a small, windowless room, she would see patient after patient suffering with mental health issues. Many presented with similar ailments – schizophrenia, psychosis, bipolar disorders, brain injuries from physical traumas, plus a large number of people with 'personality disorders', that catch-all term, the exact meaning of which is often under review in various diagnosis manuals. But there was one element that Sara kept seeing over and over again, so much so that she started to keep her own tally, noting down when she saw the signs: Adverse Childhood Experiences, or ACE. 'It's the theory that things that happen to you as a child or young person remain in your body into adulthood,' she explained.

To get to the heart of the issue, Sara would ask her patients ten questions, those that make up the official ACE test, thing's like 'Before your eighteenth birthday, did a parent or other adult in the household often or very often: swear at you, insult you, put you down, or humiliate you? Or act in a way that made you afraid that you might be physically hurt?' Or, 'Before your eighteenth birthday, did you often or very often feel that no one in your family loved you or thought you were important or special?'

Each affirmative answer equalled one point. At the end of the conversation she would add up the responses. An ACE score of 4 or more is concerning. Of the group of homeless patients she saw, around 80 per cent were scoring 8, 9 or 10.

'Oh God, but that's terrible,' I exclaimed, when Sara told me the scale of the issue. 'That means some people are doomed from childhood!' Sara smiled, gently disagreeing. 'Not at all. The advantage of knowing that someone has experienced that kind of trauma is you have greater awareness to understand future behaviours, you can get an idea of how to deal with the consequences.' If you could identify that these people who had ended up sleeping rough all had a pattern of experiences, then perhaps a model could be created to identify and target those at risk earlier on, before things got too bad. 'If we're talking about someone whose amygdala – the part of the brain that is responsible for the fear response – is overdeveloped because of childhood trauma, then perhaps just finding them accommodation and leaving them there is not enough. In that case you'd need to support them to feel safe, and that goes beyond just a lock on the door. You need to help them develop the internal and external sense of being safe.'

The importance of what Sara had told me was now sinking in. This could be a solution: if it was possible to diagnose people harbouring childhood trauma early, before they had even become homeless, then we could identify people and help them before it was too late. And there were clear examples of that idea working. In the city of Geelong, Australia, officials had put in place an Early Intervention Programme which worked with students in school to identify early on those most at risk. The young people deemed to be struggling with mental health or family issues were given extra support. The work had resulted in a 40 per cent drop in youth homelessness in the area.[23]

However, in the UK, despite this growing realization that childhood trauma was a significant factor in homelessness, little was being done to address those underlying issues later on and prevent things getting so bad.

Without finding a real, holistic solution, I was coming to realize, the vicious cycle continued, with people becoming homeless due to mental health crises, then remaining that way because there was no provision to support them to live safely and independently again. It was a frustrating process made all the more tragic by its seeming inevitability. Of course sleeping in a doorway or hostel dorm room will cause anxiety, of course losing your home will trigger depression, but pre-existing mental health conditions weren't being caught when the person still had the luxury of a roof over their head. And now a survey revealed that 70 per cent of outreach workers had said getting access to mental health services for people sleeping rough was more difficult than it was five years earlier.[24]

Back at my desk in the Bureau of Investigative Journalism's office, I saw from my scrawled notes how much I had been taken by Hamid's story, spending days researching more than

I needed to simply confirm his basic details and add him to my list of names. But now my quest had become much larger. It wasn't enough to simply try and log how many people were dying homeless. I could see that sleeping rough was not an isolated incident but simply a point on a long trajectory of misfortunes that had dragged people down. Now I needed to understand how they had slipped through every gap in the net that was meant to save them.

This was going to be my mission: the sad jigsawing of scraps of information to get to the truth. I wanted to understand the people behind the names, to know where the moments were that they could have been saved, the times their journeys could have gone in another direction. I wanted to know if the services that one would hope were there played their part. I wanted to know how to stop more people suffering the same fate.

On 23 April we published a story about Hamid on the Bureau of Investigative Journalism's website. Channel 4 News covered it too. My list of deaths was showing that at least two people had died homeless every week that winter; ten people had passed away in the last month alone.

Writing Hamid's name, typing the letters out on the page, publishing a story about him, was some small attempt to make sense of the loss of such a brilliant mind. It wasn't going to bring Hamid back, but maybe this project could do something to change people's minds about the importance of addressing how and why people were falling into homelessness. I needed to get the attention of people in power who could make a real difference. I was soon to find out that at least one person had already taken note.

CHAPTER 7

Make them count

One Friday afternoon in May, a few weeks after I had stood sadly by Hamid's abandoned car, Myer Glickmann sat down and wrote me an email. An email that would make me squeal with excitement.

Myer had a job as morbid as my project. He is a senior statistician at the Office for National Statistics (ONS), responsible for dealing with data about death. Death by cancer, drugs, suicide; Myer presided over the official figures for them all.

But there was one group of people he'd been thinking about for some time: the homeless. Nowhere in all the data he had collected was there anything specific about them. He knew the number of those experiencing homelessness was growing – you didn't need the data to know that, he told me; the town centre of Newport had quietly filled with people sleeping rough. But, like me, Myer had realized some time ago that no one was counting how many were dying homeless, and in the face of growing public concern about homelessness, that just didn't seem right.

He had taken the idea to his workmates at the beginning of the year and the response had been pretty unanimous. They all agreed that there was huge public interest in finding this data. So when he had seen my article about Hamid and my project, Myer had been intrigued. Hence his email, which floated the idea of a potential collaboration.

I didn't need asking twice. A few weeks later, I was on my way to Newport, home of one of the ONS's biggest offices. A cerulean sky stretched over the town, brightening even the greyest concrete blocks. After months spent travelling all over the country, I was coming to understand the varying hues of homelessness. It wasn't just about people sleeping rough on cardboard mattresses. Homeless people I'd spoken to had told about a whole range of places where people would bed down for the night. José* told me how he would try and catch a nap in the constant neon glare of the McDonald's because it was open all night and the food was cheap. Chris explained how he had slept in the shed at the bottom of his unsuspecting girlfriend's garden, making sure he was up and out by the time she came out for her morning cigarette. I had met Jessica* in the empty council flat she'd just been offered after weeks in a refuge. The flat was unfurnished so she had slept on the floor, using her son's bag of nappies as a pillow. I remembered Richard on the night bus, David in his car. Homelessness, as a category, had turned out to be far more varied than I had ever imagined.

There wasn't time for too much musing. I was travelling with my colleague and data expert Charles Boutaud, and our taxi was swinging down the drive of the ONS's shiny, sprawling campus. Having passed the strict security controls, we followed Myer down a corridor and into a small meeting room. He leant forward eagerly in his chair on the other side of the table. He was excited. 'No one has tried to count homeless deaths before, but now we're thinking maybe we should,' he explained in a lilting Scottish brogue. He later said that he felt 'almost a moral obligation to make this work'. But it wasn't going to be easy.

Myer had access to every death certificate created, a wealth of information I could only dream of, but there was a snag:

there was nowhere on the certificate to record if someone was homeless when they died. No tick box, no additional form. 'I mean, maybe that's the answer: create the tick box,' I ventured.

'It's not that simple, unfortunately,' said Myer. 'There are a lot of good causes we might want to add to a death certificate, but how far do you go? It could end up with a doctor or a bereaved person being faced with a long checklist of issues. And then when do you tick for homeless, when someone has been homeless a week, a year – what? And of course, some relatives might not want the fact their loved one was homeless recorded on their death certificate, because of the stigma.'

I grimaced. I hadn't factored in just how problematic this could all be. Myer was right, but without a clear check box any analysis of death records was going to be a case of scrabbling for clues. Occasionally a coroner might mention a person's homeless state in their written summary, but that was often only if they considered it to be inextricably linked to the cause of death. I thought back to Hamid: that wouldn't have been the case there.

Perhaps the stories I had already gathered held the key to this. I pulled out my laptop and showed Myer the list of names I'd collected so far: 101. 'Maybe there's a pattern here, in the way these deaths were recorded,' I ventured. 'Something you could see from the certificates – like the last registered address. Or some clues in the description.'

Myer's eyes widened. 'Do you think you'd be able to share that list with us?' he asked.

Over the next hour we came up with a plan. The ONS team would take our database and try running it against the death records register that they had access to. That way, they could check for patterns and explore whether, in the future, homeless deaths were something they could count.

In the taxi back to the train station, my whole body was

trembling. This could be huge. If the ONS decided to take up the challenge, this project could have real impact; policies could change and lives could be saved. I knew I was getting ahead of myself, but it was hard not to feel hopeful.

With renewed vigour I went back to my search. I needed to speak to everyone who might be able to help me log how and when people were dying. I had 101 names so far but I knew there were more out there. This quest was starting to take over my life, but things were getting a little easier. Somehow, after many meetings, Jon had warmed to me and would now introduce me to his connections as 'a journalist but not like the others. This one's OK'. I took it as high praise. Now his name would flash on my phone at all hours and at weekends, his mile-a-minute patter pouring into my ear with ideas and suggestions. And there was one person who stood out in Jon's monologues. 'There's a guy down in Brighton; you need to talk to him,' Jon had told me. 'Go find Jim.'

I squinted at my mobile phone screen, angling it against the mid-morning sun. I had typed in the address Jim had given me for his office but this couldn't be right: the online map had brought me to the town rubbish dump instead.

I was just about to turn back when I saw a man striding across the dump's forecourt in a T-shirt and khaki camouflage trousers, his faded, mottled tattoos creating a similar effect on his arms. 'Alright there?' shouted the man. 'You looking for Jim? He's in 'ere.'

On the first floor of a sprawling warehouse, right next to the dump, Jim Deans was busy juggling tasks. This was what it was like most days. As soon as he had the chance to wedge his bulky frame into the chair in the narrow space behind his overcrowded desk, his mobile would start up again, or some lost soul would appear at the warehouse doors looking for advice on dealing with the council, guidance on where to sleep that night or simply looking for a plastic bag packed by Jim, full of Pot Noodles and tins of soup to keep them alive that week.

I glanced around, making a mental note of the piles of papers, batteries, torches and bags that littered Jim's desk and spread across the rest of the office into the warren of smaller rooms throughout the warehouse. Five years earlier, Jim had set up the space as a 'one-stop shop' for those suffering hardship, filling it from floor to ceiling with tents, sleeping bags, dried food, generators, clothing, plus other odds and ends like ice skates, fire extinguishers and a cardboard box of porcelain figurines – but mainly, anything and everything that Brighton's most vulnerable might need.

Lacing his sausage-like fingers behind his head, he lent back, casting his eyes to the ceiling of the bric-a-brac wonderland he had built. Each day he arrived at the warehouse, he was struck by the unfairness of it all, he told me, his Glaswegian accent getting thicker as he angered. 'You go into a school and say, "Who fancies ending up homeless, pushing a shopping cart of your things down the seafront?" No one puts their hand up. It's not a plan, no one chooses that. Society is failing them. Something is happening there.'

Jim had taken it upon himself to care for the town's poor and hungry, and there were a lot of them. The streets of Brighton seemed to fill more and more each day with people bedding down in dark corners or begging for change by bus stops. Inevitably they ended up at the warehouse, as if the wind that wafted the scent of days-old rubbish from the tip next door also blew in the country's hungry and downtrodden.

Decades earlier, a younger, slimmer, all round healthier man, Jim had travelled from his home town of Larkhall, near Glasgow, and down to the south coast of England. With nothing in his pocket and no job, he soon ran out of options and ended up sleeping under an upturned boat on the beach, crawling out of the dank, salty space to work three jobs a day in the nightclubs and bars of the city, until he could scrape enough money to pay the rent on a bedsit. 'But back then it was £75 a month,' Jim recalled. 'Not like these days, when you'd more likely pay that a night!'

The memory of those homeless nights stuck with Jim, and all these years later he was dedicating his time to supporting others in the same situation. After setting up a soup kitchen and a regular tour of the town dropping off food packages to needy folks, Jim had set up Sussex Homeless Support, but doing so had been a wrench. He didn't want to identify with the homeless charities he had no time for. Jim didn't hold much truck with the big players; within minutes of us meeting, he had pulled up the company accounts of one of the biggest. 'There – see?' he said, jabbing a finger at the screen. '£80 million in assets. Where's that all going?' It was a refrain I often heard from grassroots organizations. There was a widespread suspicion that the bigger charities pulled in massive donations, yet homelessness kept getting worse. More than once I was told, 'It's all a big homelessness industry.'

These days Jim was seeing all sorts of people turning up needing his help. There were whole families living on crammed houseboats in the marina, unable to afford the rent of anything more. 'Some of those boats are absolute shitholes. But you see children coming up the gangplanks in the morning with their school uniforms on. We've got a couple on an old fishing boat, and they both work, but they still can't afford a proper rent.' (There were roughly 14,000 households on Brighton and Hove council's waiting list but only about 700 properties were available to rent each year, meaning many people waited years for a council home.)[25]

Just then we were interrupted by an energetic woman in her late thirties, who came bounding through the door. This was Amber. Jim had been looking out for her for months. She had forfeited her job as an airline hostess when she hurt her back in an accident. Unable to work, she lost her flat and ended up staying for eighteen months in a shed on a horse sanctuary, less cared for than her equine neighbours. 'Still it was a little slice of heaven that saved me,' she told me cheerily. Jim's incredulous face suggested otherwise.

Later we were joined by Angie, who was losing her home slowly, like a terminal illness cruel in its torpor. She was still in her house but after her ex-husband left her with the mortgage to pay off, depression and suicidal thoughts had left her unable to work. The payday loans she had taken out came with an APR of 49.9 per cent, her debts had spiralled, and now the bank was threatening to take the house. She sat among Jim's jumble of boxes and camping supplies as her cup of tea went cold beside her. She had scooped up Jim's 'guard dog', a bug-eyed, bony chihuahua, onto her knees and held her closely in an attempt to keep it together. 'I feel so guilty, you know, Jim, because there are people worse off than me. I'm lucky, you know. I have a roof over my head.'

'No, I don't think you are,' said Jim standing over her, his hulking frame casting a shadow over her tired face. 'I think you're worse off than someone on a park bench. You know why? Because they've already suffered the trauma; you're suffering it right now. You're in the middle of it, trying to bail a boat out. That trauma is ten times worse.'

Angie would message Jim late at night saying she was done in, ready to end it all. Months earlier she'd been talked down from the cliffs at Beachy Head, only to be told there was no long-term mental health support for her because she wasn't deemed to be sufficiently in crisis. It seemed she was extremely unstable. 'I wanted you to meet her in case . . . in case the worst happens,' Jim told me, shakily. 'Stories like hers, they need to be told.'

Angie was one of an ever-growing group Jim had taken on as his responsibility. He was available to them pretty much day and night, ready to help where the system had failed. He would sit people down, go through their options, then pick up the phone, calling one of the many contacts he'd made over the years in council services or the police. He knew the process for what happens when you're getting kicked out by the landlord or when you've run out of money to pay the rent. He knew the council might try and find ways to tell you they don't have to help. They're moving the goalposts all the time, he said. In Brighton, to get long-term support like a council flat, you used to have to prove you'd lived in the area for two years – that's gone up now, he'd warned; to get support you had to prove you'd had a tenancy in the area for either six months in the last year or for three years out of the last five. Sleeping rough for years in the area didn't count.[26]

Many didn't meet the criteria to be supported.[27] Either they didn't have a local connection, they were in the country illegally and couldn't access services, or, in some cases, they had turned down the mould-coated bedsit the council had offered and were told that, in doing so, they had made themselves 'intentionally homeless', and thus warranted no further support.

Those people found themselves trying to get into one of the seven shelters across the city. Between them there was room for 273 people and it wasn't always easy to get in.[28] All but one of the shelters required you to be formally referred there, which meant going through the council housing services. The only shelter in Brighton that didn't require proof of either a local connection or a referral from the council demanded that those staying there needed to have been clean from drink or drugs for at least one month. Others would only accept people if their immigration status meant they were eligible for public funds.

This wasn't specific to Brighton. Across the UK, shelters had different rules for who could stay. Forty per cent of them demanded proof of a local connection; the same percentage would only accept people referred to them by selected agencies.[29] In Northampton I'd met a young man with a suspected learning difficulty who had been kicked out of a shelter when they found out he owed a little over £100 in rent arrears. It was a preposterous decision; who seeking emergency shelter wouldn't have some kind of debt? The man had slept outside in the snow and lost most of his toes to frostbite.

Other shelters turned down people whose needs were deemed to be too complex. These were the kinds of decisions Jim was seeing every day. 'It's a bit like being a plumber and not being able to stand the smell of shit,' Jim joked. 'Get a different job where you don't have to fix toilets. If you're going to be involved with homelessness, where most suffer from some form of trauma or mental health issue, you're going to have to deal with it.'

Those who couldn't get into the shelters ended up in tents around the city, but they were hardly welcomed: the council regularly confiscated those tents in clean-ups and demanded a fee of £25 to return them.[30]

Frustrated that the official services were turning people down, Jim had taken matters into his own hands once again. A friend had spotted a double-decker bus being advertised on eBay. A rickety old thing with no MOT, it was in quite the state, but it was enough to get Jim excited. A bid went in: £1,200; and then a further £5,000 in refurbishment costs – but soon Jim had his own, portable, shelter.

Excited, he parked it up by the seafront. Twelve people could sleep here, sheltered from the brisk sea winds that whipped in off the Channel. There were still remnants of what it had once been, with pale and peeling stickers, like faded cave paintings, reminding people that there was 'No eating or drinking allowed on the coach' and that 'Seatbelts must be worn'. Every now and then, if you pushed it hard enough, the bell would still 'ding' a ghostly signal to the long-gone driver.

Jim and his team covered the windows on the top deck with shiny insulating boards and ripped out the seats, replacing them with sturdy bunk beds constructed from thick planks of wood. Each nook, the size of a single mattress, was cordoned off with short, blue curtains. The bus was almost always full of those needing a safe haven for the night.

As I left Jim in his warehouse sanctuary, I felt a strange sense of unease. The need was there, I could see that, but should people really be staying in a converted old bus?

I had always assumed there was a safety net to protect people when they fell. A system designed to prevent people falling into destitution, a plan to keep people alive. But where had that safety net been for Hamid and for Tony, who had been on the radar of all kinds of services, but died alone. And where was it for Angie or Amber?

Jim was trying to catch people mid-air, a trapeze artist with arms flung out desperately trying to reach a few more inches, panicked in the knowledge that if he didn't people would fall. He wasn't the only one. Jon was doing the same, and up and down the country men and women were up late at night patrolling the streets, or racing home early from work to cook huge pots of stew or curry to feed the queues that were always waiting.

But was it really necessary? Wasn't there supposed to be a network of services, supplied by our taxes, to do just this sort of thing? Where were they?

CHAPTER 9

Missed

Two hundred miles north of Jim's makeshift shelter was the town of Stafford, which lies between Birmingham and Stoke-on-Trent, almost smack in the middle of England. The town, like much of the Midlands, had suffered a financial downturn in recent years, and below the buildings' quaint, Tudor facades, many of the high-street shops and establishments were shuttered up. A few pubs and slot-machine arcades remained dotted among chain stores.

With less money and fewer jobs, people in Stafford and the surrounding countryside were suffering. Around two in ten children lived in poverty,[31] and one in four people was struggling to make ends meet.[32] Meanwhile, the cash-strapped council had cut services ranging from drug and alcohol support to domestic violence refuges and mental health provision.

The number of people presenting to Stafford council as homeless, and those sleeping rough, had hit a five-year high in 2016. And for one reason or another the council was agreeing to help fewer and fewer of those who came to them for support. It was in this environment of cuts and reduced help that Jayne Simpson had been struggling.

On a cold December afternoon in 2017, things had come to a head.

*

Beneath Jayne's fingers, the tiles were cold and white. A jagged ring pull lay at her side. On the wall outside, an inscription: 'Libraries are cathedrals of the mind, hospitals of the soul, theme parks of the imagination.' It was here, in the ladies' toilets, tucked away behind the bulwark of books in Stafford Library, that Jayne had come to die.

Or perhaps not.

At that precise moment, Will Morris had made a wrong turn on a drive that should have been second nature to him. He was on his way home from the homeless day centre he ran, where each hour would see him ricochet from one emergency to the next. He'd been musing about one of the day's many melodramas when, unthinkingly, he'd flicked the indicator down and not up and turned left instead of right.

He was silently cursing his stupidity when the phone buzzed. It was Pam,* Jayne's mother. Pam only rang in an emergency. Jayne had called her, Pam explained. 'She says she's done something stupid.' Will stared at the road in front of him. By some blind luck, his wrong turn had brought him just a few streets from the place where Jayne lay.

Fingers twitching with adrenalin, Will drove as fast as he could to the library, a shining, glass-fronted new building yards from the blue glow of the Christmas lights on Stafford's high street. As he ran through the door, the staff gave him a surly look. They were often calling him, complaining that 'one of yours is in here'. The homeless community would come for the building's warmth and for use of the free toilets. Now, Will found himself pounding on a locked toilet door. No answer. Stepping back, he braced himself and threw his thin frame against the door again and again until it fell in.

There was less blood than he'd feared. Jayne had dragged the ring-pull up her arm from the wrist to the crook of her elbow but she'd missed any veins. 'A cry for help,' Will told me later. She was bundled into an ambulance and sped through the snow a mile down the road to County Hospital.

2,545 days. Will could count, to the day, how long he'd known Jayne.

Back in 2010, he'd been at a crossroads. He'd had a long career, travelling the globe from Germany to Singapore working in the glamorous world of PR. His role – overseeing publicity for Wedgwood, the Staffordshire-based porcelain and fine china company – had involved setting up events in luxurious venues all over the world, often name-dropping his boss Lord Wedgwood to ensure the finest tables at the fanciest restaurants.

But the pottery industry that had built and maintained the towns of Staffordshire had since crumbled out of existence. While Wedgwood had hung on longer than most, the company was fading fast.

At fifty, Will was bored of the corporate world. His wife, Jan, a reserved but friendly woman with short blonde hair, was a street pastor, and Will's own burgeoning Christian faith was calling on him to take action too.

So that year he quit the PR job and started again, founding his own homeless support organization, calling it the House of Bread, the name coming from the literal translation of the Hebrew 'Bethlehem'. 'It's a safe place where the homeless of Stafford can come for a hot meal and a chat. No one will be turned away,' Will explained.

It was a timely endeavour. David Cameron and the Conservative party had just swept to power, and not long after, the then chancellor of the exchequer, George Osborne, had stood on the steps of Downing Street, red briefcase in hand, ready to announce austerity measures: sweeping cuts to public services, sold to the public as akin to the necessary amputation of a gangrenous limb. 'We're all in this together,' the politicians said.

But it was a camaraderie with limits. Most evenings Will found himself out alone, walking around Stafford. He'd patrol the streets, slowly, purposefully, through the back lanes and alleys, handing out sleeping bags or cups of hot tea to the people he met, people he now considered friends. The official records said there were just seven people sleeping rough in Stafford but the crowded tables at the House of Bread shelter each week suggested the figure was a woeful underestimate. A few years later, the police would catch up with Will, issuing a warning that if he continued to hand out tents and the like he'd be given an ASBO for encouraging rough-sleeping. He kept going anyway, and later tucked the warning letter from the police, cock-a-snook, into a frame alongside a certificate of recognition for his voluntary services, awarded to him by the Queen.*

He remembered the charity's first Christmas well, he told me. They had set up a Christmas dinner in case any of the homeless people they were working with had nowhere else to go. Will was directing his small team, who were doling out turkey and gravy, when he first saw her – a short, stooped, elderly looking woman with a shock of dyed red hair. Jayne shuffled her way through the door and gratefully took a plate.

---

* From church halls opening as night shelters to local groups banding together to start community larders, I was hearing about project after project that had sprung up to try and address a growing need. Some might call it David Cameron's 'Big Society' in action, others might point to it as proof that austerity had degraded the state's safety net beyond repair. Yet others complained that the work of people like Will was facilitating rough-sleeping, making it too easy to rely on handouts. I wasn't sure what to believe, but either way it seemed like many of these groups were keeping people alive.

She was sedate that day, he remembered; grubby, in old clothes, sitting quietly at the table, where she tucked into the turkey, as did the other handful of folks there. 'She didn't really stand out then,' recalled Will. 'She was quiet – peaceful, almost.'

Soon, Jayne was visiting the centre regularly. She'd sit quietly in the safe, warm space and knit or sip tea from chipped mugs. Even when she didn't show up, she was a presence there. New guests would arrive at the door spouting the same message: 'A lady told me I should come here and get help.' After a bit of a chat, Will would realize that the 'lady' was Jayne.

Jayne was regularly sleeping rough, bedding down in the doorway of a Nationwide bank on the town's high street. Whenever Will saw her on his many night walks around the town, she'd stop him to mention some guy down the road who needed help.

'And I'd ask her, "What about you, Jayne? You need looking after too,"' Will recalled, but she always insisted, '"There's plenty worse than me."'

By Christmas 2017, Jayne was looking old. Aged just fifty-three, her health was precarious and hip problems had put her in hospital and left her bent and haggard. Her fingernails, which she'd once painted so carefully, were brittle and yellow. Her naturally red hair had faded and was replaced by a lurid bottled crimson. She shuffled around town with a wheeled walking frame, down the high street, with its shuttered shops, to the bank doorway she had made her home. Now and then she'd pull out her battered mobile phone and call her mother, Pam, miles away on the Isle of Wight. Pam would see her daughter's number flashing on the phone's screen and experience a rush of mixed emotions, she told me: grateful Jayne was well enough to call; trepidatious about what drama would come next.

As hard as it was, Pam was trying not to give Jayne money, as she knew it would just go on alcohol and drugs. Instead she'd buy clothes from Matalan or food from Sainsbury's and parcel it all up to send to her. Pam chuckled, remembering how once she'd picked up the phone to hear the voice of a takeaway restaurant server explaining that Jayne had said her mum would pay for her meal. 'I said OK and then he told me she'd said I'd pay for all her friends too – bloomin' cheek!' It was just like Jayne to try and be generous to her friends, but also just like her to try and take advantage.

At least it was contact. Weeks, months could pass without Pam hearing anything. She'd come up with her own system to keep an eye on her wayward girl. At some point Jayne had mentioned the House of Bread, and Pam had looked up the organization online and found Will's number. Now she called him regularly to check in on Jayne's progress, and together the two would vent their frustrations at her seeming refusal to accept help.

Will called Pam from the hospital that December, still a little out of breath from the race to the library. 'Jayne's OK,' he told her. 'She's going to be OK.' Pam returned the phone to its cradle and sank onto the sofa. She wasn't so sure.

The morning after the suicide attempt, as the packed ice turned to slush on the pavement, Jayne was back at the House of Bread. By chance, TV cameras from Channel 4 News were at the centre filming a piece on homelessness in the UK. Their recording captured Jayne as she sat bashfully opposite Will, her walking frame by her side.

'I need a place to stay,' she said, her voice husky.

'Yes, that's priority number one, isn't it?' agreed Will, peering out at her from under his grey-brown fringe.

After the TV cameras had left, Will called the council as

Jayne sat and sipped her tea. But there was nowhere for her to go.

That night she slept, as usual, in the meagre shelter of a bank's front porch. The estate agent Little Mansions next door mocked her with its taunts of out-of-reach homes. The melting snow left freezing puddles on the ground.

CHAPTER 10
The journey

I watched the news footage from the day after Jayne's suicide attempt again and again. Her story was there as an illustration of the spiralling numbers of those on the streets. Her back to the camera to protect her privacy, she was an anonymous visual marker for something larger than herself. But she was more than that, I thought, as I flicked the video back to the start. Who was that small, withered woman hunched over in the chair? How had she come to be there? I thought back to all I had learnt about Hamid and his life, about Tony and David and Richard, how their journeys to homelessness had been far from what I had expected.

I wanted to know who Jayne had been before she became this forgotten woman, this blur of blankets, a mound of moth-eaten clothes. Who was she before she had become so easy to ignore?

So I set out to learn all I could about her, and I knew just where to begin.

When she was a girl, Jayne loved the trampoline – the feeling of flight as she soared into the sky above, just for a moment weightless and unattached to the world below. She was an affable child, quick to make friends. Her school report cards tell the story of a young girl keen to make sure everyone was included. 'She was lovely, really lovely in those days,' recalled her mother Pam, her voice warm with nostalgia. We were sitting in her living room in her small semi-detached house on the Isle of Wight, and she smiled as she told me about the early days of family life.

Jayne had been born in Staffordshire on 25 October 1964. But her early years weren't easy. Her father was a violent man and would beat her mother. As a young child, just four or five years old, Jayne would witness the attacks. Often her father would use Jayne as a pawn in his abuse of Pam. 'When he was out, I'd see Jayne looking at me, watching me,' remembered Pam, recalling how it felt like Jayne had been conscripted by her father to keep watch. 'She'd have this look on her face. And then when he came home she'd tell tales,' Pam recalled.

I thought back to what psychiatrist Dr Sara Ketterley had told me about childhood trauma, and how it could bury itself deep, and linger.

Pam divorced Jayne's father and married again, this time to a gentle, cheery man called Ray.* When Jayne was seven, Pam and Ray moved her and her two younger siblings to the Isle of Wight, and things settled down.

Growing up in Freshwater, a village on the jutting peninsula in the west of the island, could have been idyllic. A tangle of quiet streets gave way to green fields and then the calm expanse of the sea. A couple of miles down the road, the Yarmouth ferry terminal brought boats gliding in and out of port, a constant reminder of an unseen life on the mainland.

One of Jayne's favourite places was a half-hour walk away, on the south side of the peninsula: Freshwater Bay, where chalky cliffs dropped down to white, sandy beaches below. The family would enjoy day trips there, delighting in the spray of the salt water and the sand beneath their toes.

But by the age of fifteen, Jayne was finding village life too small for her, Pam explained. She'd got herself a job working as a waitress in a small cafe run by a kindly woman called Mrs Roberts. She liked the job but there were distractions, like any good-looking man that would wander by. Mrs Roberts would cluck and tut as she watched Jayne, concerned about the way she was acting.

She wasn't the only one who was concerned. Another woman in the village bumped into Pam one day and warned her that Jayne seemed to be flirting and befriending an adult couple. 'You want to watch her with those two,' the neighbour whispered conspiratorially to Pam. But with young children to tend to, there was only so much Pam could do.

Soon Jayne was often round at the couple's house, drinking heavily. The drink shook something loose inside her, something angry. She'd stagger home and swear and curse at her mother. One night, after a heavy drinking session, she lunged at Pam, throwing herself to the floor and biting a chunk out of her mother's leg. Jayne's cousin, who had been out with her, tried to pry Jayne off, hitting her with the nearest thing to hand – a riding crop. The doctor was called and Jayne was sedated. The police suggested Pam have her charged with assault, but Pam, though bloodied and bruised, couldn't do it. 'She was still my baby,' she told me.

Teenage years can be tough on many mother–daughter relationships. One study found that teenage girls have an average of 183 arguments with their mothers every year – that's a fight every other day. As I sat opposite Pam, listening to her recall the explosive fights her teenage daughter used to ignite in the house, I couldn't help but remember my own teenage years. I'd threatened to run away a few times, over silly things like curfews and chores; I'm sure many people have done the same. I was never really serious, though. But in the worst cases those threats turn to reality.

'Family-relationship breakdown is the biggest cause of youth homelessness,' explained Paul Noblet, Head of Public Affairs at Centrepoint, the youth homelessness shelter that towers over the prime real estate of London's Tottenham Court Road. 'Fifty-five per cent of young people supported by Centrepoint in 2018 told us they left home for this reason. The causes of family breakdown are varied and complex – it might be parental conflict, financial pressures, cultural differences or poor mental health that trigger a young person to leave, or be forced to leave, the family home.' Tragically, my database so far bore a sad testament to the dangers young people faced when they found themselves homeless. I'd recorded eleven names of people who had died under the age of thirty. The youngest of those was Aaron, a sweet-faced, blond-haired nineteen-year-old who had died of diabetes in the recent winter conditions. Aaron had been living in a tent in Cardiff. He weighed just six stone when he died. It was hard not to read details of stories like Aaron's and think about how easily that could happen to any of the teenagers I knew. A little too much pride. A wall of anger between child and parents.

Despite their increasingly fractious relationship, Pam wasn't letting go of Jayne so easily. The confines of the island's border, which were becoming something of a prison cell to Jayne, at least kept her close to home, Pam thought. But as Jayne's teenage years rolled into adulthood, she found a power she was learning to wield with great effect: men's attention.

She'd already had a string of romances, and life on the island had turned into a soap opera. She'd left a trail of young men reeling in her wake. And she had a wicked sense of humour. In one case, when a boyfriend with a prosthetic leg annoyed her, Jayne made off in the morning with his fake leg in tow.

Then things took a dark turn. Jayne was twenty-one and living in a small caravan not far from her mother's house with a man called Brian.* Photographs from the time show how she had cut her flaming red hair short into an androgynous crop. Her pale skin fitted the 1980s synth-pop aesthetic of the time, and she lined her eyes with bright blue eyeliner, like someone from a music video. And now Jayne had some news: she was pregnant. But the couple had barely enough to pay the bills. Brian was scraping together a few pounds from a paper run but it was nowhere near enough to keep them going. Mrs Roberts, the owner of the cafe where Jayne used to work, took pity on her and offered her another job, this time at a holiday park she owned. Jayne would be cleaning caravans. It was hard work, but it brought in a steady wage.

The months passed and Jayne was almost due to give birth, but she still kept working each day. Worried her daughter was exhausting herself, Pam volunteered to help Jayne with the cleaning. 'Look, Jayne, you're almost ready to have the baby; I'll come with you,' Pam told her. 'You can't go on your own.'

Every day they would talk together on the bus as it wound its way out to the holiday camp. One morning, as the bus snaked its usual path over the hills, Jayne turned to her mother. 'I had such a funny dream, about the baby,' she said, her hand resting on her curved belly.

'Oh, all pregnant women dream like that,' smiled Pam.

'It was so weird. I dreamt I was at the hospital and this red-headed doctor came in and told me my baby was dead,' Jayne said quietly. That memory still stuck with Pam. It wasn't like Jayne to talk like that, and it spooked her.

A few days later, Jayne started to have pains. At Pam's request, she went to the local GP. The doctor looked Jayne over and suggested they go to hospital. The drive there was agonizing. But in the shining halls of St Mary's Hospital, things began to look better. Pam went into organization mode, striding through the halls until she found a nurse to give Jayne the once-over. The nurse was happy enough with Jayne's condition. 'You go on home and get some rest,' the nurse told Pam kindly. 'The baby's not coming tonight.'

It was around midnight when the phone rang, shrill and angry through the darkness. 'You'd better come in,' said the doctor on the other end. 'Jayne needs you.'

This time the drive to the hospital was a blur. Ray took the wheel, glancing worriedly at Pam in the passenger's seat. Just a few hours earlier she had bounded through the door exclaiming, 'We're going to be grandparents!' Ray wasn't Jayne's biological father, but he cared for her like his own, and he suffered her rages along with her mother. He desperately hoped that motherhood might smooth some of her rough edges.

Pam found her daughter lying in the hospital bed, sandwiched between other expectant mothers on the delivery ward. She had just got to Jayne's bedside when a red-haired doctor walked in.

'I'm so sorry. The baby has died in the womb,' the doctor said, looking from Pam's large grey eyes to Jayne's blank face. 'We're too far along now, so it's going to have to be a natural birth, and it's too late for an epidural, I'm afraid.' Something in Jayne's eyes changed, Pam recalled, like a light switching off. She turned her face away from her mother and stared silently into space.

For six hours Jayne pushed and strained through the labour. At one point in the early hours of the morning, she fell back against the pillow, a strange calm spreading over her face. Pam grabbed her daughter's hand. 'Jayne! Don't die! Don't leave me.'

When Jamie was born he was warm, with a small mat of soft hair on his head. 'They've made a mistake,' thought Pam. 'They've made a mistake, he's still alive.' She cradled him in her arms. Jayne rolled over – she didn't want to see.

In the weeks to come, Pam would wake in the night thinking she heard her grandson crying. Jayne didn't seem to process the loss. She wouldn't talk about it. She went back to drinking. Her relationship with Brian had broken down weeks before. The hospital mentioned the idea of counselling but Jayne didn't want to follow it up.

Pam watched sadly from afar. 'She didn't grieve so I took on the grief,' she would tell me later. 'Almost like it was my responsibility.' Pam struggled on; she started a job at a factory, where her new colleagues helped organize a fun run to raise money for a charity supporting those experiencing stillbirths. As Pam huffed and puffed her way across the line, Jayne was nowhere to be seen.

Looking back now, it felt like Jamie's death was the moment when things changed. The moment that Pam lost not just a grandson, but her daughter, too. Slowly, one by one, Jayne burnt all her bridges on the island. She got into drunken fights – physical punch-ups with people who looked at her the wrong way. 'She'd fight the world when she was drunk,' sighed Pam. Even she could see it was time for Jayne to leave.

So, at the age of twenty-seven, Jayne found herself on the ferry to the mainland, then heading up to the Midlands. She was bound for Staffordshire.

Far away from her mother's watching eye, Jayne's troubles continued. She was drinking heavily every day and her drug use was spiralling out of control. She could often become violent. One day her photo appeared in the local paper under the headline, 'Stafford's Most Wanted'. Amused by her new-found notoriety, Jayne cut out the article and sent it to her despairing mother.

After Jamie's death, she gave birth to five more children. The first two were taken in by Pam – a girl and a boy. 'I'll always remember coming up the drive where Jayne was living and looking through the letter box, and there was her little boy with a nappy wet through hanging off him,' said Pam sadly. 'And there was Jayne, drunk . . .' she added, her voice trailing off. The plan was to look after the children until Jayne was better, but things didn't change. Rather than watch the two children go into care, Ray and Pam decided to foster them, and the couple later adopted the children as their own.

The next two babies that came along were taken by social services. Pam offered to take those children too but the officials said they were looking for younger parents and had a couple in mind. They subpoenaed Pam to come and give evidence against her daughter in a family court. The children were put up for adoption. The fifth and youngest child was brought up by her paternal grandparents.

I later heard how tragically common this pattern was. St Mungo's found that half of the single homeless women they worked with were mothers, and more than three quarters (79 per cent) of these had had children taken into care.[33] 'Having children removed into care, particularly when they are permanently removed, can be deeply traumatic for women, and can often trigger worsened mental health or substance misuse problems,' writes Katherine Sacks-Jones, Director of Agenda, Alliance for Women and Girls at Risk. 'Services need to offer tailored support to these women; to deal with the trauma of losing a child, to establish contact with children, or around care proceedings.' Sadly, those tailored approaches rarely exist.[34]

Jayne was left alone, with a gaping hole where motherhood should have been. She pushed the sorrow down, smothering it with drink and drugs. After she'd given birth to her final daughter, she fell in with a group of men who were all using heroin. They'd help Jayne to shoot up, and then, when she was prostrate and helpless, they would abuse her. She was only saved, in the most brutal of ways, when an overdose sent her careening to hospital. Pam raced to visit her there. She found her on the intensive care ward, hooked up to various machines, totally unresponsive. 'They didn't think she'd make the night,' Pam recalled.

There is no correct way to deal with grief. The 'seven stages', though helpful to some, are widely regarded as a blunt tool. Hearing Jayne's story, I couldn't help but think of Hamid, and the trauma he had carried with him for decades since his time in the war. Or Tony and his pain at losing a brother.

'The people we work with are living incredibly chaotic lives,' Will told me one day as we sat in his office in Stafford. 'And when you're living that way, you're constantly in survival mode; your brain focuses in on a few things: *Where am I going to sleep, what am I going to eat, where do I get my next drink?* When you're in that state you simply can't afford to take the time to grieve, to work through your emotions – there isn't space for that,' he said, leaning back, tired, in his cheap office chair, a cup of coffee cooling, untouched, to one side of a desk.

Instead, many people he saw were masking their grief and pain in drink and drugs. Every week Will would wade into the chaos and try to keep as many as he could afloat. That day was no exception. I had watched as he had calmly dealt with a child-custody issue from one of the residents, and he was just sitting back down when a colleague knocked urgently on the door, proffering a small plastic bag of white powder.

'It was in the first cubicle in the toilets. I don't know what it is, but it doesn't look good,' she said nervously, pulling it out of the pocket of her cargo pants. Will eyed the bag up, still calm but with a twinge of nervousness in his eyes. 'Right, we're going to have to go into shut-down mode.' (Drugs were banned on the premises and any breaking of that rule led to immediate closure for the rest of the day.) Will carefully slipped the plastic bag into a small paper envelope before neatly writing 'Drugs' on the front.

This kind of thing was becoming common. Will and his team were often trying to help those who were battling addictions, people like Jayne. The county council had reduced the funding for drug and alcohol services by 59 per cent and people were really suffering as a result.[35]

Will's assistant manager was called in and the team scrambled to shut the building down. As the residents left, many grumbled. 'It's not fair. Those idiots have to ruin it for everyone,' one long-haired teenage lad moaned as he left.

CHAPTER 11

Talking to Pam, Will and friends of Jayne's, I came to realize that there had been a moment when it all could have turned around for her. In 2003 she had married again. Her new husband, Ben,* was good for her. A short, dark-haired man, his Midlands accent had a calming effect on Jayne. They had a small house in Highfields, just south of Stafford, just a little two-bed, but they filled it with knick-knacks and made it feel like home.

Jayne had got treatment for her heroin addiction, and a few years into meeting Ben had been addressing her alcoholism too. Now life had a pleasing regularity to it. Her routine of browsing the shops and pottering around the house was interrupted only by the welcome addition of her fifteen-year-old daughter Rachel,* who came to stay with her. It was the first time mother and daughter had lived together, and Jayne flourished in her company. Rachel had been fostered and adopted before her fifth birthday. Now they were reunited Jayne couldn't help but spoil her, taking her on mother–daughter shopping trips, delighting in finding new lines of mascara or eyeshadow they hadn't seen before.

But it wouldn't last. Soon after, Jayne met Karl,* a troubled man who was using heroin. She cheated on Ben and the marriage broke up. Rachel moved away. Jayne and Karl headed to Wolverhampton, and ended up on the street. The relationship turned violent and in August 2014 Karl beat up Jayne so badly he was convicted of actual bodily harm; Jayne gave evidence against him in court. He was given a sentence of two years in prison and Jayne plotted her escape from him. She was adamant that the relationship was over. Adult social services got involved, and in July 2015 an investigating worker with Staffordshire County Council met with Jayne and drew up a safeguarding plan.

The plan, ten sides of A4 paper, laid out all the ways Jayne might still be at risk, including 'retaliation from ex-partner'. It also noted a risk of 'Self-neglect as Jayne refuses support from various sources (lack of adequate diet, missing health appointments, accepting referral but not engaging with support for issues she says concern her)' and of 'Grief from recent loss of partner increasing emotional distress in all aspects of life'.

Some solutions were explored in the report: Karl could be given a restraining order on release, it noted, though 'he has not respected restraining orders in the past . . . Jayne wants to stay away from [Karl]. She is currently wanting to move from former friends/acquaintances she knew in Stafford due to risk of being drawn into increased alcohol and drug use, and due to risk of her whereabouts becoming known to [Karl] by the "local grapevine".'

She wanted out. A fresh start.

The plan was passed on to Staffordshire Police, Staffordshire Women's Aid, her social worker, and to Will and Pam.

Pam's copy of the report arrived with a covering letter from Jayne's social worker which read: 'I shall close my work now, as I have done as much as I can to keep Jayne safe from her ex-partner'.

'As much as I can' – Pam would later wonder if that was really the case.[36]

The council started working to find Jayne somewhere to stay, but it wasn't going to be easy.

A three-storey beige building marked the end of the cul-de-sac. Jayne, sitting in the car's passenger seat, screwed up her face, unimpressed. She and Will had arrived at a residential care home run by a company called Housing & Care 21. A supported-living block, it catered mostly for the elderly. As he walked up the handrailed wheelchair ramp and into the main doors, Will remembered surveying the scene: a pink and paisley recreational room full of huge, lush armchairs that dwarfed their elderly residents.

'Will, where have you brought me?' Jayne bellowed loudly.

Embarrassed, Will spoke softly. 'This is it Jayne – your new accommodation.'

'I'm not a fucking geriatric! I'm only 50!' she exploded. 'I'm not staying here.'

Will sighed. He'd spent weeks battling with the council, trying to get them to find accommodation for Jayne, somewhere where she'd be safe from the lure of drugs and the chance of running into Karl again.

Eventually the battle had paid off and the council had found her a room, but it was far from a permanent solution. In the last five years, Stafford council had spent more than £250,000 housing homeless people in temporary accommodation, and costs were rising each year. Across the country showed a similar picture. The amount spent by councils to house homeless people in temporary accommodation had skyrocketed, increasing by 56 per cent in five years.[37] Government figures show the number of people housed in bed and breakfast and hotels had increased by a third. Some people stayed there for months, and then years on end, living with no kitchen, shared bathrooms and no front door to call their own.

In Stafford, the shortage in accommodation options meant the council had placed Jayne in a centre mostly used to house the elderly and infirm. It didn't take Jayne's outburst for Will to realize this was far from appropriate.

He managed to calm Jayne down and she agreed to head to her room. She was at the centre for around two weeks and started to settle. She made friends with an elderly woman called Winnie and the two would sit and gossip together. But then Winnie was moved to another home and Jayne was alone again.

Frustrated, she started inviting friends round, friends from the old days on the street. This did not go down well with staff and she was asked to leave. 'So she was out on her backside,' recalled Will. Having been thrown out of the centre, Jayne was classified as 'intentionally homeless' by the council. Despite Will's and Pam's remonstrations, the council housing officer explained it had no further duty to find her somewhere safe to live.

'Sometimes people just are not ready for their own places,' Will said later. Jayne wasn't alone. Another man who used the House of Bread day centre was living in his tent in the front room of the flat the council had found for him. He didn't know how to live any other way.

After she'd been kicked out of the old people's home, Jayne ended up back with Karl. He was out of prison by now and, without a local support system, Jayne had run out of options. She wasn't working and didn't have money to pay her own rent. Stuck far from her family, she resorted to her old tricks with men and convinced Karl to let her stay with him. That just made things worse.

They moved twenty miles away, to Walsall, but the abuse soon started again. Staying with Karl in his flat, Jayne was trapped, totally beholden to his whims. Rachel, her daughter, heard how he'd beat her up. On the rare occasions she saw her mum, she would turn up bruised. Jayne would fight back against Karl but things would get nasty. She'd often end up in hospital.

Eventually it became too much. Jayne headed back to Stafford alone, but Karl soon followed. 'It was almost as if he couldn't leave her alone,' Pam sighed.

One day, in early 2018, Pam called Jayne and became concerned when she couldn't understand what she was saying. She sounded upset but her words were slurred. Later, Jayne texted Pam: *He's trying to murder me. I can't ring the police or he'll hear.* Pam's head spun. Panicked, she tried calling Staffordshire police but couldn't get through. Not knowing what to do, she found the number for Hampshire police and called them – they passed a message to the local Stafford force who sent out officers to rescue Jayne.

I was coming to understand just how common domestic violence was for homeless women. Thirty-two per cent of women experiencing homelessness said domestic violence was a factor, either in the cause of their homelessness or their experiences after.[38] Then there was the horrific fact that on the streets there was the near constant threat of sexual violence.[39]

I didn't know if Jayne had ever sought the protection of a domestic violence refuge. But I did know that if she'd tried she would have faced problems. Across Staffordshire the number of refuge spaces had dropped from 71 to 64 and funding had been cut by 30 per cent.[40] One refuge manager in a town near Stafford told me they were virtually always full and funding cuts had meant a reduction in staff, which in turn meant they couldn't take the women with the most complex needs: substance abuse issues or mental health problems. 'Last week we had a lady call; she had four children, and the closest space we could find for her was the Orkney Islands,' a volunteer at the refuge told me. That was 600 miles away. They have no idea if the woman took the trip – she never called back.

The tragic truth was that cuts to refuge services had left many women with nowhere to go. Sadly, women-only accommodation facilities are few and far between. Mixed-gender hostels or other forms of temporary accommodation might feel unsafe. People fleeing domestic violence, some of the most vulnerable people in society, were being offered only impossible options. Many ended up on the streets instead.

Jayne couldn't seem to find a safe place to escape to. She kept falling prey to brutal men.

By mid-2018 Jayne was alone again. She'd spend her days sitting on a bench outside Costa coffee, watching the world go by. Her nights she passed in a bank doorway.

She had at one point tried to get herself back on track. Picking my way through official records, I found how, in 1999, aged thirty-four, she received treatment for her heroin addiction; then, in 2005, she was treated for alcoholism. In 2015 Will had encouraged her to get more help, and she'd trundle her way along the high street and up to the double-fronted red-brick building of the One Recovery centre. Nothing seemed to work for long.

But Will kept going. He knew Jayne needed help and had been encouraging her to go to professionals. The suicide attempt in the library bathroom wasn't her first, and she had been battling depression for some time. Just three months before she'd spotted the ring-pull and locked the bathroom door, Jayne had twice gone to the local psychiatric liaison team, looking for help, but still she was left struggling. Elsewhere in the town, local services were stretched. The local Citizens Advice's mental health team had been lost due to budget cuts. Waiting lists for other mental health teams were long.

Beneath a tough exterior, Jayne was struggling to cope. On 18 May, at Will's advice, Jayne went to her GP. She was at her wits' end.

The doctor took one look at the pale, withered woman in front of her, heard the desperation in her voice, and decided something needed to be done. She clicked on her computer screen and typed up a letter, referring Jayne to the area's specialist mental health team. The letter stated Jayne was 'a chaotic lady with history of alcohol and drug misuse. Ongoing anxiety and depression. Never engaged previously but desperate now. At risk of drug overdose and sudden death.'

'Desperate.' 'At risk.' The letter was sent. Help was on its way.

Or so she thought.

The GP's letter arrived at the mental health service soon after. A clinician read it over, noting the GP's alert that Jayne was 'at risk of drug overdose and sudden death', and called the doctor back, querying whether the urgency really was appropriate – after all, the clinician reasoned, Jayne didn't have any 'clear plan to end her life'.

So instead of emergency intervention, the mental health service set up a routine appointment. A little later, after struggling to reach Jayne on the phone, they decided it should be a face-to-face appointment rather than a routine telephone triage assessment. It was scheduled for 26 June, just a few weeks away.

The appointment date came and went. Jayne didn't turn up. The clinician managed to get her on the phone and she asked for another appointment date. That's where things went wrong. The clinician who spoke to Jayne on the phone failed to send the email inviting her for another appointment. The appointment was never booked in.

By July the summer days were hot and long. Across the UK, people sweltered in the unusual suffocation of a protracted heatwave. Crowds gathered in the pubs of Stafford, collectively holding their breath as the England football squad battled against the odds to the semi-finals of the World Cup. The joyous celebrations were dashed when, on 11 July, the team lost to Croatia, instantly dousing the nation's misplaced hopes for victory.

That same night, as St George's flags fluttered sadly on the high street and hardened men wiped tears from their eyes, Jayne made her way to the end of the street towards the top of the town. It had been two weeks since she'd missed the appointment with the mental health team. She hadn't heard anything from them since.

Pam still isn't sure what happened that night. It is only through piecing the CCTV footage together that anyone has any idea.

Jayne wandered along Greengage Street and stopped in front of a bank. She sat down by the doors and fiddled with her mobile phone. She was texting a friend she often hung around with. He was staying in a bail hostel nearby and she was messaging him asking him to transfer money into her bank account so they could score.

By 1.29 a.m. Jayne had slumped to one side, her head resting on the ground. Ten minutes later a gaunt, swarthy man with a bald head wandered into shot. Karl. He was accompanied by his brother. The men nudged her and lifted her head up, but she sank down again. Scattered around her were packets of drugs, both prescribed and illegal. The men walked off into the night.

At 1.57 a.m. and again at 3.09 a.m. Jayne moved slightly. Enough to show she was still breathing.

A woman found her early the next morning, at 6.35 a.m., Jayne's body limp in the doorway. She was dead. A 999 call reported 'a female, unconscious, who has vomited. Her tongue is swollen and skin is a blue colour.'

Later, I sat in the bland coroner's tribunal room and heard how Jayne had taken methadone, morphine and diazepam as well as alcohol. She had thrown up, but the drugs had damped her gag reflex and she had choked on her own vomit.

She was fifty-three.

Weeks after Jayne died in a doorway, a staff member at the mental health trust checked their records and realized Jayne's case had slipped through the cracks. They tried to book a new appointment to get the help she was asking for. They discovered it was too late.

The day of the funeral, the summer heatwave broke and a grey sky cast a sombre mood over the streets. I couldn't shake the sense of foreboding as I made my way towards the crematorium building. Pam, Ray and their adopted daughter Katie* had got up at 5 a.m. to take the ferry over to the mainland before a four-hour drive up to Stafford. As I walked up the long path to the small church building, I spotted Pam sitting on a park bench, surrounded by a field of well-wishers – and gravestones.

Rachel and Katie, long-distance biological sisters with matching cherry-red hair, whispered together not far from Pam's side. They cast furtive glances at a shy, skinny fourteen-year-old with braces and a wavy, ginger mane that frizzed down her back. This was the first time they'd met Lizzie,* their half-sister. Jayne's youngest child had been adopted at birth, but unlike the others, Lizzie had been kept separate from the family, sheltered away by her paternal grandparents. Now, she was meeting her extended birth-family for the first time, at their mother's funeral.

I was quietly chatting to Rachel when her eyes turned stony and she sucked in her breath. 'You're fucking joking! He's here,' she hissed. Katie followed her sister's gaze. Standing a little apart from the chattering group of mourners waiting to enter the service was a haggard-looking bald man wearing a creased shirt, speckled on the back of one shoulder blade with a mist of blood droplets.

'How dare he show his face here?' Rachel growled. 'He made Mum's life a misery. If Gran sees him, she'll go spare.'

Karl. The family didn't know then that he had been the last person to see Jayne alive. Pam eyed him warily from her spot on the bench, the lines on her face furrowing into a scowl. But just then she was distracted by a hand on her arm. 'It's time to go in now,' Will said, leaning down to help her out of her seat.

Inside the hall, mourners filled row upon row. At least eighty people shuffled into lines before the simple, light-coloured wood coffin, covered with floral tributes. Will faced the room. He wore a dark-grey suit, tiny hedgehogs on his tie – an attempt at levity. As he began to speak, his voice caught with emotion.

'We are here today to remember a lovely lady,' he started, 'and because we all know a Jayne: someone who needs help, someone who needs our support. What Jayne went through could happen to any of us, and so today we remember that too.'

Next Rachel stood up, visibly nervous and trying hard to keep it together. 'I love you, Mum. I'll never forget you,' she managed, before the tears choked her voice.

As the mourners filed out past the coffin, the loudspeakers blared the mournful wail of Celine Dion's 'My Heart Will Go On'.

'She was such a nice lady, she just made some bad decisions,' one woman told me. 'She was doing well for a while, then it all went wrong again.'

As I walked down the sun-dappled hill, away from the crematorium and through row upon row of gravestones, I thought about all I knew of Jayne, this composite sketch I had pulled together from family anecdotes, official reports, interviews with those who had worked with her. I had often assumed that people who were homeless were completely isolated from society and cut off from anyone else. But here was Jayne with her large and loving family. Some people, it seemed, were surrounded with love and care but, for whatever reason, just couldn't escape the streets.

I had so much that I wanted to ask Jayne. I wanted so much to have met her while she was still alive, to try and understand what more she needed, how she could have been saved. I knew Pam and Will were feeling something similar, a desperate sense of trying to work out where things had gone irreparably wrong.

Funerals are often meant to put a full-stop on a story, but this one had left me bursting with yet more questions. And, sadly, it wasn't the last funeral I would go to that year.

'Nice day for it,' said the man in the pink-and-blue tie-dye T-shirt as the late-July sunlight bounced off the white stone walls.

The town crier watched the hearse roll by, his three-cornered hat held respectfully to his chest. Red, white and blue bunting fluttered over the terracotta brick of the historic high street of Stony Stratford, a town outside Milton Keynes. The crier was just replacing his hat when a mop of pink hair leant out of one of the cars following the hearse. 'Ay up!' cried a voice.

The street had been the site of Fabian's patch, the place where he'd sold the *Big Issue*, accompanied always by his good-natured dog, Pippet the whippet. It was a writer at the *Big Issue* who had alerted me to Fabian's death. I had set up an online form where people could report any homeless deaths they'd heard about and I'd spread the word to a network of journalists.*

I'd been working in the office when a direct message pinged through one morning from *Big Issue* reporter Liam Geraghty:

---

*   I work as part of a team that coordinates a network of more than 1,000 local journalists, and others, to dig into stories in their area. It is called the Bureau Local, and the network was an invaluable asset in finding the names and details of the homeless people who died all across the UK.

'Just a heads-up that I've filed one of your "Dying Homeless" reports on Fabian Bayet, one of our vendors who passed away recently,' he wrote, going on to explain that the funeral would be held soon and that it was open to all to attend.

Keen to hear more, I had taken the train up to Milton Keynes that morning. As I stepped out of the station, blinking in the bright morning light, a jumble of objects caught my eye. Right by the station entrance someone had set up virtually the entire contents of a bedroom: a thick double bed constructed from wooden pallets and blankets, a set of shelves, even a vanity table. In front of it the owner had erected a cardboard sign: 'Homeless not hopeless.'

Homelessness was at unprecedented levels in Milton Keynes; the number of people sleeping rough had increased six-fold between 2013 and 2017. But it was, in the main, restricted to the city centre. Fabian was different: he'd lived in a small town on the outskirts, where rough-sleeping was rarer.

The crematorium was a short taxi ride from the station and, as the car pulled into the secluded car park, I found myself immediately guessing which group was there for Fabian. I'd read a little about his hippy ways and was drawn to a gaggle of people in bright, tie-dyed T-shirts. One white woman had thick blonde dreadlocks. A man stumbled towards the group with a can of Special Brew in his hand, his pink hair half hidden under a flat cap.

As mourners filed into the crematorium hall, Estella, a slim woman with tanned skin and a neat bob, pulled off her sunglasses and whispered furtively to a friend, 'He knew what to do, I told him time and time again he had to end it. But he was stubborn – but that's just Fabian.'

*

Fabian Bayet knew he had a problem. He'd drink – too much. And then there were the drugs, one thing had led to another, and then he was using heroin.

It hadn't always been this way. Growing up in Belgium, in the southern town of Charleroi, in a middle-class family, Fabian had been a sweet, gentle child. At the age of ten, when other children were dreaming of becoming astronauts or football players, Fabian said he wanted to become a priest.

I spoke to his sister Angie, over Skype, from her home in Belgium. She was a smartly dressed, well-spoken lady whose hands danced around expressively when making a point. When she recalled her and her brother's childhood she paused as her eyes welled up, and she exhaled deeply through thick lips.

Summers were filled with trips to the seaside, she had explained, where Fabian and his younger brother and sister would take part in an annual summer camp. He was a smart child, always aceing school exams despite never studying, and his independent mind showed itself even then. Once, when the summer camp was set the challenge of dressing like a football team in the World Cup, Fabian eschewed team colours or flags and instead came dressed as the football.

He grew into a healthy teenager; photographs showed his glossy brown hair glinting like the spark in his deep brown eyes. But things at home were not always easy. His mother was a troubled woman and she would take out her anger and frustrations with the world on her eldest son, lashing him with cruel words and occasionally physically beating him as well.

'He was always so gentle – too gentle maybe,' his little sister Angie explained. 'I wouldn't have taken all that, but Fabian did.' Maybe it was that aggression that pushed him to leave, to find a means to get away.

At nineteen he had joined the Belgian Navy. The promise of adventure called to his wild spirit and the travel gave him the excuse he needed to leave his mother behind. In 1989 he set off, looking smart in his uniform. He travelled to Yugoslavia, Ukraine and the Persian Gulf. I found a faded photograph from the time, in muted colours, which showed him smiling and squinting into the sun. He is crouched on the deck of a large military ship, wearing a simple white T-shirt and white shorts, surrounded by his fellow crewmen, all dressed alike. Behind them, the furled sails and wide, open sea. You wouldn't know it from the smiling man in the picture, but the navy was changing Fabian.

By 1992, Fabian had returned to Belgium. He had quit the navy, though he hadn't told his family. As far as they knew, he was in Italy on military leave. It was only when some friends ran into him on the streets of Brussels that word got back he was home. When they asked why he wasn't in Florence, he told them, matter-of-fact, that he had hung up his uniform. The friends had news of their own: his father had recently died. Fabian went home, but while he had changed, the world there had not.

His sister, Angie, thought the drug use first began while he was in the navy. Whenever it started, he was using drugs regularly then. He had been caught carrying small amounts on the international train that ran down from Holland to Belgium. When it happened again, he was faced with a serious prison sentence: the standard time for such a crime was ten years.

While Fabian was held in prison in Bruges, waiting for his court date, outside his family was scrambling. 'We couldn't let him go to prison for ten years,' Angie recalled.

'He wouldn't survive in there.' She had seen how he was suffering in the holding cells.

Furtively, she and her other brother scraped together some money. When Fabian was released before his trial they gave him the money and told him to run. 'Go to England,' the family advised. 'Wait out the ten years and then you can come back to us.' So once more, Fabian left.

London in the 1990s was awash with chemical highs. It was a party scene, the era of the underground rave, of acid house, ecstasy and sweat. Fabian ended up living in a squat, sharing the space and the one bathroom with twenty or so others. But the place suited him. When his younger brother came over to visit, he'd take him out, proudly showing off the parties, the thump of the music and the buzz of the drugs that fizzed you through the night under dark railway arches.

But back in Belgium, Angie worried about him. Fabian would change address often, moving from squat to squat, and, in a time before mobile phones, this meant she would regularly find herself with no way of talking to him. He would call at Christmas, or occasionally a few days after her birthday. She couldn't shake the feeling he was getting into trouble.

Ten years passed and Fabian's criminal debt in Belgium was over; he'd run out the clock. But Angie was shocked by the man who returned to Belgium. Fabian's skin was sallow, his eyesight was weakening and his teeth were rotten. He looked far older than someone in their early thirties. Together the family found him a place to live, got him a job and got his health seen to. But within months he was complaining. 'He'd say he found it all stifling, suffocating. He'd never had to worry about things like paying rent or sorting out council bills before, and it was all too much for him,' Angie recalled.

The call of drugs and alcohol was just too strong. Fabian wasn't alone: research suggests around a third of people who are homeless became that way due to alcohol misuse.[41] Just five months after he'd returned, Fabian left Belgium again and headed back to the UK. This time to Milton Keynes.

The years passed and Fabian found a kind of routine. Each week he'd drive or hitch a ride to Northampton to pick up copies of the *Big Issue*, which he'd bring back and sell in Stony Stratford, wooing customers with his charming chat.

Fabian was a storyteller, and he'd become quite the character in the town, where people began to call him the 'Belgian Waffle' because he'd always have a story for them. He'd tell tales so meandering, so whimsical, it became impossible to know where the truth really lay. (Indeed, there was an element of poetry to the fact that Fabian had come to make Stony Stratford his home; this was, after all, the town where the phrase 'cock and bull story' originated, derived from the names of two pubs on the high street.)

For years Fabian moved from one sleeping spot to another, sometimes sleeping in a car he'd been given, other times in the flat of his on-again-off-again partner Sandra.* He enjoyed the nomadic lifestyle; if he moved around enough, no one was able to tell him to quit the drink and the drugs.

And when life got too busy, he had a special place he could go, to escape it all for a while: the allotment. Days would pass with him sitting contentedly under a spindly apple tree, looking out at the thin, long stretch of vegetable garden before him. This was his haven, a quiet place he could come, just a ten-minute walk from the bustle of the town's high street. Here, the noise of the town was a low hum in the distance, punctuated occasionally by the cluck of one of the chickens in a nearby plot.

The allotment was often alive with colour. Towards the bottom of the plot a sea of blue ceanothus flowers speckled the ground, their scent mixing with the waft of mint emanating from a herb patch. The small shed on the allotment was just large enough for him to wriggle inside and curl up on the floor. It did fine as a bedroom in the summer months.

Sometimes friends would drop by, including a woman in her early thirties: Estella. She'd met Fabian after they got chatting when he sold her the *Big Issue*. Now she considered him a friend. Fabian would guide her through the patches of tilled land until they reached his spot. He would proudly point out the raspberries and strawberries to her as they sauntered lazily up the slight camber to the bench under the apple tree.

Those summer days stretched long and languidly into evenings, caught up in the flow of Fabian's florid stories. He'd tell Estella tales about the old man who had tended a plot here for over sixty years, or the French couple who were always looking down on him. 'The politics – he always told me about the people of Stony,' Estella recalls of Fabian's favourite topics. 'He always told me all the stories. All the things that were going on.'

The only thing out of place in this pastoral scene was the half-drunk can of Special Brew at Fabian's feet. He never really kept track of how much he drank, but there was always a steady supply of super-strong cider or spirits like vodka. (A doctor once told me the number one thing the government could do to tackle homelessness would be a restriction of these super-strong, super-cheap drinks.) Fabian would drink until he was warm. Drink until he could sleep.

I had heard time and time again that drug and alcohol use among the homeless population was tragically common. It was both a cause and a consequence of homelessness. Those with addiction problems could find their lives falling apart; jobs were lost, bills stacked up, rent went unpaid. They would slide, almost inevitably, into homelessness.

I had spent a pleasant afternoon talking to Bill, who had been a very wealthy tech innovator in the world of film and TV, having invented a revolutionary form of CGI technology. His name appeared on major blockbusters, including the *Lost in Space* film. After a divorce, he struggled with alcohol and lost everything, falling into homelessness. Following months in hospital with severe liver problems, he realized he needed to get help or die, so he found himself cycling up and down a road in West London, desperately trying to find the rumoured dry (alcohol-free) hostel with in-house support. Spotting a likely looking house, he knocked at the door and persuaded the support worker to let him it, but it had been quite a battle. Bill had had to actively seek out and hunt down the service he needed. Many didn't have that kind of energy or resolve.

But alcohol wasn't always the cause of someone's fall into homelessness. In other cases, people started using only when they found themselves bedding down outside for the first time, or as a reaction to the stress. 'I never used before I was homeless,' one man told me, 'but this is what it does to you.'

Of course, not everyone who finds themselves homeless turns to drink or uses drugs, but it is worryingly common. Some 39–70 per cent of young homeless people have succumbed to substance abuse,[42] though the drugs of choice vary. As I travelled round the country I heard of different drugs trends in different places. In Leeds and Manchester it was Spice, a synthetic cannabinoid that varied wildly in potency and had a zombifying, paralysing effect on the user. It was highly addictive, cheap and undetectable by standard drug-testing, meaning it was now rampant in prisons across the country. One academic I spoke to explained how some entrenched heroin users were so wrapped up in Spice use that they forget about heroin completely, such was the power of its addictive qualities. 'You don't even need to get up from your begging patch,' an outreach worker in Leeds told me. 'There are dealers that bring it round to them. You see dealing happening in broad daylight.'

The drug was paralysing the homeless scene in Manchester, and had become tragically commonplace. One afternoon, in broad daylight, I was walking up from the city's Piccadilly Gardens to the train station when I came across a devastating scene. A group of teenage girls were laughing and pointing their phones towards a friend who had straddled her leg across the hunched form of a man, frozen in stupor, drooling and stooped on a bench, lost on the high of Spice.

In Bradford, it was crack cocaine. One afternoon, I found myself scaling a seven-foot metal gate, my boots slipping precariously on the rain-slicked metal beneath them. Dominic, a local outreach worker, wanted to show me the place he'd found a woman sleeping just the other night. Behind the gate, in a squalid, stinking corner, hidden under a ledge of a loading bay, was a filthy nest of duvets and pillows. Something crunched under my foot. Across the ground, scattered like confetti, were dozens and dozens of syringes.

'See, those are the regular ones for injecting; these ones, with the purple tops, they're for deep veins, like in your groin, so they'd be using those to dig – and I mean dig – to get to the femoral vein,' Dominic said, seemingly not noticing my grimace.

The enclave was behind the boarded remnants of a former bar. Now, the trashed innards of the building had become a notorious crack den. As we walked away a young man popped up from behind a bench. 'You guys want a cheesy burger?' he said, hastily backtracking when he saw the look of confusion on our faces. 'That's a new one. I've heard of a cheesy bag,' Dominic told me. 'That's a bag with a bit of heroin, an ecstasy tablet and some weed – but a burger? Now that's new.'

Up in Glasgow, it was a blue pill known as 'street valium' – a counterfeit version of the anxiety medication – that was taking hold. After a run of deaths in the city, the council had taken the unusual step of issuing a public warning about the dangers of mixing the drug with alcohol or other narcotics.

Fifty miles away in Edinburgh, it had been synthetic cathinones, known as 'bath salts', for a while, but that had passed. Now it was mostly ageing heroin users injecting in more and more dangerous ways, and there was fake Xanax, a short-acting benzodiazepine used to treat anxiety, that was on the rise in the city.

In Belfast, the paramilitary gangs that had once kept heroin off the streets with violent rigour during the Troubles had been replaced by gangs peddling the drug to a fresh, new market. In a tree-encircled hostel in the south of the city, a softly spoken support worker told me how she had had to resuscitate a resident just the day before. Her mind racing back to her training, she had pulled the top of a Naloxone pump and jammed it into the prostrate man's thigh. 'I didn't know what he'd taken but we see a lot of opiate overdoses,' she said. Heroin was now so prevalent in Northern Ireland that some were even calling for the government to follow Portugal's lead in decriminalizing illicit substances.[43]

Then there was alcohol. One study found that the average number of alcoholic units drunk per week by the homeless people reviewed was 153, nearly eleven times the recommended allowance.[44] I thought back to Tony, frozen in his backyard, whisky bottles by his side. He had sunk into the desperate depths of an addiction that wouldn't cut him loose.

In every place I visited, no matter the drug, the result was the same: a desperate cycle of drug highs and come-downs, the withdrawal rattling your bones so you can think of nothing else. Work, food, self-care – it would all pale against the need for the next hit. Addiction changes the brain, rewiring the neural pathways that affect dopamine release. Without the proper support, shaking addiction can be nearly impossible.

Fabian had been using drugs for years. It wasn't enough to just want to stop. He needed help.

Estella found herself thinking of Fabian often. When the weather was bad she'd look out the window and hope he was somewhere warm, perhaps back with his girlfriend or with a friend.

In early 2016, the winter turned bitterly cold. Sitting at home, Estella had a strange feeling. She reached for her phone and dialled Fabian's number. The voice on the other end sounded tired, if pleased to hear from her. 'It's pretty cold out here. Do you know anyone with a spare room?' Fabian asked. The question had stopped Estella in her tracks. She had a spare room, complete with an empty bed, and there was Fabian out in the cold. She spoke to her partner. They talked about the risks of bringing a drug-dependent man into the house, with their young daughter. Then Estella called Fabian back. 'You should come here,' she said.

But having a man with addictions in the house wasn't easy. Sitting in Estella's spare bedroom, Fabian tried detoxing. He wasn't ready to stop the alcohol but he was going to try and stop the heroin. He wanted to do it his way, alone and out of hospital. But coming off heroin cold turkey is hard – you look and feel like you're dying. That's what happened to Fabian.

Estella would sit downstairs and worry about him. She'd make him fresh juices, blends of fruit and vegetables, and leave them carefully in a mini-fridge she had set up in his room. But day after day, when she'd go in to check on things, there would be the juices, untouched. 'It was difficult,' she'd sigh later. 'He just wouldn't do what he was told.'

For whatever reason, Fabian hadn't been up for engaging with official support from the council. 'There were so many requirements and things, and forms, it was too much for somebody like that, somebody set in their ways,' Estella remembered. 'For someone who loves to be outside and with his animals, asking him to come in and fill in forms, it was really too much for him to get his head around. He's not going to last two or three appointments – he's just going to give up.'

In the end, Fabian's body began to break down. His skin turned sallow and his stomach swelled up, hard and solid to the touch. Desperately ill, he was admitted to the local hospital. He was there for weeks. It was not an unusual sight; the number of people being admitted to hospital with drink and drugs problems who are also registered as 'No fixed abode' had increased steadily in recent years.[45]

Fabian and Estella messaged back and forth as he waited to be transferred from one ward to another. 'I've just been weighted [sic]', Fabian wrote. 'Don't laugh but I'm 99.3kgs.' (That was equivalent to 15.6 stone, on Fabian's usually svelte frame.)

The doctors drained the fluid from his stomach. His torso and ankles were swollen too. Blood was taken, tests were run. The doctors warned him the drink was killing him. In the end he discharged himself.

It was early winter by then and getting colder each day. There were night shelters near Stony Stratford and emergency ones that opened up when the weather got bad enough. But they didn't like people drinking on the premises, and there was a no-dogs policy. Fabian wouldn't leave his beloved Pippet, so he stayed outside, hoping for the best. And his luck held out: another kindly Stony resident gave him a car, and he started to sleep in that.

His health slowly improved. He even managed to cut out drinking for a while. 'I have to or I'll die,' he told a friend. For a time, it looked like Fabian just might be OK.

One day in early November 2017, Estella's phone pinged with a Facebook message:

'Greetings from Nepal, top of the world!' wrote Fabian. He had followed his lifetime ambition and travelled out to south-east Asia.

'Yay, nice one Fab, you made it!' Estella replied. 'Get on the meditation and spiritual path and you'll finally find your spirit.'

'I finally did all that,' he wrote back. 'Took a while.' Fabian was on his way to recovery at last.

But from the top of the world, there was only one way to go.

By July 2018, Fabian had returned from his trip abroad and was staying in Mablethorpe, a small seaside town on the north-east coast of England. He was living there in a tent with his best friend, Mark, a soft-hearted older man with a mane of pink hair. They'd found a quiet pitch up near some grassy fields by a small church, and kept themselves secluded there.

On the morning of 7 July 2018, Fabian was acting strangely. The day before, he had been out drinking and had a run-in with the police, during which he told an officer he had taken large quantities of aspirin and ibuprofen, but he refused to go to the hospital. During the night he had vomited at least six times and in the morning he still wasn't feeling well, and now he was taking it out on Mark. Stumbling slightly, Fabian had gone to the brook nearby for a wee, but he'd lost his balance and fallen in. Mark, hearing his cries for help, had run over and pulled him out, using Pippet's lead as a kind of lasso.

Fabian was cross and snapped at Mark to leave him alone. Cursing him under his breath, Mark left Fabian and headed off to buy them some alcohol. *Maybe that'll cheer him up,* he thought. Annoyed, he found himself walking more slowly than normal, making Fabian wait.

When Mark got back to the tent, the sight waiting for him was truly horrifying. Fabian was lying, unresponsive, in a large pool of blood. There was a shower of blood droplets running down the inside of the tent canvas. The swollen veins in Fabian's oesophagus had ruptured, causing him to vomit and cough up large amounts of blood. A tragic consequence of cirrhosis of the liver.

Drug and alcohol abuse account for over a third (40 per cent) of all deaths of homeless people.[46] In fact, people living homeless are seven to nine times more likely to die from alcohol-related diseases, and twenty times more likely to die from drugs, than the general population.[47] And drug-related deaths for homeless people are on the increase.[48]

But why were things getting worse? I wanted to know, and I found myself losing days digging into the data. It turned out that in 2012 the government changed who was responsible for heroin and morphine support services, shifting the contracts from the NHS to local authorities. Heroin- and morphine-related deaths doubled over the next five years.[49]

At the same time, councils across the country had cut alcohol and drug treatment budgets by 18 per cent since

2013/14.[50] That was having an effect. By the time Fabian died, the number of people in treatment for alcohol addiction was the lowest it has been in a decade.[51]

Then there were frustrating barriers to accessing the services that still existed. 'Even the provision that is there, we can't get clients into. We get told you can't access detox services until you've had your mental health issues dealt with, and when they try to access mental health they're told they can't get help there while they are still using,' explained Mike Barrett, head of a homelessness charity in Canterbury. 'And we know all too well that addiction issues and mental health issues usually come together when people are homeless. So it's a total catch-22.'

As the weeks and months passed, I heard the same thing over and over again – from a GP in Bradford, a soup-kitchen worker in Glasgow, a youth homeless coordinator in Manchester. Across the country, people were caught in a bind, unable to get help with their addiction until their mental health needs were treated, and vice versa.

Fabian's challenges did not begin and end with his addiction issues. He had EU-citizen status, which should have come with some protection in the pre-Brexit UK, but it offered a precarious existence. Those who were working in the UK legally had access to support services, but if they lost their jobs or their work visas ran out, they forfeited their EU-treaty rights and sank into the dreaded category of 'No Recourse to Public Funds', or NRPF.[52]

I had heard of another EU national who'd been selling the *Big Issue* just as Fabian had. He'd tried to argue that selling the magazine constituted work and therefore he was not NRPF, but the council had told him that to make that argument he needed to produce formal accounts of his income from an official accountant. Unsurprisingly he didn't have these so he, like Fabian, was stuck without recourse to public funds. He died in a homeless hostel.

The NRPF label meant neither had any entitlement to welfare benefits or public housing: no housing allocation, no access to official homelessness services, no housing benefit. Without support, many ended up sleeping rough. In 2018, there were more than 3,000 European rough-sleepers all across the country. Yet more came from elsewhere.

'You hear about the hostile environment with immigration,' one homeless outreach worker had told me one day. 'Well, you want to see these people who are NRPF and living on the streets – it doesn't get much more hostile than that.'

The consequences of a lack of support can be deadly. Nearly half of all homeless people who have died in London since 2010 were non-UK nationals, of which 28 per cent were of Central or Eastern European origin.[53]

On the day of Fabian's funeral, Bob Marley songs played through the speakers as mourners filed into the crematorium. Mark had travelled in a car behind the hearse, a can of Special Brew in his hand. When he'd seen the town crier's solemn vigil, he'd leant out of the window to holler a greeting. Now, he was staggering slowly as he made his way towards the crematorium entrance. He had dressed in a long-sleeved T-shirt, jeans – and a flat cap specially for the occasion. After the service, the drink would get to him and he'd fall over.

Forty or so people gathered in the bright crematorium hall. I sat at the back, trying my best to be discreet. I was feeling deeply conflicted about being there. I wanted to learn more about Fabian and those who knew him, but this felt like an intensely personal space. I shuffled my notepad out of sight and scanned the room sadly. In the front row were Angie and Fabian's Belgian family, looking formal and out of place among the other guests.

Later, Mark stood at the front of the room. 'I was older than Fabian. I was a tutor and mentor,' he said, his voice slurring slightly. 'I taught him the ways of the world. He's like a brother from another mother. I truly miss him.' Mark paused. He was talking without notes and had momentarily lost his train of thought. His watery eyes scanned the room quickly, careful not to stray to the coffin by his side.

'I watched over his back and he watched over mine,' he continued. 'He was the brawn and I was the brains . . .' He paused, waiting for a laugh. '. . . I'm joking here! I loved him. I'm heartbroken. There is not much more I can say.'

The registrar signalled that there would be a moment of quiet reflection during which a song would play: 'My Immortal' by the band Evanescence. The melodramatic chords from the song boomed out – 'I'm so tired of being here' – and people began to cry.

Then, chaos. A man sitting on the third row fell to the floor, his fitting body shaking with withdrawal. It brought the funeral to a standstill as awkward onlookers stood helpless as he jolted out a rhythm on the crematorium's cold floor.

'It's all right man, it's OK.' Mark leant over the row of chairs to comfort his friend. 'We're all here for you, man. We all love you.'

The fallen man came to, pale and disorientated, a red welt forming on the left side of his forehead. An ambulance was called and we all sat waiting uneasily while the paramedics led the man outside.

Angie and her family stood, and one by one placed white roses on the coffin. The rest of the congregation followed suit.

As the music played and those gathered filed out, I sat in my seat, frozen. How many more funerals could I go to? How was it that no one else was here piecing together what was going wrong? There must be lessons to learn from Fabian, from Jayne. There must be ways they could have been supported, saved even. Surely, I thought, surely there should be some official way to make sure it didn't happen again?

CHAPTER 13

Lessons unlearnt

It was the smell that first drew the passers-by to Cardon's tent. Shrouded in thick overgrowth, the tarpaulin may have been lying unnoticed for weeks.

The sun was hot and high that summer day in 2016. The light played on the slow waters of the River Severn as it wound its way through the city of Worcester. But something was wrong. A staff member from the local cricket club had come out to investigate, alerted by a member of the public walking by. As he walked in the direction of the bushes he smelt it; a thick, putrid odour hung in the air, quite different from the usual mix of woodland, cut grass and river water.

Inside a dark, tattered tent, surrounded by thicket, lay Cardon Banfield. Though nobody knew that then. His body had decomposed so much he could only be identified through DNA testing. The seventy-four-year-old had partially mummified in the heat.

More than 3,000 miles away, in the Caribbean climes of Trinidad, Cardon's elderly mother Doris sat daydreaming on her porch. She had lost track of her son years ago. He had travelled across to England in 1962, back when people were encouraged to emigrate to the UK from the Caribbean, many of them on the *Windrush* ship, to fill severe labour shortages after the Second World War. Now, Doris had asked her granddaughter Faith to help find Cardon. She just wanted to know he was safe. Faith told her grandmother she would try, though she knew it would be no easy task as she didn't have many clues about the fate of her long-lost uncle. All she had were the stories her grandmother used to tell: how Cardon had loved fishing as a boy and that, growing up on the Caribbean island of St Vincent, his love of the neon-blue ocean was deep within him.

When he turned eighteen, he and his cousin got themselves jobs working on a merchant vessel on the Geest ships trade line, bound for UK shores. On board Cardon shared the ship with mountains of green and ripening bananas. He crossed the Atlantic three times and on the ship's second voyage he persuaded the captain to sign him off, as he was going to stay in the UK.

Setting out on his new life, he moved to Hackney and married a Jewish lady called Sylvia. A photo from the time shows a skinny Cardon with tan-white skin stretched across his young face, his smart dark suit contrasting nicely with his new wife's pale-pink dress.

They had a son, but then things unravelled. Back in the Caribbean the family lost touch with Cardon. They had no idea what happened next. Cardon's mother buried herself in work to survive, travelling long distances to other islands to work as a cleaner. Faith started to notice the toll her uncle's absence was taking on her. 'Seeing my mother and grandmother crying and talking about him as I got older, I decided to look,' Faith explained.

She stared at the handful of photographs her grandmother had of him. Cardon, a boy of about eight, his hair combed to a small quiff, a long thin nose that turned up at the end, giving him an almost snooty aspect, with a serious, adult-like look in his eye. Who had that boy become? Where was he now? Intrigued, Faith had sent registered letters to the two addresses they had for Cardon, both in east London, but the letters were returned undelivered. So she had set up a profile on the genealogy website Ancestry.com and when that had yielded no results she'd resorted to asking the Red Cross for help – but that too proved a dead-end. 'I looked up records in the UK for deaths and any news that would link me to him. I came up empty-handed all the time,' she recalled.

Back in the UK, the coroner's office had finally managed to identify Cardon, matching his DNA to a police file from a robbery he had committed years earlier. Stories appeared in the local newspaper and the police appealed for next of kin, but they found no one.

So while Cardon was put to rest with a council-paid pauper's funeral, questions remained around how an old man could come to die such a horrifying death with no one looking out for him, no one caring.

But while it may have been too late to save him, Cardon was about to get his own personal champion.

These days Hugo Sugg could be mistaken for any hip, city postgraduate. A backwards-turned baseball cap and large ear-piercings helped him blend in to the hyper-trendy north London neighbourhood he lived in. But Hugo was not like many of those around him. He was a staunch Conservative for one thing, a fact that marked him out from many other twenty-somethings in the area. As did the fact that he used to be homeless. Ten years ago, when he was in his late teens, he had become very familiar with the homeless services in Worcester, where he was living.

Years later, once he'd found a home, Hugo continued to volunteer at the Worcester YMCA night shelter that had saved him. That's where he met Cardon. Hugo would be manning reception and Cardon, who was staying there at the time, would stop by for a chat, telling him meandering tales of his time in the merchant navy in the Caribbean. Cardon had been homeless for decades. He moved from place to place, having done so since 1966. 'He was a really interesting guy, really talkative,' Hugo remembered later.

Cardon left the YMCA not long after, and that was the last Hugo saw of him. But he never forgot the quiet, elderly man who had told him such colourful tales.

Years later, Hugo opened up the local newspaper to find the shocking tale of a man mummified and forgotten, dead in a tent. *I know that name*, Hugo thought, staring wide-eyed at the page: *that's Cardon from the shelter*.

That's when it started. A quest that would last for years: Hugo's attempt to get justice for Cardon.

In October 2016, days after the coroner had officially identified Cardon's body, Hugo went to the local press. 'What happened is not good enough,' he told a reporter at the *Worcester News*. 'I understand that people die, but that isn't the issue. The biggest issue was that he died when there was a service that was meant to support him. Lessons must be learnt. There is no excuse for what happened, absolutely no excuse. I'm not going to let this go, because otherwise Cardon will have died in vain.'

Incensed, Hugo wrote to the county council and at first it seemed as though they'd taken note. Council members referred the case to the local Safeguarding Adult Board, a body made up of council staff, police, doctors and social workers that looks into possible negligence or concerns around the deaths of vulnerable people. They usually focus on things like deaths of those in care, but they would be perfectly placed to ask questions about what had happened to Cardon.

But just a month later, Hugo's hopes were dashed. A letter arrived in the post from the board: they were turning down the request for a review. 'Firstly, Mr Banfield was deemed to, at his own choice, only have had very limited involvement with services in Worcestershire,' the letter read. 'Secondly it became very clear from the information gathered that he had actually spent very little time in Worcestershire prior to his death . . . It would therefore not be appropriate to commission a safe-guarding adults review, as we don't believe there to have been a lost multi-agency opportunity to work with the gentleman.'

Hugo stared at the letter, his mouth agape. So that was it? No more questions asked? No lessons learnt?

Seven months later, the Board reconsidered the decision, but once again they decided there was no cause for a review.

It was in the basement office of a London-based charity that I first got to grips with the idea of Safeguarding Adult Reviews.

Since Jayne's and Fabian's funerals, I had found myself on a mission to understand why no one was learning any lessons from these deaths. My questions had brought me to Jeremy Swain.

We sat in his warm office, the sounds of children playing drifting in from the nursery building next door. 'You want to be here when they start singing "The Wheels On The Bus",' Jeremy joked. 'It can get stuck in your head for hours.' Jeremy was head of Thames Reach, a homelessness charity that runs hostels as well as having outreach services. Although we didn't know it at the time, Jeremy would soon be seconded to the government, where he'd become Deputy Director of Homelessness & Rough Sleeping Delivery at the Ministry of Housing, Communities & Local Government, part of a team tasked with fulfilling the government's goal of eradicating rough-sleeping by 2027. When I met him, he was angry.

Jeremy had worked in homelessness for thirty-eight years,

and people dying while homeless was, sadly, nothing new. There was a way lessons could be learnt, however; a method that was being missed. 'Safeguarding Adult Reviews – that's how you do it', said Jeremy, matter-of-factly. 'And the solutions come from what you find.'

He wasn't the only one calling for them. Many experts had suggested these reviews could be the mechanism through which homeless deaths were looked into. After all, bringing together social workers, council officers, police and doctors would be a way to piece together, in a fractured system, just who was supporting the homeless person and what more help could have been offered.

But such investigations take time and resources. A simple review can cost around £8,250 – if the case is complicated, then the cost rises. Many boards were working with councils whose budgets were stretched. And the statutory government-written guidelines did not explicitly say reviews for rough-sleepers were mandatory – simply that they were recommended if there were suspicions of neglect or that council services failed in their duties.

But they just weren't happening. 'I can think of one or two,' Jeremy said with a sigh. 'But look, it's enormously disappointing that there are so few examples. It unfortunately leads me to the disturbing conclusion that the death of someone sleeping rough is viewed as less important than that of a housed person, or can be waved aside because of a misapprehension that the person has made an informed choice to sleep rough.'

I left obsessing over that idea. Was it really the case that reviews weren't happening?

Back in my office I got researching. It turned out there was no centralized database of reviews, so it was almost impossible to know if and when they were happening. I was stuck. But then I realized I had something that no one else did: a list of people who had died homeless that year – my database held scores and scores of names at that point. I could ask each and every council where a homeless person had died if there had been or would be a review.

So I got started, sending a message to every council where there had been a homeless death, asking how many of the cases had been officially looked into and how many reviews had taken place over previous years.

Weeks later, as each reply came in, I stared at my screen in dismay. It turned out not a single official review had been started or completed for any of the deaths I had logged. And across all the councils in England and Wales, there were just eight official reviews into homeless deaths by any Safeguarding Adult Board since 2010, an average of one a year.

Cardon's was not one of those.

As the months passed, Hugo became more and more of a thorn in the side of local councillors. He was demanding an official review into Cardon's death and he just wouldn't take no for an answer.

Hugo would call people out on Twitter, bombard them with emails or post sections from email correspondence online. On his website he had gone further. 'Due to incompetence shown by the following names, we are calling for the resignation or dismissal from their positions with immediate effect,' he wrote, followed by a list of names and email addresses of people he believed to be in some way responsible for Cardon's death.

I couldn't help but feel uneasy with the way Hugo had been going about his mission. He was driven, that was clear, but there was a lot of emotion there too. That kind of thinking can cloud your judgement.

But I had to give it to him. He was tenacious, and he was meticulously mapping the officials' attempts to shirk any responsibility. He had forwarded me a local news article in which a council spokesperson had been anonymously quoted as saying: 'Sadly Mr Banfield was not known to the city council as he never approached us for housing support.' That had not sounded right to Hugo; he knew Cardon had stayed in the YMCA when he was working there in 2014, and that most people paid the £29-a-week charge through housing benefit. So he had put in a Freedom of Information request to the council and, weeks later, in his inbox, there it was – proof: Cardon's application to the council for Housing Benefit, marked as April 2014 and with the address of the YMCA.

'You see!' Hugo told me. The form showed Cardon had been known to the council, at least in the years before his death.

In fact, it turned out Cardon had been on the council's books for years, popping up repeatedly over the last decade. He had been registered for housing benefit in Worcestershire in 2004 and 2005. Back then he was staying in the Berwick Hotel, a B & B in the city, which had since closed. In early 2005 he left that property and may have moved thirty miles south, to Gloucester. After that he went to Birmingham, where he stayed in B & B accommodation used by the council before moving into a shared house. He left when he had 'had enough'.

He slept rough for three years, and by May 2013 he was back in Worcester and on the radar of the local homeless outreach team. By 2014 he was in the YMCA, chatting away to Hugo.

While Hugo remembered Cardon to be a friendly old soul, others recalled that he had seemed troubled. Cardon could be offensive to the staff and other residents, using racist slurs, and he had been told off for trying to bring cannabis into the dry shelter. One day he sat scrawling on a housing benefit letter, covering the page with notes about religion, brainwashing and various disjointed and random subjects, the angry scrawl hinting at mental health troubles.

Putting all this together, I couldn't help but wonder why this man, in his seventies, was being housed in a hostel environment, where his needs must have been lost among the fifty or so guests and the handful of staff. Surely there were more appropriate places to support him – a council flat or supported-living facility?

I could never be sure, but it was poignant to me that in the years before his death the UK government's hostile environment policy had started to target those who had arrived as part of the Windrush generation. People like Cardon, who had been in the UK for more than forty years, were being told they had no right to remain. Some ended up homeless and sleeping rough. Healthcare was being denied, deportations had started. I don't know if Cardon was affected or whether it stopped him from accessing services, but it wasn't beyond the realms of possibility.

For those who found themselves homeless and without legal immigration status, deportation was a real threat. The Home Office had seconded immigration enforcement officers into many councils' housing departments, and national homeless charity St Mungo's had come under fire for passing the details of rough-sleepers to immigration enforcement teams, leading to deportations.* I kept hearing how all that had created a feeling of fear and suspicion of authority for those

---

*   St Mungo's apologized after initially refuting the claim. The *Guardian* reported that 'an internal review found that one of [St Mungo's] 18 outreach teams continued to share information with the Home Office between July 2016 and February 2017. Sharing information about rough-sleepers was in contravention of St Mungo's own policy at the time.' Diane Taylor, 'Charity Says Sorry for Giving Rough Sleepers' Details to Home Office', *Guardian*, 5 November 2019, https://www.theguardian.com/uk-news/2019/nov/05/charity-st-mungos-says-sorry-for-giving-rough-sleepers-details-to-home-office

whose immigration status might be at risk. It was pushing people underground, further and further away from any kind of help.

As a result, many non-UK citizens who found themselves homeless were being driven into exploitative situations. In Bradford it was working on chicken farms. In Northampton it was long hours and poor wages in packing factories. In Luton people were trying to pick up the odd labouring shift here and there while sleeping in old warehouses on the outskirts of the town, where tuberculosis and other illnesses were spreading like wildfire in the unsanitary conditions.

Had Cardon been turned down for services because his immigration status had been called into question? Or had he taken himself out of contact because of his own mental health issues? I couldn't be sure.

What I did know was that Cardon was last spotted at Maggs Day Centre, which provides food and a place to rest, on 16 March 2016. Right around that time, the council was changing their homeless outreach team providers. The old service, known as the Worcestershire Homeless Intervention Team (WHIT), had stopped taking new referrals earlier than was planned and the new provider wasn't ready to take over, leaving a gap in provision. The new service had never heard of Cardon, so when he disappeared no one was looking for him.

His mummified body was found on 5 July. There was no sign of what happened in the four months in between.

Faith was on holiday when she heard. An email dropped into her inbox from Yasni.co.uk, a site that helps you search for mentions of someone online. Clicking on the email, she saw the bad news: the newspaper report about Cardon's death. And there in the story, someone voicing the sadness and outrage she felt: Hugo's name. Curious, she found Hugo's email address and reached out.

Other than Hugo, no one else spoke to her or her family about Cardon's death. 'I wish they had tried harder to find his family but I don't know what information he gave or if he was ever asked,' she told the *Worcester News*.

Faith didn't know what to do. She was scared of telling her frail, ninety-four-year-old grandmother, for fear the grief would be more than she could bear. It was hard to offer Faith any comfort. I didn't want to tell her that I had heard of more people that had died like Cardon, left rotting to the point that they had to be identified through dental records or DNA, in that year alone. Kenneth, a sixty-four-year-old who was found in a field by his tent in Leeds. Or sixty-nine-year-old Philip in Bristol, whose skeletal remains were found in an abandoned building. All of these people dying in terrible circumstances and no reviews happening.

But Hugo wasn't going to give up on Cardon. He was determined to get an official review into the pensioner's death. 'I see it as a personal mission now,' he told me. 'I can't let them get away with it. I'm not going to let it lie.'

Sometimes it takes just one person to take enough interest to make the difference between people being forgotten or getting justice. And soon I would hear how sometimes it also takes just one person to keep them alive.

The night was cold and wet when David, the army veteran, decided he'd had enough – David, who had tried to do everything right, who had presented to all the right people, all to no avail. The council had turned him down months ago and he had been living in his car ever since. But it was all too much. He couldn't see a way out. Earlier in the day he had returned to the council offices, but they couldn't help him with a place to stay. He still wasn't 'priority need'.

He hadn't eaten in at least a day. His soaking clothes hung heavy and oppressive on his thin frame. His mind was foggy, his body moving as if of its own accord. He didn't know quite what drew him down the dark path to squeeze through the gates and into Isledon Road Gardens, but he found himself there at around 4 a.m. It was cold at that time of early morning, just before dawn, when the temperature drops to its lowest. The courtyard in the gardens was quiet, its brick walls shielding the space from the outside world. The trees softly waved their skeletal branches in the wind. Hungry, cold and alone, David sunk down onto one of the courtyard's benches. It all came rushing out, all the pain of the last few years, the illnesses that had sucker-punched his body, one after another: the stroke, cancer, HIV. He felt the sorrow come shuddering out of him in bursts and sobs. He cried and rocked until an idea formed in his mind, as clear as the moon appearing through the clouds. There was a way out, the only option he could see: he was going to put an end to it.

David scrabbled in his pockets. Earlier in the day he had bought a stash of crystal meth from a dealer down in Finsbury Park, north London. It was more than he needed, and enough for this. Shaking, David pulled out the needle and tugged at his wet coat sleeve. The sobs kept coming. The needle was poised.

'What the fuck are you doing?'

David's head heaved upwards up at the voice. There, walking quickly towards him, was a man in a luminous vest. A park enforcement agent called Gavin Judd.

Gavin shouldn't really have been there that day – it wasn't a park the wardens usually had issues with, so he rarely checked on it. 'But for some strange reason that day I decided to do that park,' he recalled later. As he'd made his way down the path he had become aware of the shaking shape on the bench opposite, a man messing around with something in his hand. Gavin realized it was a syringe. Instinct kicked in. 'Here, what are you doing?' he called out, in his east London twang.

David couldn't reply, the sobs were still shaking his body, he told me later. He couldn't even look Gavin in the eyes. But he lowered the needle.

'Come on, what's wrong? I might be able to help you,' Gavin said to David.

'No, you can't. No one can help me,' said David through the tears.

But over the next hour or two, Gavin sat there, on the bench beside him, and the two men talked. David told him everything. The heartbreak of his partner leaving him, the shame that had led him to flee from the unpaid rent and his flat, the sleepless nights in the car, the stroke, the medical complaints that had crashed down on him like waves. Gavin listened quietly. He saw a lot of homeless people in the parks he looked after; he had the numbers for local hostels saved in his phone. And he had come to realize that, more than anything, most people he came across just wanted to be seen, to be recognized as a person. 'I don't think I did anything that overwhelming,' Gavin confided to me later, giving a sheepish laugh. 'I just sat down and talked to him.' It turned out that this was all David needed.

'There was something unique about him,' David would later remember. 'He wasn't bullish, he just was calm and sat with me.' Hours passed. The sun rose tentatively behind them.

'Come on,' Gavin said, pulling himself up from the cold bench. 'Here's a tenner, let's get you some food.'

The pair walked down the road, shivering in the cold, to a nearby supermarket where David gratefully bought what he could. While he shopped, Gavin found the number of a local shelter and called them up. 'If he can be at this address at 6.30 p.m. tonight I can help him,' the manager had told him. David was dumbfounded. Suddenly he had been offered an option, a choice.

Later, standing outside the shelter, he remembered feeling petrified. Going in felt like accepting failure, but if he didn't do it he knew it was only a matter of time before he ended up back on that park bench. Breathing deeply, David walked forward, pushed open the door and walked inside.

It was years later that I sat with David in that same park courtyard where his story had almost ended. The sun was high then, the grass resplendently verdant, and David was sketching in his notepad when I arrived. He had drawn a scratchy image of the children's play area that stood just beyond the courtyard's walls, dark lines etched onto the white paper. 'I hadn't noticed it that night I came in here. I don't know if it was the dark or what, but I didn't see it. That still haunts me now,' he paused, tearing up. 'The idea that . . . that it could have been a child that found me . . . I can't forgive myself for that. It was so fucking selfish.'

David credits Gavin with saving his life. The conversation that night turned everything around. 'I asked him, "Why on earth did you stop?" I'm not sure I could have done that. He just said that there was something about the way I was that wasn't right, he knew I was in trouble. Still . . .'

While staying in the shelter, David had been put on another waiting list for military veterans' housing. He had been expecting the same kind of waits he had been warned of previously, so he was bowled over when, a few weeks later, he was told he'd been found a flat, a little place near Euston station.

In his new home, David grew stronger. He put on weight, he got his head clear. Life was looking up; the heartbreak, the illness was surmountable. He marched in the London Pride parade soon after, happy to put aside his concerns about the commercialization of the event to support the Outside Project, an organization for LGBTQ+ people experiencing homelessness that would later set up the first LGBTQ+-specific homeless hostel.[54]

From there, David had built his career as an artist. As his strength grew, so too did his creativity. He exhibited photographs he had taken while sleeping in his car and painted powerful oil paintings of the people he had met while homeless. The work was well received.

He started working with Clothing the Homeless, who use art as a way to help people experiencing homelessness, and with them David created a catwalk collection of garments he made from materials he had found on the streets, like the covering of an armchair, plastic sheeting, things he'd spotted and snatched up like a magpie in the days when he had nothing. He set up the One Festival of Homeless Arts, a space to exhibit the work of other artists who had experienced homelessness. One September day he and others from the project walked the length of London's Southbank, putting on their own impromptu fashion show. Crowds gathered and then began to follow David's path. At last people were listening.

In January, just as I was starting my mission to count homeless deaths, David was displaying his work in the Tate Liverpool gallery. He set up mannequins in army fatigues and berets, with gaffa tape over their mouths, and lined them up facing the bold, white wall of the gallery room. On the back of each of the army jackets he had printed text, stories of veterans who had struggled on leaving the forces and ended up homeless.

Later he worked with an organization called the Museum of Homelessness on an exhibition displaying important possessions from people experiencing homelessness. (I had been tickled to see Richard turn his used inhalers into artwork for the event: the L-shaped plastic forms were arranged in a loop, creating a circle, one nestled in to the next. It was entitled *The Roundabout* and was displayed alongside other objects that told stories about homeless people's lives.)

Life was looking up for David, and it had all started with a conversation, with someone seeing him.

*

The sun was bright and Stony Stratford high street was awash with colour and noise. An old-fashioned fairground ride blasted out cheesy, garish versions of out-of-date pop hits. Down the road, a group of Morris dancers lined up, jingled their bells, waved their handkerchiefs and trotted out their dances. It was an unusual scene, a simulacrum of British life. But it was not the fair that had brought me back to this Milton Keynes town.

Down the road, battling to be heard over the drone of a merry-go-round, Estella was prompting the town crier forward, the same man who, months earlier, had come out to herald the hearse carrying Fabian's body to the crematorium. He was pleased to do it, he told me; he had felt a kinship with Fabian, having spent time living in squats himself. 'It was like going back and meeting an old friend. There was nothing selfish about Fabian,' he said. 'When you don't have anything, you have nothing to be stolen, so you give yourself to everyone. He was such an open bloke.'

He stepped forward and swung a heavy bell, its peal cutting through the noise of the fairground rides that surrounded us. 'Hear ye, hear ye!' he shouted. 'Good people of Stony Stratford and welcome visitors, please fall silent for the unveiling of the new plaque dedicated to the life of Stony's very own celebrity and personality, Mr Fabian Bayet.'

Taking her cue, Estella cut through the ribbon strung across a large, sheet-covered frame attached to the wall. Reaching up, she pulled down the sheet, revealing an attractive black and white painting of Fabian and his dog Pippet. A murmur of appreciation passed through the crowd.

'It really does look like him,' one woman smiled.

'Do you remember the whippet?' a mother asked her young daughter.

Estella and her friends were determined that they were not

going to forget Fabian. This artwork would be a lasting memorial to the man who had brightened up their lives. Fabian's image would remain there, watching over the same spot where he had sold the *Big Issue* magazine for so many years.

But Fabian was unusual. There were scores of people just like him who were living and dying without anyone taking half as much notice. As Estella stood back to admire the picture, across the road stood a dark-haired, solemn-looking Eastern European man with an armful of copies of the *Big Issue* magazine. Fabian's replacement. The town hadn't taken to him the way they had the 'Belgian Waffle'. Despite the crowds, no one was buying today.

What was is that had made Estella see Fabian, to stop that very first time for a chat? What compelled Gavin to walk over to David's sobbing form when he could have just as easily walked on by? It was easier to keep one's head down, headphones on, mobile phone screen up, an armour against the outside world. For years that had been my routine; living in a big city, it sometimes felt as though the only means of survival was to just shut off from world around me – the only way to stay sane. But in the days and weeks after Jayne's and Fabian's funerals, I found myself walking the streets chastened. I still didn't know what I could do to be of use, but I knew it was harder and harder to walk past people and not even say hello. Every person I saw huddled on the pavement could be a Jayne or a David or a Fabian. Their loved ones could be sitting at home worrying about them. They could be crying out for the one moment of intervention they needed to save themselves.

That shift in thinking was making walking on by harder, yet I couldn't believe I had ever felt differently. How could I have been so completely inured?

I wanted to find out. Which is how I ended up in Dr Lasana Harris's office.

*

In a cupboard-like room in the brutalist, grey, concrete building of University College London, Dr Lasana Harris, a lecturer in social cognition and experimental psychology, was explaining why a question about broccoli could be the answer to how we dehumanize homeless people.

'Sometimes it just takes a simple question like that to change the way people think,' he grinned. His big smile, coupled with a casual T-shirt, made it easy to forget Lasana was an internationally respected professor, though while we talked a student waited patiently on a plastic chair outside his office door, hoping to consult him.

Around twelve years ago, as a young doctoral graduate, Lasana had stumbled onto an idea that had shaped the course of his research ever since. Working at Princeton University, in the USA, he had been working on a project about people's perceptions of various images. He had developed a test: one by one undergraduates were shown to an MRI scanner. They lay down, their head and shoulders surrounded by the scanner's tomb-like tube. Images would flick up on a screen before them for six seconds at a time – picture after picture of people who looked archetypal: a businessman in a suit, an old person in a comfy cardigan, a homeless person with a sleeping bag. Dozens of photos. As each image flicked by, the scanner would take readings of activations in the brain, registering blood-oxygen levels. The activated areas of the brain showed which parts of the brain were being used at what time.

The experiment was designed to see if we receive unique brain signals when we see different types of people, but when Lasana ran the data what he found was astonishing.

For each of the photos, the students' medial prefrontal cortex had been activated just as he had expected, but with the photos of homeless people a completely different part of the brain had been activated: the left insula and the right amygdala. Lasana held his breath. These parts of the brain were sparked when someone sees an object, not a person. 'The neural evidence supports the prediction that extreme out-groups may be perceived as less than human,' Lasana wrote in the resulting research paper. People saw homeless people as objects.

Excited, Lasana repeated the study again and again. It kept showing the same thing. And this wasn't just particularly callous people thinking like this; it was shockingly pervasive. 'If you're a regular person off the street and we stick you in this MRI, the chances are you'll display this dehumanization,' Lasana explained.

Now, more than a decade later, he was still working on this issue: 'We weren't looking for it, which is the funny thing with science. It was just an accidental finding, but it ended up being something significant, and I've spent my entire career following it. It's called dehumanized perception. It's the idea that, typically, when you encounter other people, you spontaneously try to figure out what they're thinking, and you do this for a couple of reasons. Firstly, it allows you to explain and predict their behaviour, but secondly it allows you to impression-manage – you get a sense of what they think of you. As human beings we care a lot about what other people think of us, even strangers. What dehumanized perception captures is a failure to do so, so that's what we see typically when we see homeless people. We think it is because people engage in empathy avoidance – you make a prediction that thinking about that person's mind is going to be uncomfortable, or sad and depressing; you may not feel like you have the capacity to help them. So instead of feeling guilty and terrible, you just fail to think about their mind at all.'

I thought back to the first time I had gone to meet Jon at a Streets Kitchen event. That had been me, scared to know what I'd find, panicked about how I would talk to someone who was sleeping rough. Their lives were so totally different to mine, I didn't know where to start. I knew for sure that had Dr Harris scanned my brain that first day he would have found me switched off to their humanity, seeing things and objects far different from me. And then I'd met Richard and David and Angie. And I realized how much we had in common, how we weren't existing in two different worlds, but one.

'It is a strangely culturally specific phenomenon,' Lasana continued. 'We see this dehumanization happening towards people that are homeless in Western meritocratic societies, and it may be something to do with that idea that if you are struggling it is your own fault.'

'The pull yourself up by the boot-straps idea?' I chipped in.

'Exactly,' he smiled, explaining how, in the USA and the UK, the pervasive narrative is that you are the master of your own destiny, an idea often proffered as the positive 'American dream' but one which comes with the insidious underbelly of blame if things go wrong.

Elsewhere things were different. 'In Japan the studies show a much higher level of empathy towards the homeless, manifesting not as disgust but pity. And that might be because it is a country that has experienced extreme economic and natural disasters. Many people have found themselves homeless so they can empathize with others.'

The issue, Lasana explained, was that the empathetic void, that lack of recognition of another person's very humanity, can manifest itself in different ways. 'The dehumanized get both active and passive harm: we ignore them – that is the passive harm – but we will also actively attack them.'

It was this kind of dehumanization that could explain the terrible things humans do to one another: the Rwandan genocide, colonialization, human slavery, the Holocaust. 'Yes,' I interjected. 'I've heard about that dehumanizing model being applied – you know, on the far end of the scale, to describe how people come to commit atrocities, crimes against humanity.'

'It is not that far, actually,' said Lasana, 'They are all part of the same psychological processes – we think they are exactly the same. The processes you have when you pass a homeless person on the street are the same processes that we think are active when you're committing genocide. The behaviour may seem very different, but in terms of what is happening in the brain, we think they are exactly the same.'

As Lasana spoke, my mind drifted to the haunting image of a red outline on a brick wall. Michael Cash, a skinny, bearded thirty-two-year-old had been sleeping rough since his mother's death twelve years earlier. He was sitting outside a shop in Teesside when a man walked up to him and sprayed him with red paint from a water pistol, leaving a halo of red and a ghostly patch of negative space on the wall behind him.

The assailant, Aaron Jones, had posted a video of the attack on Facebook. In it his voice could be heard saying: 'This is how we deal with the beggars on the street. He's not even a beggar. There he is, sprayed to death.' He didn't know how true those words were. Four days later Michael killed himself in a nearby graveyard. He had refused to report the incident to the police.

Aaron Jones was convicted of assault. The judge heard how he had taken umbrage at people begging in the town and had posted a photo of Michael before, with the caption: 'It's about time this spice head got moved, smile for the camera.'

I could only imagine that Aaron hadn't seen a person when he aimed his paint-filled water pistol at Michael – he'd seen a beggar, 'a spice head', an object. The attack seemed to be as much on the concept of 'the homeless' as anything that Michael had personally done.

I had heard story after story of similar cruel acts. The man sprayed with water by train station attendants. The drunken party-goer who drop-kicked his entire weight into an unsuspecting person's tent. The people that urinated on those sleeping rough. Those that set people's sleeping bags on fire, their victims prostrate and unsuspecting inside. An Instagram account, set up under the name Local.nittys, that posted video after video of homeless people being verbally assaulted or hurt. One man sprayed a homeless person with a fire extinguisher while friends, filming on phones, laugh hysterically. In another, a man used an acoustic guitar to whack a homeless man slumped unconscious and unsuspecting on a bench. The anonymous account garnered 12,300 followers before it was taken down.

The lack of empathy Dr Lasana was documenting explained a lot, but the fact that it was so common, almost a natural occurrence, scared me. Were we hardwired to dehumanize the homeless? I took a deep breath. 'Is there . . . Is there some way to retrain our brains?' I asked nervously.

As it turned out, the way to get a different result was baffling in its simplicity. While his participants in the MRI scanner looked at the photographs of rough-sleepers, Lasana asked them an easy question: whether the person in the image would like broccoli or carrots. Suddenly the data changed, the subjects started to see the homeless people as humans. 'To think about the vegetables, you have to get inside of their heads,' he explained, 'and that is the crux of empathy.

'The vegetable question showed the issue isn't hardwired

in the brain – it is exactly the opposite. The brain is extremely elastic and can adapt very easily. So if you're in a soup kitchen and you're feeding people, you're going to see them more as people.' Indeed, after taking subjects to soup kitchens between scanning their brains, Lasana noticed massive differences in his result.

I sat up straighter. That finding excited me. If you could reawaken people's perceptions of homeless people as human, maybe you could improve the lives of those who found themselves on the streets.

As I left Lasana's office, I thought about how guilty I had been of dehumanizing those who I walked past. How often I had switched off my human empathy, perhaps as a coping mechanism to allow me to simply walk down the street without my heart breaking. Now I realized that the consequence of that shutdown was taking its toll on society. As inequality rose year on year, we had started erasing from view whole subsets of our neighbourhoods.

That same thinking, the lack of compassion, had tipped over into public policy. I had heard how legal action was being taken to regularly castigate people living homeless. People were being arrested and charged for sleeping rough, or for suspected begging.

Often, the criminal justice system was relying on the Dickensian Vagrancy Act 1824, which made it a criminal offence to sleep 'in any deserted or unoccupied building, or in the open air, or under a tent, or in any cart or waggon, not having any visible means of subsistence'. The law had been introduced to deal with growing homelessness after the Napoleonic wars but had later been criticized by abolitionist William Wilberforce for being far too broad and blunt a tool. It had been repealed in Northern Ireland and Scotland but still remains in force in England and Wales.

In recent years things had gone further, with the introduction of Public Spaces Protection Orders (PSPOs) in 2014 which made it possible to ban people from certain areas of a town or city. Now those orders were being routinely used to stop people from sleeping rough or begging, and led to a £100 on-the-spot fine or a prosecution and £1,000 bill if you couldn't pay there and then. Those banning orders could keep people from the very areas where the few homeless services were offered, preventing them from accessing soup kitchens or medical help. Across the country, 10,000 on-the-spot fines of up to £100 were handed out in one year alone.[55]

In Conwy, Wales, a fifty-five-year-old woman was sent to prison for six weeks for begging outside a shop after she'd already been banned on a criminal behaviour order. Jon had been furious when he had heard about that case. 'There were no complaints of anti-social behaviour about this woman. She was banned from sitting down for ten minutes. That's probably where her social life is,' he told a national paper. 'This is happening more and more across the UK. They say they're trying to rid the town centre of the blight of beggars and whatnot, but it's mainly an attack on homeless people. It's just to remove poverty from the streets.'

I feared he was right. I had collected a long list of similar cases. Like the man in Gloucester who was sent to prison after he repeatedly broke an order banning him from begging in the city centre. The judge at his trial admitted he was conflicted in the ruling: 'it is a persistent disobedience of court orders but I will be sending a man to prison for asking for food when he was hungry,' he said. He did it anyway.

In Carlisle, a thirty-three-year-old man had to pay £105 in court costs after he was found to have been begging. The man argued he had just been sitting in the city centre when a child dropped two £1 coins into his lap.

Another man had been fined £150 after the police caught him begging – in court it had been referred to as 'gathering money for alms'. The fine was being taken out of his benefits, leaving him with less and less money each month, ironically pushing him closer to begging again.

So people sleeping rough were being fined, taking the little money they had, or imprisoned.

The consequence was that many of those sleeping rough no longer trusted the police or wider authorities to look out for them.[56] Their very presence had become a crime.

Danger was all around, from the public to the police. People sleeping rough were being beaten up, fined, ridiculed and imprisoned.

But I was soon to learn that the threats were not just external – they came too from other people also experiencing homelessness. Across the country, people were bedding down knowing those around them had mental health issues or else were high on drugs or drink. Each night became a gamble. Sometimes you lost.

CHAPTER 15

Violence on the streets

Sergio smiled calmly, his face projected large on the TV screen as the judge leant towards him, checking she had heard his plea correctly.

'You are pleading not guilty?' she asked.

'Yes,' said Sergio, and there was that smile again, seemingly knocking the judge off guard.

'Thank you very much,' she replied.

'You're welcome,' beamed Sergio, as if the whole exchange had been nothing more innocuous than asking for the time.

It was mid-August and Lewes Crown Court was buzzing with action. I had just about caught my breath as I pushed open the door of the building. The walk from the station had involved a steep hill, and I was worrying about running late as I hastily tipped open my bag for the security men at the door. The white stone exterior of the building hid a rather shabbier inside. As I had scrambled up staircases and marched along corridors, I had noted the grey gaffa tape holding together the fraying edges of the claret-red carpet.

These halls had held murderers and innocent men, top barristers and newly qualified lawyers. It was in this court-house that the killer of Sarah Payne was tried and convicted. In the 1940s it had been the place where justice had finally caught up with John Haigh, a serial killer notorious for disposing of his victims' bodies in a bath of acid.

Courtroom Three was bright. I found an empty spot on the hardwood benches at the back of the chamber and scrabbled around in my bag for a pen and notepad. Around me, people filed into the public docks.

'It's cold in here,' a middle-aged blonde lady said to the man sat next to her, crossing her arms tightly against the breeze from the hard-working air conditioner.

'I'm still fuming about that satnav taking us through Tunbridge,' her husband replied.

A digital clock behind the judge's bench clicked to 10:00. A door opened and in bustled Judge Christine Laing, a round-faced woman with dark hair and rosy cheeks.

I shifted uncomfortably in my seat. For an hour my pen remained poised above my notepad as the court dealt with a series of administrative issues: the tardiness of a psychiatric report needed for a future trial; the consequences for a young man who had missed a probation hearing. I have often found in my reporting that courtrooms are not the high-stakes, nail-biting theatres of drama that television might lead us to believe. There is no gavel-banging (British judges don't use the things), rarely screamed accusations. No, instead it is calendar-checking, paperwork-shuffling, and British reserved politeness.

So I had almost started daydreaming when the court clerk announced the next case: the plea hearing of Sergio Lemori. He had been charged with murder.

The manicured gardens of Brighton's Royal Pavilion museum nestled around the ostentatiously sculpted domes of the Pavilion building, its towers and minarets making it Brighton's very own Taj Mahal. The grounds always stayed open throughout the night so there were hours when the paths were traversed in meandering zigzags by merry partygoers heading home to bed. But by the early morning it was often just the occasional fox, snuffling through the hedgerows, that kept the late-night security guard company. That and the handful of men that would sleep out there, tucked into dark corners.

One of them was Andrew O'Connell.

The evening of 7 August 2018 was warm and balmy. Martin, the security guard on duty that night, wasn't long into his shift when he saw Andrew rolling out his sleeping bag and settling down in the doorway of the Pavilion's museum. It wasn't unusual – Andrew would often sleep there. The roof of the doorway's porch stuck out a good two metres, its edges replete with scrolled, ornate carvings hanging down like icicles. The spot was sheltered and provided not only a warm little enclave out of the elements but an impressive view of the Pavilion's main domed roof, bulbous and glowing in the grounds' uplights. And there, built securely into one of the porch's corners: a CCTV camera casting a watchful eye across the whole doorway.

Andrew had been using the spot for a while. He had an understanding with the security team: it was fine for him to sleep there in the doorway as long as he was up and gone by the time guests arrived in the morning. He had always been polite to the staff – 'humble' was how one of them described him to me. When the Pavilion gardens had been cordoned off for the annual Pride festival the week before, Andrew had gratefully thanked staff anyway, before heading off to find somewhere else to stay. The festival had finished two days previously so now Andrew was back in his usual spot, curled up in his sleeping bag. He was fast asleep.

So, as Martin made his usual way round the gardens, he thought nothing of it when he saw Andrew that night. But when Andrew was still there in the morning, Martin was confused. He checked the time – it was almost 7 a.m. Andrew was usually long gone by then. The security guard walked slowly over to the bulky shape in the doorway and called out to him to get up. The sleeping figure did not respond. It was only then he noticed the paving stone, a chunk about a foot long and three inches thick. Mottled grey with some light mossy patches, it lay incongruously near the opening of the sleeping bag. Then he spotted the blood, lots of it, matted into Andrew's dark hair and down his face. There was more coming from his left ear.

A low groan emanated from Andrew's lips. He was still breathing. He stirred slightly but didn't open his eyes. An ambulance was called. He was rushed to hospital.

The CCTV caught the whole thing on camera. At 12.56 a.m. it shows Andrew sleeping soundly in the porchway. Then, out of the darkness, a slim black man comes into shot. He is wearing shorts that show off a wine-glass shaped tattoo on his lower left leg. His T-shirt has a distinctive 'I ♥ London' logo on the back. He is carrying a brown holdall; it appears heavy.

Slowly the man walks towards Andrew's sleeping body, treading carefully, seemingly keen not to wake him. He places the bag on the floor and pulls from it a heavy hunk of stone, perhaps a piece of paving slab or something old, like you'd find in a graveyard.

Without waking the sleeping man, he lifts the stone up and brings it down heavily on Andrew's head.

The man then walks away a few steps before stopping, looking around and then turning back. Again, he lifts the stone up and brings it crashing down. He does so twice more.

Between the third and fourth blows the camera shows Andrew moving slightly. The fourth blow is the hardest. Andrew stops moving. And then the man walks away.

Andrew O'Connell was a wanderer. The fifty-four-year-old had a flat, a small place in Maidstone, Kent, but he had left it a while back, taking off during the summer months to travel around the UK. He'd arrived in Brighton a few weeks earlier, just before the annual Pride march, an event that draws visitors from far and wide. Since then he'd kept himself to himself.

He was affable enough. One police officer recalled speaking to him a few days before the attack. He'd told her his name and that he was 'travelling round the world'. Each Sunday Andrew would make his way to a soup kitchen run by Jim Deans. 'He was a friendly chap,' Jim told me. 'A really nice guy, you know.'

Jim had arrived at the Royal Sussex hospital in the evening following the attack, at around 10 p.m. Scanning the corridors, he saw a familiar face, a trauma nurse who he knew well. She hurried up to Jim. Andrew wasn't going to make it, she told him bluntly. You don't receive those injuries and walk away. Jim remembers standing there in the corridor in shock.

Andrew had undergone emergency neurosurgery but the prognosis was bleak. He lay in a coma, surrounded by tubes and machines. Outside, in the corridor, his son and daughter-in-law had spoken, bewildered, to a local clergyman, Pastor Andrew Ramage, a man who often worked with homeless people in the area. It's so senseless, they had said, a million-in-one thing. Pastor Ramage gritted his teeth – he didn't want to explain just how common it was for people sleeping rough to be attacked. He knew people who'd been stamped on, had their sleeping bags set on fire; in one case a man had told him how he'd woken up to find a guy defecating on his sleeping bag. Frequently it was members of the public, but those on the streets often had their own mental health issues and could be dangerous too. (In one sickening case I followed, a man who was sleeping rough suffered more than 160 injuries at the hands of three other homeless people. He died in a stairwell.)[57]

It was early the next day when Jim got the news he'd been expecting: Andrew had died. He wasn't sure who in the local community he should tell. As he'd left the hospital the night before, the police had pulled him to one side and asked him not to make anything public. That still grated on Jim, months later. 'The police didn't release anything for thirty hours, and the story going round Brighton was there was a guy going about with a hammer attacking homeless people. If it had been anyone else, they would have said there's been a serious assault leading to death and we've got the assailant in custody. Instead of that, people thought there was someone running around targeting people sleeping rough. Folks were petrified.'

In fact, the police had already found their man. It was a brazen crime, and the trail of evidence led them straight to him.

When the police found Sergio he was sat atop a large tombstone in the grounds of St Nicholas's Church, less than half a mile from the murder scene. At his side was the brown holdall. He was still wearing the 'I ♥ London' T-shirt.

PC Barratt turned on his body camera when he spotted him. He approached Sergio and arrested him on suspicion of attempted murder. 'Your description, the way you look, the way you are dressed, meets . . . Looks like a person who has attempted to murder, has attempted to kill,' the police officer told Sergio.

'It's me, it is me, the person you're looking for,' the dishevelled man replied.

Sergio was homeless too. He had been sleeping rough and had come to the UK from Italy, where he had citizenship. Jim remembered seeing him around, but no one knew that much about him.

Later, at the police station, he changed his story, giving another name and denying everything. 'I was in the church yard all night,' he lied.

The first day I saw him in court, albeit via video link from the prison where he was held, he was relaxed, playful almost – completely at odds with the seriousness of the charge being put in from of him. His lawyers had told him there was CCTV evidence; he said it wasn't him. He thought he could get away with it.

A trial date was set, and Sergio was led back to his prison cell.

A few weeks after Andrew died, people gathered by the clock-tower in the centre of Brighton, the shadows it cast pointing like a compass hand out to the sea, which lay grey and flat down the hill below.

Jim spoke to Andrew's son and daughter-in-law. 'They just kept talking about his plans, how he was this, how he was that. They just couldn't get to grips that he was dead,' Jim recalled.

The pastor who had comforted them at the hospital surveyed the crowd before starting to speak. 'Like many of you, I am both saddened and angry about the loss of Andrew O'Connell. In fact, I am furious. Usually at events like these, the church person will say something from the Bible, talk about God's will and how the deceased is in God's loving hands. But I am too angry just now to talk about those things.'

A woman was leaning forward, filming what he was saying on her phone. *Probably from the council,* Pastor Ramage thought to himself. *Well, screw them. Let them sue me if they don't like it. Let them take me to court.*

Pastor Ramage's relationship with the council was fraught, to say the least. He had watched the fallout as they had reduced funding for homelessness provision by a third (taking inflation into account) since 2010.[58] Adult Social Care and Mental Health services had been hit too. Pastor Ramage adopted a term he'd heard a homeless man coin when referring to the council: 'a fuckmuddle'. If they weren't going to support the homeless population, well, that is where he stepped in.

'Many lives have been lost on the streets of Brighton and Hove, lives that could have been saved by a safe place to sleep, a place to go and talk, to sit and be heard, supported and cared about. The council have had the resources and the money to provide such places, yet they have chosen not to support projects that offered to set these up. That is the source of my anger – that those we entrust with the management of public assets and finances make decisions that cost lives, and yet it is the grassroots organizations that are out there every day, who have to pick up the pieces, to face the grief and witness the true impact of those decisions.'

The crowd listened sadly. None of this was going to bring Andrew back.

Months later I was back at Lewes Crown Court. Inside the courthouse, things were all of a fluster. 'The computers have frozen up on us,' a court clerk apologetically told a barrister, who was sitting on the carpeted step outside Courtroom Three, his wig by his side. Down the hall, a gaggle of police officers looked from one to another in confusion. 'You don't have a laptop on you do you?' the clerk asked one of them. 'Classic Sussex Police – we can't even play a DVD!' another joked.

The computer system failure meant the judge, who was still in her chambers, had not yet been able to review the CCTV footage from the night of the attack.

Finally, a police officer with a laptop turned up (though with only enough battery for fifteen minutes) and the court-room doors were opened.

Andrew O'Connell's daughter, Tara, had travelled to the town for the trial and now sat sandwiched between her sister-in-law and Pastor Andrew Ramage, the latter looking solemn and official in his dog collar. Tara had worn a blue suit jacket that hung a little too large on her thin frame. Under that she wore a bright red blouse – the brightest thing among the muted tones of the wood-panelled courtroom.

The public benches, where Tara and Pastor Ramage sat, were positioned to the side of a large, glass-encased box, a space large enough for three chairs to sit comfortably side by side. Once the judge was in place, she summoned Sergio Lemori, who rose from concealed stairs below the court, into the glass box. Tara lent forward in her seat, nervously sizing up the man who had killed her father.

Sergio was dressed in a lavender-coloured fleece pullover, and below that the scrappy ends of a sky-blue T-shirt poked out. His skin was dark and tanned, and his hair a frizz of short, dark waves. He barely noticed his surroundings as he turned in his place, affording Tara a brief glimpse of his impassive face before he sat down.

The proceedings were short and perfunctory. The prosecution barrister, a white, fair-haired lady called Kate Ludsom, flew through the facts surrounding the case: the sighting by

Martin the security guard, the CCTV, the police interactions with Sergio later. As she went to describe the evidence picked up from the concrete slab, the judge interjected carefully. 'I don't think we need to go into all of that,' she said in her Scottish accent. I can only imagine she was trying to spare the family hearing about the dark red stains that dotted the rough corners of the stone, the DNA, the skin crushed into the weapon.

Instead, Ludsom went on to explain how the defendant's DNA had been found on a drainpipe near the murder site, the very spot where the man on the video had rested a hand after the murder.

As the barrister continued, in measured tones, to describe the act of the killing, Tara stared hard at the ceiling, willing the tears that had flooded her eyes not to fall. She flinched at the details from the autopsy: 'severe facial bruising, skull fractures, bleeding over the surface of the brain.'

All the while, Sergio sat with his eyes downcast, looking serene, almost bored. There was no indication of a motive, no suggestion the two men had even met.

When it was time for Tara to take the stand, she carefully unfolded the impact statement she had printed. Without looking up she read it clearly and slowly for the court, stopping briefly when her voice became thick with emotion. 'I keep picturing him smashing my father's head in as he lay there sleeping. My father never hurt anyone, he was a lover not a fighter,' she told the court. 'As a family we are heartbroken and I don't think we will ever be the same again.'

A psychiatric assessment of Sergio had been undertaken but the expert had found no underlying mental illness. He had, however, noted the likelihood of an antisocial personality disorder, having noted Sergio to have 'abnormal mental processes' and to be 'disassociated from reality'. As Sergio's own defence lawyer attested, 'This case is quite bizarre in some senses. He made no effort to cover his tracks, and the assault took place in a location where CCTV is known to exist.' At this, Sergio yawned widely, making no attempt to cover it up. His eyes closed and his head tipped to the side. For a second I wondered if he had fallen asleep or if this was some strange show. I couldn't tell if the judge had noticed, but Sergio snapped awake as she called him to attention.

'Sergio Lemori, can you stand up please,' the judge intoned.

'The circumstances of this crime are truly shocking.' As the judge spoke Tara started to sob, audibly. Pastor Ramage placed a hand on her shoulder. 'The CCTV recorded the crime in unsparing details and I must say it is one of the most shocking pieces of footage I have seen in all my years in the justice system.'

Tara pressed a balled-up tissue to her mouth.

'I believe you intended to kill him, and this was a brutal, callous and sustained attack . . . There is no evidence to suggest you'd ever met him and no evidence that you suffer from any mental illness,' she added. 'Your lack of remorse throughout these proceedings, of which I have been present for all, suggests to me you might have psychopathic tendencies.'

Sergio scratched his left hand and casually checked his nails.

He was sentenced to a minimum term of twenty-five years. As he turned to be led out of the dock, Tara glared at him, through tear-soaked eyes, with a look of pure horror and incomprehension.

I have slept outside a few times in my life. I spent a night on the rapidly cooling pavement outside Milton Keynes train station after missing the last train after a gig. Halfway through the night my friends and I moved to the comfort of a grassy bank nearby, only to be woken when the sprinklers came on. Another time, while backpacking around Europe, I slept in parks waiting for youth hostels to open, or on train platforms waiting for the first, cheap route out in the morning. Looking back now, I can see how ill-informed that was, and hearing about the senseless violence meted out on Andrew's sleeping body, I feel sick with the worry of what could have been.

But those experiences were in no way a comparison to what it is like sleeping on the streets night after night. In a meeting I had with a homeless charity in south London, the press officer there suggested I do so again, 'to get a sense of what people go through'. I nodded, uncommitted, and tried to steer the conversation in another direction. That had always felt like entirely missing the point. Sleeping rough was not a one-off experiment, nor was it a wild, youthful adventure on a balmy summer eve. It wasn't one night of feeling the cold and opting to stay awake just until you can get up and go back home again. No, it was the constant, exhausting cycle of trying to find the safest place you can get to. Of staying up through the night, vigilant to the dangers of drunken passers-by who can rain down unprovoked violence at any time. Of fearing those sleeping around you, too. Of feeling invisible, unseen, an object. Of the constant fear that, like Andrew, you might never wake up.

Pastor Ramage remained shaken by what had happened to Andrew for a long time. But there was no time to stop; there were always people to support, new faces and old needing his help. So he was somewhat distracted when I walked through the door of the train station cafe, weeks later. I spotted him immediately, a solid wall of a man in black bike leathers, the flash of his dog collar incongruous. The pastor had parked up his Triumph Bonneville motorbike outside the station and was fitting in a coffee with me between flitting from one commitment to another. His last stop was still on his mind.

'I've just come from seeing this lovely bloke. He's dying, sadly. And all he wants is to get back in his flat.' Pastor Ramage smiled forlornly, his pointy teeth flashing. The pastor had been helping an elderly man, seventy-three-year-old Alfie, through a complicated and long-standing problem. Alfie had been in and out of court, fighting to be allowed to stay in his rented flat, but during the process he had fallen seriously ill. Now he was in a hospice on the outskirts of Brighton, but he couldn't give up on the idea of getting back to his flat.

'I'm seeing him again this Tuesday. You should talk to him,' Pastor Ramage told me. 'It just seems so wrong that we can't make his final wish happen – you know, give him the dignity of dying at home if that's what he wants.'

A few days later I got a text from the pastor. He'd checked

in with Alfie, who wanted to talk to me. So I found myself heading back down to Brighton, on my way out to Martlets Hospice, a bright, hospital-like building nestled among neatly tended gardens.

At the reception desk, the woman's face lit up when I told her who I was going to see. 'Ah, Alfie, he's a love. I think he's out, though, isn't he?' she said, turning to her colleague. 'Yeah that's right,' the colleague confirmed. 'Saw him going out a while ago. He's off to see some flats. He'll probably be back soon, though. You're welcome to wait.'

Perturbed, I found a seat in the small waiting area and flicked through an out-of-date women's magazine, worrying I'd got the date and time wrong. Minutes passed, then half an hour. At one point the glass automatic doors near the waiting room slid open with a hopeful judder, but it was only the hospice's tortoiseshell cat, who languidly sauntered down the corridor as if she owned the place.

Concerned I'd travelled all that way for nothing, I texted Pastor Ramage. *Hi. Could I get Alfie's number?* I typed. *He's gone out to see some flats (the reception think) and they're not sure when he's due back.* Soon an answer pinged back: *He thought he would be back before 4 LOL.* I glanced at the time on my phone: 4.30 p.m. already.

At that moment, the doors slid open again and in came a skeletal man, swamped in jeans and a jumper which hung from his thin frame. 'Ah, here he is!' one of the receptionists beamed. 'This is your man!' I sprang into action, eagerly approaching Alfie, my hand outstretched.

Alfie had been staying here for a few weeks already. I followed as he shuffled through the magnolia corridors, beaming a hello to the health workers as they passed. His sunken cheeks were covered with a wiry, ginger-white beard, his big eyes blinking behind the frames of his glasses. He was sharing a room with three other people, the movable hospital beds spaced around the room and separated by curtains. The chair and locker next to Alfie's bed were strewn with the clothes and bags he had with him.

In a common room down the hall, Alfie fished out a handful of change from his pockets, enough to pay for two small plastic cups of latte, 20p each. 'Not a bad milky coffee they do here,' he said, a hint of pride in his voice. We settled ourselves at a table, studiously trying to ignore the shell-shocked sadness of an elderly man whose partner was trying to explain to him how he wouldn't be going home again. Martlets, for all its bright corridors and cheerily painted walls, was a place where people came to die.

And yet, despite all the odds, Alfie was flourishing here. So much so that the staff were encouraging him to move to a retirement home. That's why he had been late, he explained; he was out visiting some options, though he said he was only doing it to please the staff. He was adamant he didn't want that. 'I'm old in body but I'm not a fuddy-duddy yet,' he said. 'I'm not ready for dominoes by the fire, you know.'

Alfie was unusual in many ways. He'd had a colourful life, he told me: he'd been a master cabinet maker and joiner, and told tales of days mixing with people like artist Duncan Grant of the Bloomsbury set in London. They would meet at Grant's creeper-covered home, Charleston House, out in Lewes, the same place he had entertained Virginia Woolf, T. S. Eliot and John Maynard Keynes, back in the day. 'We used to have dinner together and that was great fun, and that was all out of me wanting to learn how to draw and paint back when I thought I could,' Alfie smiled. (I have no idea if such stories were true, but he certainly told them to many people.)

For decades Alfie had rented a flat, in the centre of Brighton, that he called home. It was a small place, a one-bed on the second floor of a grand old townhouse just metres from the bustle of the town centre and Brighton Pavilion. Above him lived a doctor and below the tenants would come and go; at one point there was a band there. 'They were absolutely fine – not what you'd expect at all,' he recalled with a toothy grin.

He'd been renting the flat for years, though, according to those who knew him, he spent a lot of time sleeping elsewhere. Sometimes he'd bed down in a garage, other times he'd stay on the sofa of an elderly friend – that was, until she died. 'I'd find somewhere nice and warm,' he explained. 'Car park places. Anywhere that was warm and dry. Away from the seafront, because it's dangerous to be on the seafront for anyone, male or female.' He had been in his late sixties at this point, older than many of the rough-sleepers that lined the doorways of the city. This wasn't an old man's game.

One of the reasons Alfie would sleep out, rather than in the warmth of his own flat, was that it was full. Full from one wall to another with things he'd collected over the years. To him they were treasures: a polished wooden box, scratched records, glinting mirrors. But others didn't see it that way. Alfie was a hoarder. A magpie.

'He believed everything he had was valuable,' chuckled Sara Emerson, who had known Alfie for about seven years and had come to care about him. During that time she'd worked at various different homeless projects around the city: lunch drop-ins, evening shelters. Inevitably, Alfie would turn up, often with some pilfered gift in tow. Sara would hold her breath as Alfie would rummage inside his rucksack. 'I've got a present for you, Sara the Carer,' he'd say with a smile. 'I saw it and just thought of you.' Sara would think, *Yeah, right – you've spotted something on the street and thought, 'I'm having that.'* Once, he fished out a heavy glass paperweight, presenting it to her with great ceremony. Sara couldn't help but smile.

Despite his funny ways, he was an absolute joy to be around, she told me: 'He never presented like a rough-sleeper; he never carried his stuff round with him. He had a lot of friends and he was very personable, so he kind of got around off the back of that really.'

Alfie was well known among the homeless community in the city. He could regularly be found at the soup kitchens and day centres that supported the homeless. Every Saturday he'd sit with his friend Phil, another homeless man, and enjoy a free meal at the Safe Haven centre. On Wednesdays it was a meal at the Salvation Army, which is where he had met Pastor Ramage.

He lived life by his own rules, coming and going, dropping off his treasures in the flat, sleeping there some nights then bedding down outside whenever the mood took him. This went on for years, but then his carefully woven patterns started to unravel. After one too many months' missed rent, and worried about the state of the place, the landlords started proceedings to kick him out. There were repairs that needed to be made, damage to the walls and things left mouldering, but Alfie wasn't letting people in to patch it up. Plus, this was prime real estate, slap bang in the centre of town. Rents around here had skyrocketed but Alfie's tenancy was unusual in that it was rent-controlled, meaning his rent stayed the same. If they got him out they could charge the next person much more.

But the fact that the flat was rent-controlled also meant it was protected by all kinds of legal safeguards, and Alfie wasn't letting go easily. He took the landlords to court and, after a long hearing, the judge ruled that they'd have to let Alfie back in, with the stipulation that Alfie give the landlords access to clear out the junk that had accumulated there.

'That's not how he remembered it later, though,' Sara told

me. 'He saw it as them taking his precious, priceless artefacts. The truth is, it was old broken speakers and things he'd found on the street.'

The stress of the court case had proved too much. Alfie had a heart attack. He was rushed to the hospital and fitted with a pacemaker – or a 'peacemaker', as he would joke. It was there that officials decided he couldn't be discharged back to his flat. The homeless team in the hospital ran an assessment: he just couldn't be trusted to look after himself, they reasoned.

Instead, Alfie was put in temporary accommodation: a room in a hotel, a ramshackle old building just a hundred metres from Brighton's seafront. It was far from temporary, however: he ended up staying there for about eighteen months. 'It was nothing more than a slum-dwelling, really,' he explained later. 'Disgraceful. It was an old house – two houses joined together actually – but absolutely rotting away.' Alfie was in a small room with no cooking facilities. He wasn't allowed a portable hob and, too weak to go out for food, he just stopped eating. 'I survived on fresh air,' he recalled.*

According to Alfie, while he was staying there the place was fumigated to treat an insect infestation. He'd received a letter telling him to be out at a certain time but had felt too unwell to move. The place was fumigated around him.

Sara went to visit him there one day. He came hobbling out of the hotel, barely able to stand. He had hardly eaten in

---

* The hotel was sold by its former owners in July 2019. A spokesperson from the owners when Alfie had stayed there assured me 'that facilities are certainly not slum-like' and that there were kitchens on each floor with microwaves and fridges. She also noted that the facilities were used as 'short-term emergency accommodation', though Alfie recalled being there for many months.

a week. Sara told him to get his things together. She was taking him to hospital.

The hospital tests found his oesophagus almost completely blocked by a cancerous tumour. They put in a stent and then, later, another. Now Alfie talked with a croaky gurgle, his soft voice occasionally masked by a bubbling hiss.

Lying in the hospital, Alfie had got to musing on his life. He and Pastor Ramage had sat for hours, cosy and safe in the hospital, discussing the scriptures, spiritualism, faith. One day, when the ward was clear of people, Alfie turned to the pastor grave-faced. He had a favour to ask. *Oh God, what's he going to ask me to smuggle in?* the pastor had worried to himself with a gulp. But Alfie surprised him: he asked the pastor to baptize him.

He also started talking more and more about his son, telling Pastor Ramage memories of the last time he had seen him. They had been estranged for many years. Alfie had only been with the boy's mother a few months, back when they were both too young to be serious about anything. The relationship hadn't lasted the pregnancy.

Alfie remembered seeing his son every now and then when he was small, stroking his hair and cooing, 'Lovely, lovely boy.' But as he grew into a teenager and then a man, they lost touch. Now he regretted he hadn't played more of a role in his boy's upbringing. 'I thought it was a good, character-building thing, but now, later in life, you reflect on things and your mistakes, and that was one of them. But you know, I love him deeply as a son,' he told me later.

Alfie lay in his hospital bed and wondered where his boy was now.

Weeks passed and eventually the doctors said they were ready to discharge him. They had put in a second stent to keep his tumour-riddled oesophagus open, but there was nothing more they could do for him and they needed the beds.

Terminally ill homeless people have no legal rights to housing. I had heard horror stories of people discharged from hospitals and into homeless hostels, the already-beleaguered staff there left to nurse men to their deaths, doling out medicines or helping people to wash when they were too sick to stand. Too often, terminally ill homeless people fell between the cracks of the NHS, social services and council housing departments.[59]

So in many ways, Alfie was luckier than most. Sara was trying her best to get him into a hospice but, after winning his court battle, he was adamant he was going back to his flat. But Sara was still worried about him. He seemed to be in a lot of pain, unmanageable pain.

On a crisp July morning, Alfie made his way down to the Old Steine Gardens in Brighton's centre. He'd dressed in layers – a thin black jacket over another dark-green one – trying to keep the cold from his willowy frame. He was heading to his baptism.

Pastor Ramage had set up a gazebo right in front of the grand tiers of the Victoria fountain, there in the middle of the park. They'd chosen to do it as part of the weekly Street Ministry the pastor held for the homeless community, held in the gardens. The proceedings had been caught on camera and I watched them back later, smiling fondly at Alfie's shyness.

Dressed in a black T-shirt and shades, Pastor Ramage looked more like a bouncer than a priest, and he joked as he raised his voice over the din of the public place. 'Dearly beloved, we are gathered here today . . . No, we're not having any of that old rubbish,' the pastor laughed, beckoning Alfie forward.

As Alfie shuffled forward to be blessed with holy water, he was lighter on his feet than usual. There was something about rebirth that appealed to him, he told me later: a fresh start, even at the end. A chance to be clean.

'You are claimed by God and made new again in Christ,' Pastor Ramage smiled, his hand planted firmly on Alfie's frail shoulder.

'That's how I got saved,' Alfie later told me. 'And I'm glad I did.'

But despite the spiritual relief, his old body continued to break down. The cancer spread. In the end the pain was too much. Sara succeeded in persuading him to go to Martlets. 'The pain made him relent,' Sara remembered.

Once there, he liked the hospice. It wasn't home but the people were nice and the environment suited him. 'Yeah, it's all right here,' Alfie confided to me when I visited him there, 'but it's not home, is it?'

We sat and spoke for well over an hour but Alfie's croaky throat was getting tired. It was getting late, too. A porter had brought Alfie's dinner, a bowl of soup, and he was tucking in hungrily. But still he was dreaming of his flat, just a couple of miles away. The one place he wanted to get back to, the one place he called home.

As I left him to his dinner, he smiled sadly at me and said: 'I just want to go home, to my garret, where I can look through the window, read, write, whatever.' He just wanted to go home to die.

A tired, grey sky stretched over the Solent as the *St Faith* ferry slid across the water. On board, in the passengers' area that looked like a hotel lobby, I watched as Will – from the House of Bread in Stafford – carried a lacklustre coffee over to his smiling wife, Jan. It had been forty years since they last made this trip. Back then it had been a time of new beginnings: they'd been visiting the Isle of Wight for their honeymoon. Four decades later, it was an ending that had brought them back. In the boot of Will's small car parked on the deck below, among bags of clothes and other paraphernalia, was an urn. Jayne's ashes were going home.

Less than an hour later, after a drive that twisted and turned through the Isle of Wight's small towns, Will parked the car and retrieved his precious cargo from the boot.

Pam, Jayne's elderly mother, greeted us enthusiastically from the doorway of her small, red-brick semi-detached home. Her short, plump figure leant against the doorframe, the sunlight catching the grey and white of her wavy, shoulder-length hair. This was only the second time she and Will had met in person, but after six years of phone calls they felt like old friends.

'You made it!' she beamed.

Once indoors, we hovered nervously before Pam guided us to the sofa with a waft of her crooked fingers. 'Now, just a second,' she said warmly, 'I want to get this sorted first.' She flipped open the cover of an iPad and brought up the menu for the local fish-and-chip shop. Once selections were made, Ray, Pam's balding, bespectacled husband, was dispatched to collect the order, leaving Pam smiling sadly at us from across the room.

We sat a little awkwardly together, Will and Jan bending their tall, slender bodies into the soft folds of the low sofa. The conversation meandered from small talk about Pam's hospital visits to the conversion of the pub across the road into flats. The room was bright and cosy, full of pictures and statues of penny-farthings. A carriage clock clucked peacefully on the mantelpiece; it was a little after 11 a.m. Despite the late-summer sun, Pam had the radiators cranked up high and Will had to pull the cotton jumper from his thin frame to cool down. None of us let our eyes wander to the small urn tucked just out of view by the leg of the coffee table, but Jayne was never far from anyone's mind.

A few weeks earlier, at the House of Bread, Will was trying to work out how to help Jayne's friends through their pain. 'Our friends here, they're not like you and me,' he told me as I joined him in his office. 'You know, I go home and cry, often. But they can't do that,' Many of the people he was working with were stuck in survival mode, so preoccupied with worrying where they were going to eat or sleep from one day to the next that there was no time to process emotions or work through grief.

And I had come to notice that many of those working in the homelessness sector were in the same position. I was struck by what a strange job Will had chosen for himself, taking on the burden and trauma of working with people on the edge, taking on their pains himself, mourning their deaths and racking his brain for where and how he could have done more.

I'd seen the same thing in Brighton, after being invited to a session for homeless outreach workers on dealing with grief. Dr Tim Worthley, who I'd met all those months ago in his surgery, was there, radiating his calm GP demeanour. As hostel workers and drug rehab staff sat in small circles around the church hall, Tim led his own group in talking about how they dealt with the stress and the loss.

'It's hard,' said one woman softly. 'I mean, often you know these people better maybe than their own family do, you see them every day and they confide in you and stuff, but then I never know if it is appropriate to go to the funerals . . . I'm not their friend, I'm not their family, but I still care.'

'Yeah, and then how do you explain what you're feeling to your own friends or whoever,' another lady chipped in. 'I mean, you want to be professional, and it is part of the job, so it is hard to explain why you're crying, why you're upset.'

'I think it's important to own that,' said Tim, leaning forward, elbows resting on his thighs. 'Working with these people, people who have been let down by everyone, who are naturally suspicious of the system, you have to open your heart wide to them, to be able to do your job. So of course you care more than you would, say, treating a housed patient. So when they die, you feel it.'

Tim felt it. I knew Jim, with his bus, did too. And Jon in London. And Estella in Milton Keynes. And Hugo in Worcester.

And now I could feel the pain and sadness blanketing Will.

Will had been the one to drive Rachel, Jayne's daughter, to the morgue to identify the body of her dead mother. It had been a few years since they'd been together, and Rachel had been shocked by her mother's wrinkled skin and dirty nails.

She remembered their trips to the manicurist and the pride Jayne had taken in her hair. Will had tried to support Rachel through the shock.

The day I visited him at his office, our chat was punctuated by a call from Pam. 'I found myself sat on the sofa, just doing nothing, and suddenly I was thinking of Jayne and crying,' Pam had told Will, half-embarrassed, her West Country accent lilting down the phone.

'That will happen, Pam,' said Will softly, closing his eyes as he spoke. 'You need to let it out. It's important.'

Jayne had never let the pain out, I thought. I was beginning to understand that better now. The grief at losing her first child never dissipated. It folded in on itself, concentrated to a point that occasionally burst forth in fits of anger or self-loathing. She carried it with her to the end. If only someone could have reached her before it was too late.

A month later, on the Isle of Wight, Will, Ray and I were sat cheerily making small talk around Pam's kitchen table. We had just finished our fish and chips, as well as a huge portion of apple pie.

Pam had left for a moment but shuffled back into the room, two envelopes in hand. 'These are the photos we collected together,' she explained, handing them to me, and I gingerly slipped out nine shining photos of Jayne, from smiling teenager to a series of her beaming in a white wedding dress.

'And this is the letter from the hospital I mentioned,' Pam added. On NHS-headed paper a doctor has written how she will be performing her own review into the care Jayne got at the hospital in Stafford, to see if there was more that they could have done. The Mental Health team had reviewed their interactions with Jayne, too, noting how they had failed to make her another appointment despite the fact that her GP had flagged just how precarious a situation she was in. But there were vital errors in the report they presented to Pam, and in the inquest. The report noted that Jayne's baby had died 'in the last 12 months', when in fact it had been decades earlier. Reading through the documents gave Pam little comfort. 'How are they still getting things wrong?' she asked me.

After carefully looking over the photos and letter, Will glanced at the clock. It wasn't long until we had to get back on the ferry and return to the mainland.

'Shall we do this now?' he asked Pam.

She smiled sadly. 'How shall we do it?' she asked. 'I have a Tupperware here.'

'Make sure it's not wet,' her husband Ray chipped in.

'I know, I know. I'm not daft.'

Carefully Will picked up the urn from the sideboard, where it sat next to our plates covered with the remnants of chips and mushy peas. 'If you have a scoop of some kind, this would be easier,' he said gently.

I watched awkwardly as Will decanted half the ashes in the urn into Pam's Tupperware. The half that was left he'd take back up north, to Rachel.

As we left Pam and Ray that day, I found myself wishing Jayne had found her way home, had cut herself off from life in the Midlands, and settled here with her mother.

So often, we think of those that are sleeping rough as completely detached from loved ones, cast adrift in life. But what I saw in Pam was a mother who cared desperately for her child, who tried everything she could to keep her safe. 'I try to remember the good times, I really do, but they were so few and far between,' she told me sadly. 'I think maybe I failed her, but I tried, I did try.'

As we drove away from Pam, Will wondered aloud whether knowing more of Jayne's life could have somehow improved the help he had offered her. 'It's something I've just come to recognize now,' he said as he swung the car round and made in the direction of the ferry. 'If we know more about the people we're trying to help, about their family lives, what they have been through, perhaps we can do more to support them.'

I couldn't answer; I was lost in my own thoughts. By now I had attended inquests, interviewed people's families and friends, scoured the local papers for deaths and enlisted the help of dozens of journalists to help me find more names. Piece by piece I was coming closer to the true number of those who had died while homeless. It had become a bigger mission than I could ever have imagined. I'd written up names from lists recited from memory, from scraps of paper in doctors' surgeries, from shaken day-centre workers. I'd extracted figures from the handful of councils that collated them and travelled the country to try and get others to start their count. I'd heard so many tragic stories of people whose lives could have gone another way if help had come at the right time. All of these names – they were adding up, weighing on me. Cardon, Hamid, Tony, Fabian . . . Name after name, life after life. The stories were haunting me.

But there was something about Jayne's story that stayed with me, beyond the hundreds more names I came to learn about that year. Perhaps it was the fact that the pale, smiling, red-haired woman in the youthful photographs Pam showed me didn't look hugely different from my own mother's family. Or was it the sad fact that it was a mother's love for her still-born baby that destroyed Jayne in the first place, and her own mother's love that kept Pam holding on, year after year, bloodied and bruised in body and spirit by her wild daughter – desperate to save her, right until the end.

Later, Pam wandered down to the sea, flanked by the chalky cliffs of Freshwater Bay, Jayne's favourite place to play as a child. *She was happy here – for a time, anyway,* Pam thought as she remembered her skinny, happy daughter soaring, carefree, upwards on a trampoline. And then she slowly, sadly, released her daughter back to the sky.

PART THREE

There Are Lessons to be Learnt

By early autumn my heart was heavy. When I had started out, I had wanted to get to a figure, to fill in a void in the data, but I cared so much more deeply now. I felt like I'd held a magnifying glass to society and I was appalled by what I saw. It was easy to feel desolate.

But something else was gnawing at my stomach. A frustration, an anger. It wasn't enough to fixate on the tragic, I reasoned, pulling myself together; I needed to look for solutions, too. I wanted to know what more could be done to stop people dying, to help them out of homelessness. I knew there were models out there, examples we could be learning from, and I wanted to understand the options better. I found myself thinking back to the man who had been my spirit-guide for so many months, someone who had hit this point of desperation himself and found a way out. I needed to talk to Jon.

It was unseasonably warm when I found myself walking through the leafy greenery of Finsbury Park, my heart stirring with nostalgia to be back in what used to be my old neighbourhood. I was heading to Streets Fest, another of Jon's brainwaves and an exciting prospect: a small music festival designed specifically for people experiencing homelessness.

I was excited. I felt in desperate need of positive action, some beacon in the gloom, and this could be it. For months now, Jon had been calling at random hours of the day, his voice spewing forth in a torrent of ideas and energy, the thick cadence of his accent forcing me to ride the conversation like river rapids. At first I wasn't sure what to make of these calls – they were hard to explain to my partner, who did a much better job than me of leaving his work behind at the office. But I had come to realize that these issues were not simply nine-to-five concerns for Jon, they consumed his entire waking life. And they had begun to do the same to me. My weekends had filled up with funerals, my evenings with soup kitchen runs. And now, this.

In a clearing of the park about the size of a football pitch was a huddle of stalls, tents and people. Clusters of friends sat or stood around the edges of the expanse, and at the far end of the field a larger group bobbed and swayed in front of a large stack of speakers blasting out hip-hop beats.

Scanning the area, I couldn't see any sign of Jon, but there, standing in a small group next to a stall where hair-dressers were cheerily tidying people's hair, was Stephen,* the toothless man I'd met months earlier at the Streets Kitchen meal.

I made my way over to him. 'I remember you,' I said. 'We met in Hackney a while ago.'

'Oh yeah,' smiled Stephen. 'I go up Hackney on Tuesdays. What's that?' he gestured at my dictaphone. I explained I was a journalist and had been following Jon's work for some time. Stephen's eyes lit up at the news. 'They were here before and took my picture for the *Islington Gazette*,' he beamed proudly. 'I told them to take my picture for the publicity. I've been on the telly six times. I love publicity, it adds to my legend.'

Stephen's white hair flickered and fluffed in the light breeze. He exuded a happy glow. That day he was wearing a navy-blue fleece jumper, with two watches strapped over his left sleeve. He'd got them two-for-a-tenner from a friend, he told me, but his favourite was the one with a brown leather band and a sepia-toned world map on the face. A suitable timepiece for a traveller.

While Stephen's friend, a shy, mousy-haired woman, nervously waited for a haircut from one of the volunteer hairdressers, Stephen explained how he had travelled all over the UK. He had lived with his father into his mid-twenties but everything had changed when he came downstairs one day to find his father's body laid out in the dark: dead. That image had haunted Stephen ever since. The shock changed him forever. 'I smashed up the house and then I was on the streets,' said Stephen, his large eyes widening as he leant towards me. 'It's still affecting me now,' he said. 'I was making love to a woman once and I forgot I was making love to her because I was thinking about my dad,' he giggled nervously. 'It's comical but you know . . .'

Since then, Stephen had sofa-surfed and slept rough. For a time he had his own flat but then things went wrong with his benefits – despite his mental health issues, he was assessed by officials and told he was fit to work. With that swift decision his Employment and Support Allowance (ESA) was stopped. 'I have nightmares,' Stephen fretted. 'I have PTSD. I see my dad's body everywhere. I don't go to sleep. And they were calling me a liar.' For three years Stephen lived without the ESA benefits, he said, living on the streets. All the while the government was telling him he could, and should, get work. Finally he had got to tribunal and a magistrate ruled his bene-fits should be reinstated, but he hadn't seen that money come through yet. After three years with not a penny to his name, adjusting to the new possibilities the money could bring would be hard.

His friend's haircut was finished now and, as the hairdresser held a mirror up for her to inspect the work, a small smile spread across the woman's lips. 'Oh, very nice,' Stephen boomed happily. I was distracted; I'd just spotted Jon talking animatedly with a huddle of people in high-vis vests. 'Ah, Jon's a diamond,' smiled Stephen, following my gaze. 'He's one of those people that's got a good heart, which is very rare in this world.'

Standing among the people and the music, Jon was in his element. Somehow he'd managed to gather housing teams from local councils, dentists, hairdressers, a mobile library, musicians and homeless outreach workers all in one place. The idea, I heard him telling a volunteer, was to give homeless people all the things they needed in a 'one-stop shop, and let them have some fun while they're at it.'

As Stephen wandered off with his friends, I saw what Jon meant. Too often the services that are available to homeless people are perfunctory, if efficient. They're all about getting the basics covered – very rarely is there time for fun or enjoyment. There at the festival, people were relaxing, meeting friends. In a far corner a drum circle had formed. Elsewhere, artist and veteran David Tovey was helping others create squares for a patchwork banner, each one bearing a message.

Richard was there, too, wheezing his way around the stalls. He'd eyed up the stall offering free burgers but wasn't so sure about the rest. 'It felt a bit like a Homelessness Conference – everyone lining up to talk about how good they were,' he moaned to me later. But then, through our many chats, I'd come to understand that Richard was a hard man to please entirely.

While there were plenty of services on display, there were

other, softer connections being made too. Diarmaid Ward, head of housing for Islington council, wandered cheerfully among the crowds, his high-vis vest and lanyard the more obvious signs marking him out from the festival's other guests. I watched as he settled himself down on the ground by a skinny, older man: 'Irish Willie', the man who had worked security at the Sofia House squat in the depths of winter.

'Ah, hello! I know you, William!' Diarmaid boomed happily, his freckles fading into the pink flush of his cheeks. 'How are you doing? Look at you – you've more layers on now than you do in the cold!'

'Ah, here's a good man,' exclaimed Willie with a smile, his Irish accent matching Diarmaid's. 'I've been in hospital, accident and emergency, for three days, would you believe that?' he said, tugging down his khaki-coloured cap.

'Ah, no, what's wrong with you?'

'Whatever I eat and drink came right through both sides!'

'Good God!' boomed Diarmaid.

'Ah, but I'm getting better now,' replied Willie, his thin frame sagging among his layers of T-shirts and other tops.

Willie was well known in the Islington area. Though he had a flat of his own, he could often be found helping out in squats or supporting the Streets Kitchen team. When Sofia House had been closed down months earlier, he kept an eye out for what happened to the former residents.

Diarmaid smiled as he took in the rows of stalls that bordered the field. His colleagues were out in force, talking to people, making connections, suggesting they come in and visit the council officially to try to get help. But Diarmaid later told me that at the back of his mind had been the nagging concern that, despite all their best efforts, the council, like the rest of the country, was woefully under-resourced when it came to having places for people to stay.

Diarmaid told me of his frustration at how hard it was to build new council houses. All around the park, stretching out across the borough, were blocks of flats that had once been council-owned, but all that had changed. Almost 3 million council-owned properties had been sold off since Margaret Thatcher introduced the Right to Buy scheme in the 1980s, allowing council residents to buy the properties at a much-reduced rate. Councils had been expected to replace each property sold with a new one, but this was made impossible by a stipulation in the Right to Buy plans. 'We only get 75 per cent of the money from the sale back,' Diarmaid explained. 'The government takes 25 per cent, and we can only use that Right to Buy receipt for up to a third of the cost of a new home – we've got to find the other two thirds from our own funds. So the entire system is stacked against building council homes.'

Things just kept getting worse. In 2012, the government increased the discount residents could get when buying their home, whittling down further the amount in the council's coffers for rebuilds. 'The replacement one-for-one idea is complete nonsense,' Diarmaid told me, sighing. 'If councils had been able to replace council homes one-for-one then we wouldn't be in a housing crisis right now.'

Add to that the fact that councils had been banned from borrowing money on their assets to build new homes. So with just a sliver of the profits coming in from the sale of council homes, and the ban on borrowing, councillors like Diarmaid were in a bind. 'We have about 38,000 council homes that we manage ourselves. There's also lots of housing associations in the borough. But there's still a waiting list of just over 13,000 households,' he explained. The majority of those would be people classified as homeless, or those in overcrowded and vulnerable living arrangements. So Diarmaid wandered the field that day, chatting to people like Willie, encouraging them to come and connect with other council services, all the while knowing there just weren't the council homes needed.

In another corner of the field, Jon was still going a mile a minute. I wandered over to say hello and in breathless starts he grabbed my arm and led me over to some person or other 'you just have to talk to'. I scribbled down their stories and then, with my notepad full of names and information, I said my goodbyes and headed off, the sound of the drum circle and happy chatter echoing in my ears.

A few weeks later I was back at the park, beckoned once more by a message from Jon. His eyes were sparkling with mischief as he pulled open the door to the Lodge, a ramshackle old building on the edge of Finsbury Park. 'Not bad, is it?' he said, surveying a hallway scattered with boxes, including a sealed plastic crate labelled 'Rat proof'.

The council had loaned him use of this old building as a temporary headquarters for the festival but the weeks had passed and no one had come to collect the keys, so Jon had drawn on his squatting instincts and was making it home-base until he was kicked out.

'If they've forgotten to ask for the keys back, I'm not going to remind them,' he beamed, scurrying down the hall and into the kitchen, where a pot of spaghetti and another of bolognese sauce were bubbling furiously on the small stove.

That afternoon he was really excited, almost flustered. A new pilot scheme had started across London in an attempt to reach out to some of the most vulnerable, entrenched rough-sleepers around, and Jon had been asked to help out.

'So far, whatever I've asked for – they've said yes!' he chattered excitedly. 'I mean fucking hell, I said look, why don't you get them new clothes and they were like all right, yeah, tell us how much you need for that. And the food too . . . so look, I've bought them the good stuff, you know, proper nice mince for the sauce. Fuck, I mean I'm going to keep asking for stuff until they say no. You know what I mean?' He laughed. I couldn't help but smile at his infectious blend of distrust and excitement.

Across the country, pilot projects were being set up, prompted by the eventual realization that rough-sleeping and homelessness was out of control. Central government had announced a pot of funding that councils could bid on to pay for homelessness projects. It was a good PR move, prompting positive headlines, but those on the ground were dubious. One-off pots of funding were no substitute for the myriad cuts and long-term decimation of services. When I read the announcement of the funding I had thought immediately of the people whose stories I had come to know already that year, how complex and interwoven their needs were. Could this funding also replace the cuts to mental health provision that had left Hamid stranded, or the drug and alcohol services that had impacted Fabian? Would they improve hospital discharge care to look after Richard or pay for reviews to learn lessons from people like Cardon? It seemed not.

In London, some of the funding was going to a cross-borough pilot project that involved setting up a temporary shelter space for two weeks at a time, to entice entrenched rough-sleepers before moving them on to more permanent accommodation.

Despite his excitement at the council suddenly stumping up funding for this pilot, Jon was sceptical. He knew how set in their ways many of the area's rough-sleepers were. 'A fort-night's stay isn't going to change that,' he told me. Still, he was going to help where he could.

Carefully, Jon slopped the spaghetti and sauce mix he had cooked into a large, portable cool box, which he lugged onto a small trolley. Navigating his way through the corridors of the building, he made his way outside and we juddered our way to the bus stop.

'The plan is that I'm going to drop this off at this pilot shelter, and if anyone asks, we just say you're coming with me,' he said as he dragged the trolley into the pushchair bay. No one had told Jon not to bring guests to the pilot shelter but he knew that St Mungo's, the organization running it, were nervy and Jon was not one for jumping through bureau-cratic hoops to get permission. So as we dragged the cool box full of food up the steps of the church building that was housing the shelter, I couldn't help but feel a little tremor of concern about what he was getting me into.

As we got to the door we bumped into two dishevelled men, both in their fifties and one with a bushy matted beard and a hunched back that accentuated his rough appearance.

'Come on, lads, don't be going out, there's food here,' said Jon cheerily. He recognized the men from around the Finsbury Park area – they were both foreign nationals and, ordinarily, wouldn't have access to housing support from the council because of their immigration status.

Inside, the church hall was clean but sparse. Two rooms had stretcher cots laid out, the only sign the building was being used for anything other than prayer groups or other church functions. The blue canvas cots with their spindly legs reminded me of photographs of hastily constructed humani-tarian relief shelters, the aftermath of some terrible natural disaster. Some sat empty, untouched, others sagged under the meagre possessions of their occupants: a scuffed rucksack here, a few books there.

The shelter had room for twelve but it was an unseasonably warm September day and that meant many of the hoped-for residents had opted to stay outside. Jon doled out the food to four men milling about the place. The still-hot spaghetti bolognese sagged on the perilously thin paper plates. 'Cheers, yeah,' smiled a bearded blond man as he retreated back to his cot to eat the meal.

Wandering round the centre later, Jon was critical. 'It's a bit soulless, isn't it,' he said, eyeing up the plain walls and the empty tables. The hall was certainly functional rather than homely. On the walls of a side office – which adjoined the main hall by means of a hospital-ward-style window – the team had stuck up whiteboards with neat rows detailing each of the centre's guests: a list of Polish and Romanian names with concise notes for each one. 'I mean, it could do with some pictures or something. Next time I'll bring some flowers in, to brighten the place up a bit,' Jon harrumphed.

I glanced around the sparse room, trying not to stare at the handful of men now eating Jon's fare. This particular shelter was meant to support the people who were hardest to reach, those who either didn't qualify for regular services or were so used to living on the streets that they couldn't handle the alternatives. Some of the main targets for the scheme had been those sleeping under a nearby railway bridge. That stretch of road, by Finsbury Park tube station, had become something of campsite, with eight people regularly sleeping there. Some of the residents had made their own structures out of pallets of wood and tarpaulins. One had a mirror attached to the outside. Others had simply set up sleeping bags on top of layers of compressed cardboard. Walking past, thinking of Richard and his tales of Cardboard

City in the 1980s, it felt like we hadn't come so far after all.

A few days after I'd surreptitiously visited the centre, I made my way back to the settlement under the bridge. It was 10 a.m. and a street-sweeper vehicle was parked at the nearside of the bridge, its bored driver waiting next to it. It seemed that as well as the 'carrot' of the shelter, there would be a 'stick' too – the council were asking people to move on and the area was being cleared out.

Under the bridge, in his high-vis vest, Diarmaid Ward, the council housing officer, was talking to a woman who had been sleeping there. Other council representatives were working their way up and down the bridge, encouraging people to come with them to the pilot-project shelter.

Laminated posters stuck to the side of the bridge read: 'We need to keep the streets safe and clean. Any outstanding items left on the pavement will be taken and kept in the storage until 3 October – you can reclaim your belongings by telephoning 020 . . . Our housing outreach team are on duty every day. We want to help everyone to get safe and secure accommodation.' The bridge was cleared out. The people living there moved on. (There were 253 other clearances of encampments across the country that year.)[60]

But weeks later, when I visited again, it was as if nothing had changed. The mattresses were back, so too were the wooden structures. First one, then more.

'Our outreach teams helped about thirty-eight people into accommodation from that area, but it hasn't solved the problem,' Diarmaid Ward told me later. 'It is a very, very difficult situation, and you can't make people accept help. One of the issues is the open access to Class A drugs in that area.' (I'd heard the same from other people, that dealing was common and that the quality of product going round that neighbourhood was seen as superior to elsewhere.) 'If drug dealers are acting with impunity then you have to look at how come the borough has lost three hundred police officers in recent years. You've got to think about what are this country's priorities?' Diarmaid said, sighing.

The pilot shelter project was shut down after two weeks and moved to another borough. Some of those that passed through were found places to stay, others were back on the street.

Walking through the bridge underpass weeks later, Jon was disheartened. A two-week pilot was never going to work, he told me. You needed to find a safe space, a long-term, friendly place where people felt welcomed, where they would have the time to readjust and work out what help they needed.

But where could that be? Sofia House, the squat in the depths of winter, had been too short-lived and precarious. 'The Lodge', which he had now in the park, was a place to store goods and cook food, but it wouldn't work to put people up – there wasn't the room. He needed a space, a place he could set up his own way and with none of the hoops or red tape that the big charities brought along. But where?

Two weeks after Streets Fest, Richard had had an operation at the Royal Free Hospital; a catheter that had been bothering him had been removed. The surgery had gone well – one less thing to worry about. '[Richard] is experiencing some social issues relating to his accommodation,' the doctor wrote in his discharge papers. 'It is understood he has no fixed abode and has been homeless for most of his adult life. He has been deemed suitable to return to the hostel.'

In a bid to understand how this was happening I had spoken to medical professionals, off the record, who told me how troubling it could be to discharge people like Richard, people who clearly had nowhere safe to go but who simply were not sick enough to take up a much-needed hospital bed. Resources were tight, beds were at a premium, one medical expert explained – there's only so much you can do. What perhaps weighed the heaviest was having to discharge those who were terminally ill, knowing there was nothing more the hospital could do but worrying you were sending them off to die in a hostel bed or worse.

On the other hand, some doctors explained, there were always the folks who were not ill but simply looking for a warm bed and a free meal – what to do with them? Hospitals are not hostels; there had to be some limits to who got care. Indeed, I had seen notices sent out warning hospital admissions staff to refuse entry to certain homeless people, warnings with mugshots and bold letters stating that some people would fake illness to have a bed for the night. For doctors in hospitals across the country there were hard decisions to be made every day.

There was a solution, though. In some places I had heard of intermediate care beds, often located in hostel facilities but with medical staff on hand to keep an eye on people. These worked brilliantly for those too ill for the streets but not grave enough for hospital: a warm, safe place to recuperate and take medicine in peace. But they weren't without complications. They involved doctors agreeing to be legally responsible for people still in their care but away from them, outside the hospital ward. And then there were the complications with getting medicines with high street-values out to unsecure locations. Still, Dr Dana Beale, the doctor in Westminster treating the homeless, had several such beds at her disposal and found them hugely useful when treating her homeless patients.

Richard didn't blame the doctors. He had become quite fond of some of the hospital staff, and occasionally spotted nurses from the ward at his local food bank, picking up supplies for themselves.[61] But he wished there was somewhere other than his cold hostel bed where he could recuperate. As autumn drew in and the weather got colder, he was finding that even having a roof over his head was not enough. He had been living at the hostel for months and now he wanted me to come and see what he was complaining about.

It was midday and cold as I jumped out of the taxi. I had agreed to meet Richard at the bus stop outside the hostel so he could accompany me inside, pretending I was an old friend. 'They'll get funny otherwise,' he said.

I wasn't sure if this was paranoia on Richard's part but there was good reason the hostel owners wouldn't look kindly on a journalist snooping around. A few years earlier, a local paper had exposed the conditions there, running a series of stories on the place, including a front page about how someone had died in one of the rooms and gone unnoticed for days.

'Better to keep a low profile,' I had agreed.

Signing into the guest book, Richard started his performative monologue for the uninterested staff member behind the perspex window, telling some elaborate story of an imaginary friend he and I had in common who he was planning to see later. I nodded mutely, feeling the itch of the woollen hat I had pulled down low over my forehead in an attempt to look less like a journalist.

Once past the reception desk, we shuffled up the steep stairs, going as fast as Richard's walking stick would allow, and then there we were, on his corridor. I pulled my hat lower, suddenly aware of the CCTV cameras that dotted the hall. A voice behind me stopped me in my tracks.

'Hey . . . Hey you . . . What's your name? Come on love, tell me your name.'

I wheeled around, nervous, but it wasn't a member of staff – rather, a fog-eyed man, a resident there, perhaps high or drunk or something else. His lumbering gait was bringing him closer and closer as I mumbled some nondescript reply . . . 'Er, I'm just here to visit my friend,' I stuttered, ducking into Richard's tiny room.

Inside, we both perched on the narrow single bed, now covered in a thick royal-blue throw. There was nowhere else to sit; the room was really just the bed and a narrow space alongside it. At first I made the faux pas of suggesting I could take the flimsy plastic stool-type thing in the corner but Richard hastily declined. Only later, after placing my bag down on it, did I realize this was his commode.

Scanning the room, I noted how few possessions Richard had to his name. I could scribble most of the details down on half a sheet of my notepad: a small, wheeled suitcase stuffed with a few changes of clothes, the boxes of medicines branded with exotic-sounding names like metformin and amoxicillin, and a plastic bag stuffed with hospital paperwork. It was strange to see him in this tiny room; he looked smaller here somehow, more brittle. Out on the streets or in the glow of McDonald's lighting he had had a more commanding presence, a surety of his surroundings. Here he looked like a little old man.

He was miserable, he said. He'd wake most mornings at 5 a.m., the cold air permeating the old, thin window frame that rose from the end of his bed like a gravestone. The fleece throw he had covered the bed with did little to help. The cold air was thick and claggy in his damaged lungs, and he would wake gasping for breath.

He had complained several times to the manager or whoever was on duty, but the answer was always the same: keeping the heating on at night rattled the pipes and was so noisy the other residents complained. Really the old building needed a new plumbing system entirely, Richard told me, 'but good luck getting the cheapskates to pay for that'.

Instead the staff had provided a small electric fan heater to try and warm his room, but it had done little to help and he found himself coughing and sputtering with the dry, re-cycled air in just the same way he had with the cold.

Richard was visited by a social worker once a fortnight, and whoever came would write neat little notes in his visitation book, which he showed me eagerly. He had started adding his own, not satisfied that they were listening to his complaints: 'WOKE UP EARLY 4 a.m. HEATING OFF!'

I read the reports a little concerned. This hostel was far from ideal but I didn't like the idea of him complaining so much that he was asked to leave. I didn't want to see him sleeping on the night buses again.

Once, at one of our meetings in McDonald's, I had put it to Richard, as bluntly as I dared, that it was unusual for someone to be street-homeless for quite as long as he had been. 'Do you think there's anything about your case that makes it different?' I asked, letting the unspoken question sit between us: *Could it be somehow your fault; could you be sabotaging the help that is offered to you?* Richard stirred more sugar into his already sweetened coffee and grunted. 'I think maybe some of it is of my own making. I'm so used to being homeless, I've accepted it,' he murmured thoughtfully. 'You hear that word "entrenched" . . .' He trailed off. I sat back, surprised. Was Richard really saying that in some way this was a life he was choosing? But later, after leaving him, I had realized things weren't so simple. I got the impression that, after being let down time and time again by society, Richard had lost all faith in the system to help him. Now, his apparent refusal to take up the help even when it was offered was perhaps some way of maintaining control of his own destiny.

And it wasn't as if the help he was offered was all that helpful. Yes, Richard could be curmudgeonly, but there was no doubting this environment wasn't beneficial for a man with his medical conditions. Indeed, his doctors had agreed with him about the cold in the hostel being a problem and had written letters to the manager and to the council but still the heating remained off at night.

For an hour we shuffled through his pile of hospital paper-work, while he told story after story about hospital stays, impatient nurses, perfunctory discharges back to the streets.

Twenty-four hospital admissions and discharges in the space of just twelve months. Sometimes he stayed for hours, other times it was days or weeks.

I took photo after photo of the paperwork Richard had collected and then, keen not to overstay my welcome, scurried out of the hostel and into the street, keeping my head bowed so as not to catch the receptionist's eye. It took a few blocks before my heart rate slowed.

For weeks I had been trying to get my head round why so many people were being discharged from hospital back to the streets. I thought back to Jayne, sent back to her doorway bed, her wrists in bandages after her suicide attempt.

Then there was Darren, who'd been a rifleman in the British army for seven years, seeing action in Northern Ireland and Kosovo, only to end up living rough in London, deep in the midst of a heroin addiction. He had put off going to hospital for weeks, well aware of the looks of distaste he was bound to get from the staff. 'They all think I'm just there for a free bed or the drugs,' he told me. So he stayed where he was, bedding down in London's West End, outside the Piccadilly Theatre. When the theatre staff left at the end of the day they'd leave the music playing through the external speakers, so Darren fell asleep most nights to the incessant refrain from 'It's a Hard-knock Life'. It wasn't until his friends called an ambulance for him that he realized how sick he was. He had serious blood poisoning and was in hospital for three months.

And there was Sue,* a hunched woman in her fifties with a thick east London accent. She had been discharged from hospital after months recovering from a horrible illness, only to be packed off without the bus fare to get her to the temporary flat that had been set up for her. With no means of getting across town, she dragged her walking frame, laden with bags, for miles, back to the doorway she had slept in before being admitted to hospital.

I had assumed that people were dying homeless because they were totally off the radar, because they had failed to go for help. But here they were, people approaching doctors, asking for help, and yet they were still in trouble.

More than that, analysis of medical records showed a huge spike in the need for medical services often preceding someone falling into homelessness.[62] This could be a clear warning sign that someone needed help; the moment to get support to them.

Hospital could be the perfect place to catch people like Richard, Sue, Jayne or Darren, and turn their lives around. In the three months he was in hospital, Darren kicked his heroin habit with the help of a methadone programme and got clean, Sue got stronger and ready for a fresh start. These were like *Sliding Doors* moments, points where someone's story could have gone a dramatically different way. But instead of intervening at this crucial stage, the system was just spitting people back out onto the streets, often at incredibly short notice. Patients might be told that they were being discharged in just a few hours, sometimes with nothing more than a Post-it note with the address of the local council's homeless office. And things were getting worse. More and more people were being discharged from hospitals registered as 'No fixed abode'.[63]

Soon it became clear why. I had been talking to academic Michelle Cornes, who was producing guidance on the safest way to discharge homeless patients. She had explained that back in 2013 there had been solid investment in homeless hospital discharge schemes: £10 million was ring-fenced by the Department of Health and Social Care and fifty-two schemes were set up all across the country. It had all been in

response to shocking figures that had shown 70 per cent of
homeless patients were being discharged onto the streets. The
government had been chastened into action.

And the pilot schemes had done a lot of good, quickly
saving the NHS millions of pounds by avoiding people
bouncing back to hospital soon after discharge. But, all too
inevitably, the funding had run out and one by one the schemes
had shut down. Now, twenty-seven schemes existed, and some
comprised nothing more than a solitary staff member trying
to plug the gaps. With scant resources and a lack of buy-in
from other departments in and outside of the hospital, many
of the schemes that were left were struggling.

One day I got a worried call from Michelle, her voice tense
and agitated down the line. The goalposts had been shifted:
guidance on how to safely discharge people had been quietly
changed. Previously the NHS England guidance had stated:
'Too often discharge is seen as freeing-up a hospital bed rather
than acting in the patient's best interest to move them swiftly
to a safer, more familiar environment that will encourage
supported self-management, speed recuperation and recovery
and have them feel better. We must make every effort to shift
understanding to this reality.'

'But now that really helpful phrase has been taken out,'
Michelle sighed.

In its place, the new guidance told hospitals: 'Where
patients do not meet the eligibility criteria for care and support,
or the local authority housing priority criteria, it may be necessary to discharge them back onto the street.'

'That's a loophole. A totally retrograde step,' Michelle cried.

This new guidance encouraged hospital staff to get people
like Richard out as soon as possible. It encouraged them not
to ask or register whether someone was homeless or not.
Forget the previous prompting to work 'in the patient's best

interests', now the official policy was to patch them up and ship them out.

I was worried for Richard. Worried the winter was closing in and he was losing patience with the cold hostel. Worried that each time he went to hospital he was spun around and sent right back out again. How much longer could that sorry dance go on for?

I was beginning to feel more and more like the powers that be simply did not want to know the scale of the problem before them. Beyond no one counting when people were dying, I had heard how safeguarding boards were refusing to investigate deaths, how official shelters were turning away people who didn't fit their criteria, how councils were finding ways to deny that someone was really homeless and in need.

I needed more evidence. I needed data. And as luck would have it, the closest thing to a homelessness census was just about to start.

The Overground was winding its way to Highbury and Islington station when a man shuffled into our carriage.

'I'm sorry to bother you, folks, but I'm trying to get some money together for a hostel, so if anyone can spare any change or a bit of food it'd be much appreciated.'

I slipped off my thick gloves and scrabbled in my bag for one of the flapjack bars I'd stored away there, thinking back to the days when I would have pretended not to see this guy. I still wasn't quite sure what was the appropriate thing to do in situations like this. Embarrassed at the meagre offering, I passed it over.

Outside, the night sky was inky black already. It was winter, a Thursday night, and Islington's fancy Upper Street was buzzing with drunken revellers. I wove my way through the smokers, huddled in their exiled packs, and the couples hungrily kissing on the corners, onwards to the bright glow of number 222, Islington Council's office building.

Through the glass front I spotted Jon right away. He was there, trademark flat cap on, talking with housing officer Diarmaid Ward and four others. It was about 11 p.m. and I was already feeling a little sleepy. I wasn't sure I'd make it through the night.

I had been waiting months for this. Across the country I had been joined by local journalists all digging into the number of homeless deaths in their areas. From Bristol to Belfast my fellow journalists were asking questions and logging names in my database of those who had died. We were doing it, building the first data set of its kind.[64]

But the more I had learnt about homelessness in the UK, the more I realized how flawed the official data was that we already had. Which was why I was in north London that chilly evening. I was there because I wanted to find out more about how we hold data on rough-sleepers in England and Wales. The official figures had shown a massive increase since 2009, when rough-sleeping had all but disappeared in the country. Since 2010 the numbers had shot up by 169 per cent. But recently there had been a shift from councils supplying estimated figures to more snapshot counts, where officials would go out on one night of the year to count how many people they saw bedding down. I had heard mixed things about the practice. In Belfast one charity worker worried the figures were being too heavily relied on when they were wildly out of sync with reality. 'The figures say there are just sixteen people sleeping rough in the city. We know that's just not the case,' she said.

Jon was suspicious of the figures too. 'See, them – the councils – they don't know where they're looking, do they?' he'd told me some days earlier. 'You see some of these councils saying "Oh, we only have four people here, the count says so." Do they bollocks; they're just not trying to find them.'

That was why Jon was there that night, swigging gulps from a large can of Monster energy drink and talking a little too loudly in the council room crowded with volunteers. He'd approached the council saying Streets Kitchen would do their own, alternative count, on the same night, to check the council's work. The council had upped the ante and invited Jon and his team along, meaning he could see first-hand how they were undertaking the task. He'd invited me to join him.

This was the first live count the council had undertaken since 2009. In the intervening years, outreach officers had supplied estimated figures based on what they were seeing day in, day out. The year before they had estimated there were twenty-seven people sleeping rough, the year before that just eleven. I thought back to the encampment under Finsbury Park tube station bridge. I had heard how thirty-eight people had been moved on from sleeping there alone, so those estimates didn't seem quite right either. Perhaps a snap-shot count was a more accurate method after all?

I made my way through the reception area to a large open-plan office, a space lined with desks where, just hours earlier, council workers had been hard at work processing the steady stream of those who came through the doors presenting as homeless. The room was warm and people were already stripping off the layers of clothes they'd worn against the cold. Everyone was chattering away; a kind of expectant excitement washed over the room.

Jon had ambled up beside me and tapped my elbow, pointing to a slim woman with a brown bob and kindly face who was trying to get people's attention. 'That's Georgina. She works for the council. She's all right, in my opinion,' Jon whispered to me.

Georgina Earthy was the Rough Sleeping Lead and was coordinating the count. 'Thank you, everyone. I'm absolutely amazed at the turnout. It makes tonight much easier,' she said, raising her voice to he heard above the chatter. 'Sarah is somewhere walking around with the document packs. Some of you will go out in pairs, some of you will go out in threes. No photos, no selfies with people bedding down . . . Jon knows what I am talking about . . .' she said, smiling. (Jon had a real pet peeve about people posting photos of homeless people. 'Those photos can haunt them for years,' he'd told me, explaining how a photo of someone at their lowest point could prove embarrassing or even dangerous if they ever managed to escape the streets.)

'So we just wanted to run through the definition of what a rough-sleeper is, for the purposes of the count,' Georgina continued. She went on to explain what we were looking for and how we all had to check in with her during the night and come back to be officially signed off at the end. I nervously looked around the room. We'd been split into small groups and the leader of each one had a pink, plastic A4 folder with the team's names written on it in marker. I was not on Jon's list.

Feeling like a child on my first day of school, I wandered round the room before spotting my name written in bold letters on one of the folders. I was to be in a team with Kevin, a council outreach worker and former employee of St Mungo's. I didn't know my luck. Kevin had worked in outreach in this area for around nine years – he knew these streets and the people living on them well.

Next to my name on the folder was another. 'I need to find C. L. L. R Williamson,' Kevin said, and before I could explain that the letters stood for councillor, he wandered off asking around for someone called C. L. L. R.

Finally, Kevin found who he was looking for. The final member of our team was Labour councillor Flora Williamson, a young, cheery woman whose energy was to keep me going through the night.

Inside the plastic envelope was a map showing the area we were required to search. 'Bunhill . . . Never heard of it,' I said.

'I know there's a cemetery there. It's quite famous. It's down near Old Street, right?' Flora replied.

Kevin drove us to the area and found a spot near Old Street

roundabout to park. He flicked on the car's inside light and pulled out the folder we'd been given. 'OK, so we know what we're doing. This form here is where we fill in details, so we want to know name – if they want to tell us – nationality, and we want to know how long they've been out and what services they are accessing. So you can let me take the lead if you like,' said Kevin, cheerily, passing the forms to me.

Soon we were stomping down dark, cold streets. A hundred metres away the city hummed with life on the main roads of Old Street, but the quiet side streets felt like another world. I couldn't help but think back to Andrew O'Connell, who had found himself a well-lit doorway covered by CCTV in Brighton, only to be murdered while he slept. I told myself that my shaking hands were just down to the cold.

Now we were there, I realized I knew the area fairly well. In the daytime, you could walk down any main street around the area and see people sitting out, their bags and blankets left near them, but now it was dark those still out on the streets had squirreled themselves away in safe corners. I was suddenly incredibly grateful for Kevin's knowledge; I would have had no idea where to start if I had been alone.

We zigzagged from street to street, trying to work our way as methodically as we could across the yellow-highlighted section of our photocopied map. I barely saw the dark red bulge in the shadowy doorway as we walked by. It was nearing 1 a.m. now and the temperature had dropped.

'You OK there, mate?' asked Kevin confidently. The red bulge shifted and formed itself into a man. He sat up stiffly and rubbed his tired eyes. This was Gezim.* He scratched at his dark beard as he spoke, his eyes puffy and tired, almost hidden behind the cowl of a dark hooded jumper. He was just thirty-one but he looked much older.

Kevin, who had crouched down on his haunches beside

him, calmly began to draw out bits of information. Gezim was Albanian, he said, and had been working legally as a builder until his visa ran out. 'I was on the building site, a foreman. Now I have this,' he said, handing over a tattered plastic wallet covering a piece of paper with a Home Office logo. Under his phone, name and birthdate, a box had been checked: 'You are liable to be detained as it has been ascertained you are liable for deportation.'

'So I couldn't work, I was renting a place round here, near Moorfield hospital, but with no money I cannot stay there anymore,' he explained. 'I've been sleeping here for two weeks but have been other places for about a year before that.'

'Have you visited any drop-in centres locally? How do you survive now you're not working?' Kevin reeled off a list of questions while I did my best to get my cold fingers working to fill in the details on the form. The data, we had been told, would help outreach teams find these people in the future.

Gezim explained he didn't want to go to a hostel: 'There are drugs and things there,' he explained. Rocking back on his heels, Kevin gave out the name and number of a day centre in the area. 'They are open on a Friday. They've got case workers there, they've got warm food, showers – you know?'

We finished our conversation and struggled to our feet. Walking away from Gezim felt wrong. He curled himself back up in his sleeping bag, a thin layer of cardboard underneath him, framed by the MDF of the boarded-up doorway he was sleeping in. We kept walking.

About half an hour later, on another street, we were stopped by a drunk couple. 'Hey mate, do you know the way to XOYO – the nightclub,' the young man asked me hopefully as his girlfriend teetered on his arm.

'Er, no, sorry, not sure,' I muttered back.

'Ah, whatever,' the girlfriend piped up, looking annoyed at

the map in my hands. I'd forgotten about that. But giving clubbers directions was not what we were there for. About thirty metres down the same street we found two men laid out in sleeping bags over long air vents in the ground. The warm air rising around them was welcome comfort to my cold hands.

These men were Polish – builders, they said – with papers allowing them to work here. Only one spoke English – the other curled his face away, not wanting to talk to us. Soon they were joined by a third man, who came staggering over to us, a plastic Coke bottle that smelt of booze in his hand, his bright blue eyes shining angrily in his lined, bulldog face.

'What you do?' he asked accusingly. 'You immigration? We have papers.'

Kevin tried to explain but the man wasn't listening; he just squared himself up to Kevin's tall frame. 'Ah . . . You help?! How help, how help, you give money?'

A note of frustration in his voice, Kevin started to explain about the day centre. The man wasn't listening, he just shouted louder.

'OK, you're getting aggressive now, so we're going and if you follow we'll have to call the police,' Kevin warned. The man started lurching after us down the streets and wasn't showing signs of leaving. I pushed the light at the zebra crossing and was cursing how slowly it was taking to change to green. I was scared this guy was going to start swinging at us.

Finally, the crossing light flashed and we made our way over the road, only to hear the dull thunk of a lobbed plastic bottle hitting the ground behind us. Fighting the urge to turn around, we kept walking.

I wasn't completely surprised by the aggressive response. I had expected a certain level of suspicion. Many on the streets worried about being turned in to immigration officials and deported. I started to wonder if people were avoiding being seen for just that reason – how many dark alleys, bin stores and basements were we missing as we wandered the streets? Were there more people out there?

We kept going, past darkened shops and the locked-up cemetery. Flora and I tried our best to be helpful, straining our eyes in the shadows, but every time we saw something it turned out to be just discarded clothes or rubbish bags. The batteries in the small torch the council had provided had died and Kevin was using the light of his phone as he pulled open doors to bin lockers and wandered round the back of buildings and down dark alleyways. I thought of a man called Russell Lane, who had climbed into a large, industrial bin to sleep and not heard the bin men as they banged on the sides the next morning, checking if anyone was inside. At his inquest I had heard how he had been tipped into the bin lorry, his legs mangled in its crushing jaws. It was only when they heard his screams that the bin men realized what had happened. Safe sleeping-spaces were hard to come by.

We found two more people that night. There was Alex,* with his punch-flattened nose and dirty red hair. That was not his real name; Kevin knew his real name and called him it by mistake. When I later repeated it Alex flew into a rage: 'Don't call me that name, right? That's what my fucking stepdad called me when he was raping me,' he spat out angrily. Just seconds before we had been laughing amicably. I was thrown. 'I'm . . . Oh, I'm sorry,' I spluttered.

Along with him there was Rob,* who was on his feet and planning to walk into the West End to keep himself busy and warm until morning. Both were self-confessed alcoholics and had cans of extra-strength Polish lager in their hands.

We noted down their details and walked back to the car, only to find, much to Kevin's chagrin, that even at 2 a.m. on a quiet side street, the parking attendants had been out and had issued him a ticket.

We had counted five people in our patch and would later find out that a total of forty-three people had been counted across the borough of Islington that night.

As I sleepily headed home in a taxi, I was a little confused. We had found fewer people than I was expecting. But when I thought about it more, that wasn't hugely surprising. It was the depths of winter, and in the next borough, Hackney, the winter night shelters had opened up for the season, so many people who usually slept rough in the area might have gone there. And we had Kevin guiding us – the teams without his expertise were at a disadvantage. Plus we had been told not to go into dark and dangerous alleys or into basements, but how many people had we missed there? What about all those hidden away that night?

When the official figures were collated and announced a few months later, there was some surprise at the numbers. Nationwide, the statistics now suggested there had been a 2 per cent drop in rough-sleeping, the first drop of any kind in seven years. In Brighton and Hove, for example, the number of people registered as sleeping rough fell from 178 the year before to just 64 people.

But that just didn't tally with many people's daily experiences. It didn't ring true to Jim Deans, who ran the bus-turned-shelter and fed people every week, nor to Pastor Ramage or Dr Tim Worthley who, day in and day out, were seeing as many rough-sleepers as ever. 'It produced a figure that was under half of what the city's rough-sleeping campaigners estimated as the real number,' a local councillor for Brighton complained.

In South Derbyshire, the constituency of the then national Homelessness Minister Heather Wheeler, the council had logged zero rough-sleepers in the whole area. That figure had come as a surprise to long-time and well-known rough-sleeper, the self-styled 'Ebenezer Goode', who was found by an ITV documentary crew[65] in the centre of a South Derbyshire town. Ebenezer told the TV cameras he had been sleeping rough in the area for thirty-two years, yet on paper, according to the count, he did not exist. 'I know there is more than me. False count. I don't know how they missed me,' he told the documentary makers.

So if the constituency of the Homelessness Minister had failed to reflect the real picture, how could the countrywide figures be trusted?

A friend, fellow journalist Patrick Greenfield, had been looking over the areas that had recorded drops in figures and found that the vast majority were places where they had changed from supplying estimated figures to the snapshot count from one night. The methodology had changed and then the numbers had dropped.

That's what had happened in Brighton and Hove, and more than thirty other councils. When contacted by Patrick, several of the councils said they had made the counting change after advice from the Ministry of Housing, Communities and Local Government, who were doling out money through the Rough Sleeping Initiative fund.

Intrigued by Patrick's findings, I had asked several councils that had shifted to a live count after getting funding for any correspondence with the government about the stipulations of the grant. After sifting through the paperwork, I noticed government officials suggesting timing for the snapshot count and warning that if snapshot figures did not reduce between 2018 and 2019 then central officials would 'work with you to revise and refocus your proposed interventions', suggesting future funding might be in jeopardy.

Heather Wheeler insisted that switching counting methodology was not a requirement of the funding. But the chair of the UK Statistics Authority was voicing serious concerns about the changes and about the government's long time frame for improving its data. 'We would expect the department to plan for better statistics on rough-sleeping in a period shorter than nine years, to publish those plans, and to give greater clarity about the impact that the apparent change in rough-sleeping counting methods used by some Local Authorities may have had on the comparability of the statistical series,' wrote Sir David Norgrove.[66]

It was worrying. Changing the data or manipulating the figures was not going to solve homelessness. The government was shouting about grand plans to eradicate rough-sleeping by 2027 and the 2 per cent drop played into that goal, but how could progress be measured if we had no real idea of how many people were sleeping rough in the first place?

One solution was in the way Scotland collated its figures. There, when a person presented to Housing Options teams in the council they were asked if they had slept rough the night before or in the last three months. Their answers helped the government assess how many people were experiencing rough-sleeping. But even that was limited; it relied on people approaching the council and only asked for very recent experiences.

But now Scotland was exploring the idea of going even further. The Scottish government was toying with the idea of a national database for those experiencing homelessness, where someone's needs could be logged and services helping them could update what support they were providing. The same idea was being proposed in Wales too.

Something similar existed in London, called the Combined Homelessness and Information Network (CHAIN), which helped keep track of those who naturally moved from one borough to another. CHAIN wasn't without its flaws; some people didn't want to be logged on the system for fear of perceived consequences, such as deportation. But it did give a more realistic picture of who was out there and what help they were or weren't receiving. When CHAIN later produced annual figures for rough-sleepers, they had recorded 276 people sleeping rough in Islington alone, six times more than the figure we had provided (and a marked increase on previous years).[67] The area I had been searching, Bunhill, was one of the places CHAIN had marked as having the most frequent connections with rough-sleepers. Clearly our best efforts had failed to give an accurate picture of the state of homelessness in the borough – the methodology was flawed.

Those sleeping physically on the streets might be at the extreme end of homelessness, but they are just part of the picture. As I shivered my way home after the Islington count I couldn't stop thinking of all those who wouldn't be included on either the snapshot count or the rough-sleeper database. Richard in his emergency hostel. Alfie in the hospice. David in his car. There were more people out there, hidden away, I knew that. And soon, I would find even more.

In a looming townhouse on the outskirts of Bradford, up a steep twisting staircase, Grace* sat waiting for her baby. A hundred or so metres down the road I was on my way towards her, tagging along while a friend of hers pushed her ten-month-old boy, Joseph,* through the streets in his pushchair. Joseph's large, ponderous eyes stared up at us, fixed, almost catatonic. The baby made me nervous; his blank stare reminded me of children from the TV news, shell-shocked and vacant in the midst of some great disaster.

On arriving at the three-storey red-brick house, we made our way through a kitchen pulled apart by builders, past the tattered and stained sofas of the living room and up the stairs to Grace's door. As soon as Joseph saw his mother, his dull eyes lit up, his serious face broke into a smile – she was his home.

Grace was not what many would consider homeless. She had a roof over her head, after all, a room with a bed, a small fridge, and en suite shower. But it was not home. She did not want to be there and she had no idea how long she would be. She was hidden away from the world and forgotten about. And she had ended up there in the most dramatic of ways.

As we settled down in her room, Joseph gurgling happily on the double bed next to her, Grace told me the tale of how she had been lured from her home in Uganda to Saudi Arabia by the promise of well-paid work. "'You're going to have a good life, the work will bring a good salary, in five years you will be a rich girl," they told me.'

She had paid 2 million Ugandan shillings (the equivalent of £400) to traffickers with their promises of better jobs abroad, but when she got to Saudi Arabia the men that had arranged the trip took her to a rich family who confiscated her passport. She had been tricked. Grace was told she must work as a cleaner for the family, taking care of their young children too. They made her sign a contract in a language she didn't understand. Scared and confused, Grace obeyed. There was no going out without their permission, no friends. If she spoke out she was beaten. She was paid a pittance, and without her passport she had no way to escape.

For six and a half months Grace worked there from morning until midnight. She was denied even basic toiletries and took to washing her skin and hair with laundry detergent, which she could sneak away. Her skin grew ashy and dry, her hair – which she had once taken such pride in – was unoiled and brittle.

Then the family moved her to the UK, to their house in Acton, west London. In the car from the airport Grace tried to take in the tall buildings, the grey sky. She was put to work in the family's house – there were seven children and the two parents, it was cramped inside, and she was expected to look after them all. They paid her £170 a month but told her they were sending it directly to her aunt back in Uganda. Here, too, she was trapped. Her captors told her, 'Don't go outside, people here don't like black people. If you go outside they will kill you.' She didn't know what to believe.

For months Grace's home was a prison. She slept on a thin mattress in a tiny storeroom. The father of the house told her, 'I will be with you any time I like.' He would rape her.

The winter set in, cold and grey, a million miles from

home. But Grace was making a plan. One day, when the family were distracted, she saw her chance and slipped out the back door. Even if it was true and people outside did want to kill all black people, it was better than this, she reasoned.

It was February and freezing cold. She had run out without her shoes and the ground beneath her feet sent freezing darts of pain up her legs. Panicking, she tripped and fell. She scrambled up and banged on the neighbour's door but no one answered. Mad with fear, she climbed the garden fence, hitching herself up on the trellis. She tried at four more houses, desperately pounding on the doors and windows, crying out for help. At the fifth house an old woman answered.

'Mama, help me,' she pleaded to the pensioner. The lady looked at her, confused.

'Why are you shaking? Where are your shoes?'

'Please! I think people are following me!' Grace cried.

'OK, OK, don't kneel down. Let me call the police.'

The police had come. She had been taken to immigration control, where she told her story. An asylum claim had been put in. But that was all months ago.

Grace had been moved up to a safe house in Leeds and was told she would be there for forty-five days. A year and four months later they moved her to this shelter in Bradford. There she'd become pregnant and had her son. She was still waiting for her asylum case to be decided, so she couldn't access mainstream welfare benefits. Instead, her housing situation had been arranged by the Home Office. She showed me the letter they had sent. 'Accommodation is provided on a no-choice basis. You should have no expectation that alternative accommodation will be provided to you if you do not accept the accommodation allocated to you.' She'd been put into the homeless hostel for women – this hulking old

town house run by G4S.* There were fourteen women staying there, most with children, and many had long lists of
complaints.

'This is our fifth day without any hot water,' one told me.

'My room's so small there is barely space for my girl to
crawl around,' said another. 'A rat ate my baby's doll.'

'When I first saw my room, I cried so much,' said another.
'It was dirty, the little fridge smelt so bad, there was mould
on the walls. I waited for someone to come and clean it but
no one did so I cleaned it myself, but the mould came back.
It is not fit for someone with a child.'

Grace said the same. 'There are mice in the rooms, the
lift is not working.' She had tried her best to make it homely.
Joseph's cot lay next to her bed, his little clothes folded neatly
in the corner, and on the wall she had stuck some colourful
alphabet stickers. Dotted around the room were cheap, charity-
shop picture frames holding vibrant, colourful photographs
of Grace and her family back in Uganda, smiling proudly in
gold-and-red shiny dresses.

Grace's room was on the first floor and she had seriously
hurt her foot and stomach in previous accidents. As she
showed me the scars, I thought of what a doctor in Edinburgh
had told me – that many of the patients he sees who have
traumatic pasts suffer with chronic pain, pain that sometimes
has a psychological, rather than physiological, source. Research

---

*   G4S later told me they no longer ran COMPASS, the service that was in
charge of the day-to-day running of the shelter Grace was living in. A
spokesperson explained: 'Over the course of the contract, G4S' priority was
to ensure the people living in the accommodation provided were taken care
of and complaints were always taken very seriously. We conducted more
than 4,000 inspections every month and those inevitably revealed some
defects in properties and their inventory that required repair or replacement. Our asylum seekers could also access a free multilingual 24/7 service
centre by telephone to report defects.'

found a quarter of people experiencing homelessness have been experiencing chronic pain for over ten years.[68]

But Grace was also suffering from a very recent accident, and her foot was bandaged heavily. A few weeks ago she had cut her foot badly on the jagged metal frame under the bathroom door, leaving her unable even to hobble up and down the twisting stairs. She was told she needed an operation but there was no one to look after her baby boy so she had turned it down. She had asked the Home Office to move her to another space, at least while her foot healed and she was immobile. Her GP wrote to them, too, asking the same, and so had her family support worker, but all she had heard was silence. Instead, she was relying on women from the local mother-and-babies group to deliver food, nappies and take Joseph out for playtimes.

'All I have now is Joseph,' she told me sadly. 'He is my only friend.'

As I left, it had started to snow lightly outside, the flakes tapping quietly on the draughty sash windows in Grace's room. I left her there, a trafficking victim and her child trapped in her first-floor room, shuttered away where we don't have to think of them.

As Grace sat stuck in her room, down in London, Sallie* was preparing to make her escape. She was desperate: her boyfriend of seven months had turned into a controlling monster, he would scream in her face in front of her children, monitor her movements and fly into jealous rages if her mobile phone ran out of battery while she was out. When she hid with her children in a locked room he tried to break the door down. Then there was the sexual violence, the spitting, the strangulation, the slapping.

It had all happened so quickly. She and her two sons had been doing well, living in a rented flat in south London, when out of nowhere her landlord had issued them with a Section 21 'no fault' eviction notice. She and her boyfriend had started dating just a few months earlier and he had convinced her that the solution to her housing troubles was for them to rent a place together, pooling their wages to be able to afford something decent. Sallie didn't have many options – she went with it. Then the abuse had started.

'From the minute I moved in it was absolute hell. He was a total control freak, would take receipts out of the bin . . . He assaulted me outside my workplace,' she told me, the anger bubbling in her voice. It all became too much. She packed a suitcase, took her two sons and fled.

But Sallie had nowhere to go. Her mother, a retired teacher, lived far away in a one-bedroom flat. She tried calling the national refuge hotline as well as a local refuge, but no one could find her a space. One of her sons was a young teenager and tall for his age, which meant the refuges wouldn't take him.

Desperate, she approached the council instead, applying as homeless. There she and her boys were given emergency accommodation in a bed and breakfast for the night, and then invited back for a full assessment interview. The council officer had been sensitive and appeared understanding. He helped her work up her homelessness application. 'The reason for my homelessness is due to fleeing domestic violence. My children and I have nowhere to go or stay,' she had written.

The council worker reassured Sallie that they'd get it all sorted out quickly. They would place the family in temporary accommodation for now while the decision was made as to whether they would get a more permanent council flat. New legislation brought in by the government earlier that year meant the council had a time limit of fifty-six days to try and relieve her homelessness before making a decision on whether she would qualify for long-term help. Fifty-six days – she could handle that.

When Sallie walked through the doors of the shelter she had felt relief. It was far from ideal; just two rooms on the ground floor, blank walls, high ceilings and draughty sash windows which had been plastered over with yellowing newspaper to provide some kind of privacy. There were two short bunk beds in one room – a place for her boys – and a queen-sized double for her, crammed into the kitchen space. She set up her boys' suitcases and toys along the wall. This would be home for now. At least it was safe.

Six months later she was still there, still unsure if the council was going to decide whether they had a duty to house them or not. There were loud, violent neighbours, male and female, who screamed down the halls, sometimes until 4 a.m. Sallie had recorded the racket on her phone and sent it to the council: 'Living here is not pleasant as it is, and the conditions are being further exacerbated by the resident(s) above us.' No reply.

A man upstairs had schizophrenia. A woman in a room nearby also had mental health issues. There was domestic violence going on in the shelter. Sallie's neighbour had come home to find a man on the shelter steps beating a woman with a belt. Once, Sallie's teenage son was coming back from the shops when he ran into a couple fighting in the corridor. The woman grabbed his arm screaming, 'Help! He's going to stab me! Get him out of here, get him out of here!' The boy, just thirteen, was traumatized, scared every time he had to leave the room to go to the shared bathroom. He had started to self-harm and was being bullied at school. One morning, after arriving through the school gates, he went into a toilet cubicle and tried to slit his wrists. 'We left hell, the screaming and banging, and then we came here and it was the same again.' Sallie struggled to get the words out, her throat tight with sorrow. 'They knew we had fled domestic violence and they put us here.'

The building was as fragile as its residents. When it rained, water ran through the ceiling tiles in the corridor outside the shared bathroom, and sodden chunks had fallen down. The council, who owned the building, had reassured the residents that it wasn't rain but that rats had chewed through pipes. The fire alarms were always going off for no reason, and around once every month the fire brigade was out, exasperatedly looking over the property.

Another woman, who lived down the hall with her toddler, had been in the shelter for over a year. She too had fled domestic violence. 'They don't care,' she told me, listing the times she had complained to the council about conditions there. 'They leave us here like animals.' Her young boy tugged at her skirt, nervously.

'We get told it's not the worst hostel, there's worse places,' Sallie chipped in. The council's message was, in essence, be grateful you've got a roof over your head, even if it is mouldering with damp and chewed by rats.

As the winter grew colder, Sallie and her boys realized the radiators in their room didn't work. She tried buying a fan heater but it left the plug socket scorched and brown. Instead she took to sleeping in with her youngest, nursery-aged son, snuggling in among the six small teddies he had lined up by his pillow. Overnight she left the oven on low with the door open, to try and keep her boys from shivering.

Sallie worked as a security guard at a supermarket twenty-four hours a week, though she always volunteered for any overtime going. It wasn't the job she had dreamed of in her days at private school – she'd been attacked, bitten, strangled – 'but I've got children to look after, and I'm trying to improve our circumstances.' She had worked solidly since she was sixteen years old, and was now thirty-three. She remembered taking umbrage with the shock she had seen in the council officer's face when he had heard she was working. It shouldn't have been that surprising – more than half of families living in temporary accommodation were holding down jobs.[69] Shop workers, waiting staff, teaching assistants, carers at old people's homes – across the country people were finishing their working days and heading back to shelters or bed and breakfasts.

Because Sallie was working, she had to pay more to live in the shelter than those who were unemployed. Her rent was £236.17 a week (which included all utility bills and council tax), and about £100 of that came out of her pocket; the rest was made up from housing benefit. That left her with £100 a week to feed her kids, dress them, pay for transport and everything else. She wasn't managing to save much and that was worrying her. 'We've had to start over from scratch, so I'm working all the hours I can because when we get out of here we have to replace all the possessions we left when we ran,' she explained.

The days went by. Then weeks. Then months. Sallie was meant to have received a decision within fifty-six days on whether the family would be found housing. In the end it took 184 days for her to get her decision: that she and her two children did qualify for support and would be given a flat when one became available. It had been a hugely frustrating wait, but Sallie could still see the positive side: 'There are people in here that have been a year with no decision on their case,' she said, sighing.

Now she was about to start bidding on council flats as and when they became available. Each week new properties would be advertised on the council's website and she could choose which looked appropriate for her. It could be a long process.

Bidding on a place did not mean she would get it – there was still something of a lottery involved. A lady who had turned up at the shelter pregnant was still bidding on one-bed flats even now. Her baby had turned one; the little one's entire life had been spent waiting to get out of the shelter. 'It's the not knowing,' Sallie said, tired out. 'People here are scared to speak out, some don't speak English, you're scared in case the council takes what you have from you. There are so many people living like this in the UK and I just can't believe it. You know this isn't even the worst of it. I wouldn't be in this position if I had any other option. I don't want to be in this position.'

So her boys' games and toys remained unpacked. The banging and shouting in the halls went on. Sallie put her kids to bed that night not sure when they would next have a place they could truly call home. It was a thought that echoed in hotel rooms and shelter beds across the country. At that very moment, there were 125,300 children living like her sons, in temporary accommodation all across England. That winter child homelessness hit a twelve-year high in the UK.

Leaving Sallie in her shelter room, I was struck by the frustration of it all. Here was a single mother who was working hard, who had access to housing benefits, and yet was still beholden to the council for a place to live. Her wages and benefits were still not enough to cover the exorbitant rents anywhere near her sons' school and nursery.

In 2016 housing benefits (known officially as Local Housing Allowance) were frozen until 2020, in a move designed to save the government £3.5 billion. But while payouts were frozen, private rents just kept on rising, meaning more and more properties became simply unaffordable. And then there was the huge barrier of landlords refusing to rent to people on benefits. Housing charity Shelter employed professional mystery shoppers to pose as prospective tenants on housing benefits and approach letting agents. Out of the 149 letting agent branches that were approached, one in ten 'had a branch policy not to let to anyone on housing benefit, regardless of whether they could afford the rent.'[70]

Intrigued, I tried my own version of the experiment. I picked five cities across the UK and used the government's benefits calculator to work out what I could theoretically afford in each area if I was on housing benefit. The amount I could get in housing benefits varied from place to place, as it is based on market price, so, if I was a single mother looking for a two-bed flat for me and a fictional eight-year-old daughter, I could get £424 a month in Bradford and up to £1,025 a month in east London. I knew from my research that renters on housing benefit often ended up topping up their rent with their own funds, so I added a bonus of £100 a month into the budget.

Then I started my search for a place to live, hunting on a variety of rental websites for anything I could afford within that budget. I was searching for places in Bradford, London, Stafford, Milton Keynes and Salford. It was slim pickings. Time and time again I would fill in the website's search terms and hit 'Search', only to be told: 'There are no properties matching your criteria.' I found myself edging the budget up, looking further and further out of town centres.

I scanned the details of the handful of properties that would be affordable. There, buried deep in the descriptions of many of them, were lines like: 'No pets, no smokers and no housing benefit'; 'Please note housing benefit, part- or full-time, claimants are not accepted'; or simply, 'No DSS'.

In other cases it was less clear whether my fictional family

of two would be allowed to rent, so I set up an email address
and fired off a few quick emails:

Hi,

*I'm looking for a two bed flat for me and my 8yr old daughter.
Saw this one and looks really nice. Just wanted to check if landlord
accepts people paying rent through housing benefits?*

Thanks!

Then I waited. Two weeks later, out of fifty properties I had
enquired about, I received just sixteen replies. Eleven of those
had told me outright that the landlord would not accept anyone
on housing benefit, no matter what the circumstances. Only
two said they would consider it (the others were asking for
more information or telling me the properties had been let).

One by one I read through the responses I'd received, often
comprising just a line or two.

'I can advise unfortunately the landlord does not accept
tenants on housing benefits.'

'Unfortunately our company does not accept DSS/housing
benefit on any of our properties. This is due to the referencing
company we use and us having to adhere to their rules and
regulations.'

'Sorry, I have checked and the landlord will not accept
housing benefit. I do not have anything at the moment that
I can help you with.'

Some were just plain presumptuous.

'Hi, The landlord is not accepting that as your income is
too low and you would not pass the credit check the landlord
undertakes to insure the rent,' one estate agent wrote. They
hadn't asked what savings I had or whether I could provide
a guarantor for the tenancy. It was just an assumption that if
I was on benefits, I could not pay.

It had been a struggle to find properties that were even
affordable within the narrow limits of the long-frozen Local

Housing Allowance. The few that did exist would not even consider the prospect of renting to someone on benefits. I stared at my emails. It was an impossibly cruel conundrum.[*]

'We see that all the time,' a housing lawyer at a community law centre in north-west London told me. 'And it gets worse. Councils have a duty now to prevent homelessness, but all we're seeing here is them handing out a list of estate agents and private landlords where people can try and rent. When I called up every name on that list, every single one told me they wouldn't rent to someone on housing benefits.'

A few months after meeting with Sallie, I checked on her again. She was still bidding. Every Thursday the council would post a list of available properties on their website, and Sallie would sift through them all, desperately bidding on any that looked suitable from the limited information. On Sunday nights bidding ended and she would find out where in the queue her bid was. It was always horrifyingly low on the list. She had been told she and her boys would be in the shelter for a year, but at this rate she was worried it would be more like two. The bathroom on her floor had been cordoned off and was unusable, and a leak had appeared in the ceiling above her boys' bunk beds. But she was stuck.

I was worried for Sallie and her boys. And for Grace and

---

[*]   I tried repeating this experiment on a bigger scale. My colleagues Charles Boutaud, Tom Blout and I scraped the details of every two-bed property advertised on one day across Great Britain, using the property-rental site aggregator Nestoria. We then mapped these 62,695 properties against the Local Housing Allowance rates in each area. Only 3,492 (5.6 per cent) were affordable. Some areas, including Bristol, Cardiff and Milton Keynes, had fewer than ten affordable properties even though they each had several hundred listings. We then tried contacting a 10 per cent sample of the affordable properties. Of those that were still available, 49 per cent of landlords said they would not rent to anyone on benefits, while 32 per cent said they would but only if the person had a guarantor or could meet other conditions, like paying six months' rent upfront.

little Joseph. From what I knew of the impact of traumatic childhood experiences, I couldn't help but fear that the thousands of children across the country living in unsuitable, temporary homes were being set up for the homeless crisis of the future. It felt like we were spiralling. There had to be a way out, a foothold to halt this freewheeling fall. A way to rise from the ashes.

David the artist lay motionless on the ground, the light from the ambulance siren casting brief shadows on his face. Paramedics huddled over him, working furiously. Moments earlier he had been pacing the floor crying, his shaking hands desperately grasping a small notebook.

The paramedics leant back on their haunches. They stopped working. It was futile. I held my breath, frozen.

The audience erupted.

I had travelled up to Manchester to see David's opera *Man on Bench*, a heartbreakingly personal piece inspired by his suicide attempts. In a cavernous, abandoned warehouse, David and his team had constructed an incredible theatrical event. For an hour David recounted the worthlessness, self-pity, loneliness and frustration he had felt while homeless. His first line, uttered in a faltering voice, was: 'I am vermin.'

Fake tea-light candles surrounded the stage, each one marking someone who had died that year. On the side of the real ambulance he had hired for the show, David had projected many of their names and faces – I had passed the list and images I had collected to him earlier. David had remarked how easily he could have been just another name on that sad register.

Music swelled. Performers dressed in costumes he had made from items found on the streets swarmed onto the stage.

From stage right a choir of maybe thirty people strode on, the Liverpool Chapter of the Choir With No Name, a collection of people who had experienced homelessness. As they congregated on stage they began to sing a refrain from British singer Rag 'n' Bone Man: 'I'm only human after all / Don't put your blame on me.' Three-quarters of the cast had experienced homelessness. The play had spoken to many of them, and the air was charged with emotion.

Later, I asked David why he had turned the worst moments of his life into theatre, and he paused. 'For Gavin,' he said, 'because he saved me.' The park guard who had been the only one to stop and ask him what was wrong. The title of David's play – *Man on Bench* – was as much about the saviour as it was the saved. Gavin had hoped to get up to Manchester to watch the show but something had come up and he couldn't make it. He was still a little bemused by the whole thing. 'It's really surreal,' he chuckled nervously when I talked to him. 'I just think: bloody hell, I was just doing my job!'

After leaving David with some food and the appointment for the hostel, Gavin had walked away and not heard anything about David for years. 'I was wondering if he'd turn up, to be honest,' he said, smiling. Plenty of people he had tried to help would end up missing vital meetings or failing to follow them up themselves. So he had been bemused when, after such a long time, David had got in touch about meeting again for a short film he was making. 'I remembered him the minute they called. I couldn't remember his name but I could see him clearly.'

David never forgot Gavin, the man who had come to symbolize the moment his life had turned around.

But mining his life for his art had not been easy. Putting on the show had been a stressful experience. David had never meant to perform in it; he had an actor lined up but he had pulled out at the last minute, leaving David to pick up the central role. That very morning his production team had been telling him to cancel – David was so stressed he couldn't speak a sentence without bursting into tears. His friends were worried about him.

And yet he had pushed on. Now, as the audience rose to their feet cheering, David crouched to the floor sobbing, overcome with emotion. He had done it.

Five years on from his darkest moment he was thriving as an artist, and this play was his way of telling his own redemption story, of that moment on the park bench, when his life turned around and he started again.

Swallowing his sobs, David addressed the audience. 'In 2013 a man saved my life. If it wasn't for one person stepping over and talking to me, taking a chance on this, none of this would exist.

'This has broken me, this art piece, it really has. I just want people to leave here and consider other people for once. We are living in a society that's trying to get rid of compassion and empathy. But I believe art can change the world.'

The audience rose to their feet once more.

As I watched him take his bow, convulsing and trembling with emotion, I felt a rush of elation. There was hope, there was a way back. David Tovey was living proof. A man with myriad illnesses, mental health issues and shame. A man who had experienced misfortune after misfortune – there he was, surviving it all, telling his story. And it started with him being seen.

Blinking as I left the warehouse, I made my way through the streets of Manchester feeling excited. It was the second time I had been to the city in a few weeks and it was beginning to feel like the epicentre of change.

*

The previous month I had pulled my coat tighter as I made my way down the familiar sloping path towards Piccadilly Gardens, taking in the familiar sights like old friends. I grew up not far from Manchester and for much of my teenage years it had felt like my one connection to the real world, full of the culture, food and clothing I couldn't find in my small home town. But on recent visits I had been struck by the scale of the homelessness there. On the short walk from the station to the square, a ten-minute walk at most, I passed five people sitting on the streets.

Police would often hassle the rough-sleepers here, telling them to move on, threatening them with arrest for perceived attempts at begging. A little later the city council announced plans for a crackdown on rough-sleeping, introducing fines of up to £100 for those considered to be loitering or acting in an antisocial way.

Meanwhile, people were dying homeless and the council had no official count of how and why it was happening. The coroner's office here was recording a death of someone classed as 'No fixed abode' about every six weeks.[71] Those working in the various grassroots outreach teams across the city were sick of the silence. Today, they were planning to force people to listen. They were taking to the streets, to shout about the number of homeless deaths in the city.

I squinted against the bright winter sun and scanned the concrete stretch of Piccadilly Gardens, its raised corners and pillars providing neat cover for the various clusters of Spice users that sat or lay frozen around its edges. Jon had told me to meet him and the group here, but there was no sign of him.

Nervous in case I'd got the wrong date, I pulled out my phone and dialled his number.

'Ah, yeah, y'all right,' Jon shouted down the line, barely

audible over the din of shouts in the background. 'Yeah, we left the Gardens. We're marching to the city hall.'

Minutes later, panting slightly, I caught up with the group, about forty people in total, as they marched down an echoey, narrow street and onto the square before Manchester town hall. Jon had brought a large black tarpaulin daubed with white paint that was flaking off and dusting the protesters in a fine dandruff of paint chips. The sign had been misspelled but the message was clear enough – it read: 'No More Homeleless Death'. As they walked, they chanted: 'No More Deaths, On Our Streets.'

While the group assembled in front of the grand, orange-stoned Town Hall building, I pulled out my notepad and surveyed the crowd. Among them were many of the city's volunteers, the groups beyond the official charities, that had seen the spiralling homelessness crisis and had stepped up to the challenge.

There was Darryl, with dyed-black hair, mum-like in her demeanour, who ran a soup kitchen once a week. Anthony, with his woollen hat pulled low and the white paint-flakes caught in his eyelashes. He volunteered at a breakfast club for rough-sleepers – or 'Manchester's Finest' as he liked to call them. Mark, with his knock-off Burberry scarf, tan face and bulbous nose. Softly spoken with a broad Mancunian accent, he told me about the night shelter he'd set up in a disused church hall. 'We do it all from donations now,' he explained. 'There's room for twenty people and we're always full. Most come and go but there's this one lad we've been helping for months. He'd been trafficked from Slovakia to Reading. He's been with us for a year and of course the council won't help him because he can't get public funds.'

After an hour or so of chanting and singing, the group disbanded, most taking up the suggestion from Anthony to follow him to the Old Nag's Head pub, a low-ceilinged, cosy working-men's boozer tucked down a side road, shielded from the blossoming gentrification of the rest of the Northern Quarter.

Perched on a low-slung sofa, I got talking to Reuben, a balding man with a long, biker-style goatee beard and wrap-around sunglasses. Reuben knew the homeless sector well, and on the way back to London on the train I flipped on my phone and friended him on Facebook.

Over the next couple of weeks Reuben and I kept in touch, and so, when Jon told me he'd heard that Reuben was involved in setting up a squat in Manchester, I wanted to hear more.

Hey, did I see you guys had set up a shelter/squat? I wrote to him in Facebook Messenger. *I was thinking of heading up to Manchester again next weekend. Do you think you'll still be going then or is it a temporary thing?*

Will be here, came his reply.

So after watching David Tovey's heart-wrenching opera, I jumped onto a tram and headed out to Eccles, carefully following the instructions Reuben had sent. Finally I found the place. Sitting right next to a red-brick Salvation Army hall was a three-storey former GPs' surgery. This was the place Reuben and others had made their home.

It was dark by the time I got there. The winter evening had drawn in faster than I had expected, and it was with a certain amount of trepidation that I made my way round the dank alley to the car park behind the building. I couldn't help but remember the looming shadows and broken glass of the crack den I'd peeped into while in Bradford. Just what was I getting myself into? Hurriedly I texted the address to my partner, with a note: *Just so you know, this is where I am. Will call you when done.*

And then I called Reuben.

It was not what I was expecting. Inside, the building was warm and bright. A side door led straight into what had been the surgery's waiting room. Now the built-in receptionist desk acted as a room divider and makeshift shelf, gathering piles of DVDs, papers, jigsaws in boxes and a vase of flowers. Someone had strung fairy lights over the window and they sent their warm glow dancing onto the ceiling. Around the edge of the room the group had arranged a series of sofas and armchairs, and in the centre was a family-sized dining table, homely with a purple table-cloth.

It had been an experienced squatter who had first found the space. Stuart Potts, or 'Pottsy', was a force of nature. With a naughty sparkle in his eye, he reminded me of Jon.

Pottsy rubbed his stubbly black hair, pulling his hand over his weather-beaten face when he spoke about the past. He had been in and out of prison a few times, lived in tents, sofa-surfed, you name it. And on the way he had become something of a connoisseur of squatting. He had developed the keen eye of the property hunter, always on the lookout for the big buildings whose lights never even flicker on. The doors left carelessly open, the windows already smashed in. These days he kept a mental list of the places he saw sitting empty. Not houses – it was illegal to squat in those – but old non-residential buildings were fair game. This former GP's surgery had lain empty and boarded up for years.

Getting in was easy, and once he was in it was a case of making sure someone was there every night. He knew the law; he knew that to be legally evicted the owners would need to serve notice on the people staying there. 'Then we take 'em to court – buy ourselves some time – and move people some-where else. We've got a plan; we have another four places lined up to move to after this one,' he explained as he proudly gave me the grand tour.

The building sprawled over three floors, with numerous rooms, including a kitchen and bathroom on each floor. As we trudged up the stairs, I thought of Jon and his dreams of finding a space like this. I wished he could see me now.

I was just beginning to relax when a hulking monster lumbered around the corner – a cartoonishly large, caramel-coloured French mastiff dog, his thick skull like a battering ram. I clutched my rucksack protectively as he padded over towards me.

'Don't worry about him, he's a sweetheart really,' a voice came, laughing, from down the corridor. Stacie appeared smiling from round the corner, her hand outstretched in greeting.

'He's a little softy, aren't ya, Kion,' she cooed, grinning at him. 'His breed was bred for guarding mansions but here he is looking after us.'

Kion gazed lovingly up at his owner. He would plod through the corridors after her, nervous when she was out of his sight. At night he'd chance his luck and, if she was in a good enough mood, he could sneak onto the bed.

Stacie and her dog had been in the squat for a week and a half now, and she was surprised at just how at home she felt.

'People expect squats to be all roaches and people shooting up in the hallways, but it's not like that,' Stacie told me, her neat eyebrows arching to make her point. There were rules of course: no violence, no hard drugs in public spaces, and no Spice. 'It turns people mental,' Pottsy chipped in. But other than that, it was simply a case of trying to be respectful to each other.

'Are you on cooking duty tonight, then?' Pottsy asked Stacie, cheerily.

'Yep, but don't get your hopes up. I haven't tried this recipe before,' she said, turning to me. 'You can give me a hand if you like.'

Upstairs in the kitchen, Stacie hitched up the sleeves on her peach-coloured jumper, adorned with a sequined version of the Manchester bee symbol. Tonight she was making dinner for thirteen people, the current inhabitants of the 'Saving People Shelter', as they had come to name the place. As this was her first night cooking for the group, she wanted to get it right.

There was ample food in the larder to choose from. 'It looks like an Asda has exploded in there,' one of the residents joked to her as she picked out cans from the shelves. Donations to the centre had been coming in thick and fast since it opened two weeks ago. They were working through the fresh stuff as fast as they could, but what they couldn't eat was packaged up and sent out with outreach teams to people on the streets. It was a well-oiled operation, Stacie thought.

It was these very donations that had brought her here. She had wandered into her local pub one night, looking for a quiet place to stop and think. She was weighing up her options. Her boyfriend of eighteen months had just turned violent. She would later downplay the incident: 'It wasn't like abuse or anything, he just got physical.' But she knew enough to get out. She'd experienced domestic abuse before. For five years a previous boyfriend had beaten and bullied her, tracking her down when she tried to leave and kidnapping her. When this latest man showed signs of violence she knew right away she had to get out. But where to go was another issue.

She had sat in the pub, racking her brain. If she went to the council for help there was no guarantee she would be classed as 'priority need'. Around 2,000 women a year are faced with homelessness after fleeing domestic violence.[72] A refuge wouldn't work, nor would a homeless shelter. They simply wouldn't accept animals but she wasn't leaving Kion. She'd had him since he was born – before, even. She had told her friend, the owner of a pregnant bitch, 'I'm taking the third puppy out.' When Kion arrived, a sopping bundle on the kitchen floor, Stacie burst the birthing sack surrounding his tiny frame herself. *There is no way I am leaving that dog behind*, she thought to herself. It was a refrain I had heard a great deal. Let down by society, many of those experiencing home-lessness turned to the love of a pet to keep them going. Often they would prioritize the needs of the animal above their own. I'd heard of doctors' services purposefully providing veterinary sessions for pets as a way to get to their owners. 'It's a way to make contact with patients who would never come for help for themselves,' explained Dr John Budd up in Edinburgh. One vet in London told me sadly how they had lost more owners than dogs in that last year. A man who had died while sleeping rough had been identified because his loyal dog, who would not leave his side, had been registered, along with the name of his owner, with the local street-vet team.

Stacie wasn't giving Kion up, that much was clear. *I could buy a tent*, she'd thought. *If it was a good one maybe it wouldn't be too bad, and Kion would keep me warm, anyway.*

Life hadn't been easy for Stacie. She had left home at fourteen. She could just about be in the same room with her mother now, but back then every interaction had ended in screaming fits. She slept on friends' sofas or floors for a bit, and then got taken in by a neighbour, a lady who would take in the waifs and strays of the town. She stayed there until seventeen, when she became pregnant.

That was thirteen years ago now. These days, her son was living with his paternal grandmother. Stacie remembered the time, on his seventh birthday, when he had saved up his birthday money – £50 in total – and asked her if he could use the money to buy sandwiches, fruit and drinks for the homeless. Together he and Stacie spent a day handing the supplies out around Manchester. 'The only thing I've done right in my life is that child. The only thing I can safely say I am proud of is him,' Stacie told me later.

Sitting in the pub, weighing up her options, Stacie's attention had been caught by movement across the room. Wandering over she found the barmaids sorting through a pile of clothes and canned food.

'Where's this going?' Stacie asked.

'It's for a homeless squat that just opened down the road,' the barmaid told her. Stacie's heart leapt. There on the table, among cans of peas and carrots, were several cans of dog food. Could this be her way out?

A few weeks later she had her own room with a decent bed, and things were starting to look up.

They were a good bunch, the folks here. Not without their issues – but who was? – she said, introducing me to the group. There was Raul, the Romanian handyman who had taken it upon himself to fix whatever needed fixing, including giving Stacie a lock on her bedroom door. His wife Christina was smiley but mostly mute, given her lack of English. She'd sneak Kion biscuits and treats when Stacie's back was turned.

Daniel,* with his sandy-blond hair and cool-grey eyes, would lean in and listen intently as people spoke. There was something about him that reminded me of some of the boys I went to high school with – the lilting Mancunian accent, the cheeky smile. He had a calm, almost gentle demeanour, so it was a shock when I heard how he had been in and out of prison for armed robberies, sticking up post offices.

Then there was sixty-five-year-old Phil, who had been

released from prison after serving time for groping a woman. He'd been released with nowhere to go to and had ended up sleeping on a cardboard mat in the local bus shelter, cowering from drunk teenagers, who would spit at and threaten him. Other times he'd hop on the train out to the airport and sleep in the departure lounge. Since arriving at the squat, he could often be found hunched in one of the living-room armchairs. The old man would watch as the young ones hurried to and fro, huffing to himself occasionally. It could get noisy at times. Pottsy would carry a portable speaker around with him, blaring electronic music wherever he went; and some of the residents would shout down the halls to each other. But Stacie was looking after Phil. She'd take the £10 he'd offer and buy him cigarettes and strong, 9 per cent Karpackie Polish lager, and come back with exactly the right change.

'She has a kind heart,' Phil smiled at me.

Just the other day Stacie had returned with a pigeon with a broken wing in her arms. 'The poor thing's hurt,' she'd said, tucking it carefully into the protective confines of a bush by the door.

I couldn't help but smile as I watched the discarded residents of this makeshift home coo and care over the pigeon with the broken wing. Days later, when it died, Stacie announced to us all that there was going to be a pigeon funeral.

CHAPTER 23

Homelessness is a prison

Not long after my first visit to the squat, I was back in the neighbourhood, wandering past the reclaimed surgery building and the fresh pigeon grave. I wanted to drop in and say hello but I was running late. I was heading to the Salford Unemployed and Community Resource Centre, where many of the squat's residents would make use of the daily breakfast club, another voluntary affair, run out of an old garage lean-to, which dished up free hot drinks and toast most mornings.

As I walked down the grey main road, I was lost in my thoughts. I was thinking about Pottsy. The day before, he had shown me a video on his phone: a strange living-room scene set up by the side of a canal. A year earlier he had been living on a forgotten patch of canal towpath. By his tent he'd arranged a black leather armchair, a white Ikea bookshelf and a sign reading 'Bless this Home'. He'd spent his days fishing in the canal – eating the fish he managed to catch – and he washed his clothes in the same bottle-green water.

When the council kicked him off the land, Pottsy loaded all the possessions he had in the world into a wheelie bin and called his mum, who told him he could leave his things in her garden. He dragged the bin down winding roads to her house, and was struggling to pull the heavy load down the narrow passage to her yard when a man stuck his head out of the next-door window, complaining about the noise.

The complaint turned into a fight, the fight escalated, the man came outside. Pottsy, in a fit of rage, started swinging his fists around. His hand went through the rear window of his mother's car. The police were called and he was arrested, despite his mother's protestations. He got a three-month prison spell in HMP Forest Bank.

Pottsy had been in and out of prison and young offenders institutions for years – 'about ten of them, I reckon' – for crimes ranging from driving offences, criminal damage and, once, an assault. 'I beat up a burglar I found robbing my house. He got a non-attendance order' – for not turning up to court – 'and walked free. I got sent down. Then later he got done for doing the same thing to an old lady and ended up in the same nick as me, the same wing. I don't think he was too happy about that,' he laughed.

But Pottsy was getting too old for this. He was determined the stretch in HMP Forest Bank would be the end of it. After serving his three months, he found himself preparing to leave with nothing. 'I arrived there in shorts and T-shirt in summer and came out in the same clothes in the winter. The prison guards were running round trying to find me some trousers or summat. It's not really their job, is it?'

The prison staff advised him to go and ask for housing from the council, gave him £46, the standard prison discharge grant, then led him out through the prison gates.

What now? The money jangled lightly in his shorts pocket next to his mobile phone, uselessly dormant, being out of battery. No taxi, no friend picking him up. Wrapping his arms around himself to stave off the cold winter winds, he started walking, heading west towards Swinton. That was his grand homecoming. The £46 soon ran out. He spent weeks staying on friends' floors until, desperate, he opened his first squat, and then another.

Then things had started to turn around. One day, hanging out in a park trying to while away the day, he met a woman: blonde, beautiful, chatty – and they got talking. Now, a year on, they were an item; she had become his home. And they had a baby, a little boy, and life felt very different.

These days Pottsy was using his squatting skills for good, advising others, like Stacie, how to stay safe and warm. I had a grudging respect for that: out of nothing, Pottsy had found a way to do better and, rather than be bitter, he was using his experience to help people. But I also knew how easy it would be for Pottsy to end up back in prison. That was why I had made my way here, to the Salford Unemployed Centre, a two-storey building which housed a variety of services designed to help the most vulnerable in society. I wanted to find out how you break that cycle of prison and the streets.

I passed through the doors, found a seat and settled down in the musty waiting room, with its yellow woodchip walls. A murky-green fish tank stood at one end of the room, and 'Thank You' cards were Blu-Tacked to the walls like sad Christmas decorations. In the next room, I could just about make out the silhouettes of two women sitting with one of the centre's staff, trying to get their heads around the new rules of Universal Credit, which was being rolled out across the country.

My thoughts were interrupted by the appearance of a thin, balding man in the doorway, faded tattoos on his hands, thick gold hoops in his ears. This was Stuart Green, Prison Project Officer at the centre and the man I was there to meet.

'This used to be a police station,' Stuart told me, chuckling, as we made our way up the narrow staircase to his office. 'One of our key-workers actually works in the room that used to be a cell, which seems weirdly appropriate,' he said with a laugh.

Stuart's days were busy. If he wasn't going in to one of

the three prisons in the area to talk with inmates and staff, he was racing around trying to support someone who had just been released. Settling down behind his desk, squashed into a corner of the room, he leant back and sighed. The project had started ten years ago and things were just getting worse. 'We don't work with sex offenders or those who have shown gratuitous violence, but other than that, pretty much anyone we can help, we try and help,' he said, smiling.

Stuart's relationship with people started inside prison walls. Most prisons have an officer from the housing charity Shelter working inside, but ironically that tailored support is not carried over when the person is released from prison. 'I've always thought that was a joke – where the bloody hell do you think crime happens?' Stuart quipped. 'It's as if all they're doing is collecting data. They come up with a "housing plan" but that's generally "Present at your housing office at the local authority wherever you've been released to."'

Often, Stuart was alerted only when people were being released and logged as 'No fixed abode'. He was the one there when, like Pottsy, they made their way out of the gates with just their £46 discharge grant and a list of meetings they needed to attend, to adhere to their probation conditions.

I stared at my notebook, distracted. This was confusing. I'd written a fair bit about the criminal justice system in the past, about people held indeterminately in prison under now-defunct sentences, or those swept up into group convictions despite only being on the periphery of a crime. But in all those cases I had heard a great deal about the close eye probation officers kept on those who were released from prison.

'Isn't it part of the probation rules that they have an appropriate address registered?' I asked Stuart.

'Yes, that's right, according to the rules.'

I thought of Pottsy. 'So how do people wind up sleeping

in a tent next to a canal or in a squat. How can that be allowed by the probation team?'

'I don't know,' sighed Stuart, staring down at the maroon lino on the floor. 'The probation system changed. People aren't seeing their probation officers anymore, they just get a phone call every few weeks. We had a guy who came here; he'd had a year's probation license. In that year he didn't see his own probation officer once. He saw others, duty officers, but not once his own probation officer, in twelve months.'

In 2014, under the guidance of then-Justice Secretary Chris Grayling, the probation service was split down the middle. The changes were made to address the fact that data showed that nearly half of all individuals leaving prison reoffended within twelve months. In a bid to divide the caseloads into levels of higher and lower risk, the low- and medium-risk probation cases were put out to tender, allowing private companies (called community rehabilitation companies) to mop up the contracts. These private companies worked to financial incentives. The fewer people that reoffended, the more they would be paid.

Stuart had seen just what that meant on the ground. 'It's payment by results . . . that affects a lot,' he said. 'If you suspect someone is sleeping rough or if they miss their check-in appointments . . . Well, if you just turn a blind eye and don't report them for breach of conditions, they don't get sent back to prison and you get your bonus. If I was dependent on somebody not going back to prison to guarantee my pay, I wouldn't be recalling them to prison because they hadn't turned up. That's my opinion,' Stuart said.

He wasn't the only one with concerns. By 2017 it was clear the new system of outsourced, privatized probation services was not working. A National Audit Office report found many serious issues with how the new companies were working, and the whole sorry mess was being reversed, with the revisions and reversals costing £467,000,000 more than required under the original contracts.

Meanwhile, it was left to people like Stuart to pick up the pieces, stepping in where decent probation support should have been. He would regularly meet people at the prison gates, get them to their probation meeting and then to any drug or alcohol programmes they were required to attend. Only after that, it was a trip to the council to sit and wait for the housing officer to try and find a place for the night. Without the help of a lift, and with just a few pounds in their pockets, most people would never make it from the mostly rural prisons to all these appointments.

'Housing Services at the council closes at 4 p.m., so I try and get people there for when the doors open,' Stuart explained. 'I've had times where it's been five hours just sitting and waiting for somebody.' Only those people deemed to be 'priority need' would be found emergency accommodation. 'Generally my client group is male, generally healthy – depending on how you class healthy – so chances are they won't get "priority need". Then it's on your bike, sort yourself out.'

Add to that the fact that, to get any support at all, you need to be able to prove you have a connection to the area. 'You used to have to reside in Salford for six months and then you got on the housing list, but then it went up to two years,' Stuart explained.

He would try his best to work round it. Back when you just had to prove a six-month connection, he'd try and get people into a cheap hostel. He'd tell them, 'Look, you just have to put up with six months of this.' Now that Salford council had upped its requirements to two years, that solution just didn't work.

Across the country, from Brighton to Glasgow, I had heard how councils would turn people away, saying they had lost their local connection when they were sent to prison elsewhere. It was an impossible catch-22: you need support because you've been in prison for months at a time, but now you can't get support because, by being arrested, according to the council you made yourself 'intentionally homeless', plus your time in prison meant you haven't been physically in the area and have therefore lost your local connection.[73]

Without council support, the only option was to apply for benefits and try to rent privately. But the introduction of Universal Credit had brought with it further complications: to apply for benefits you had to complete an application online, but prisoners were not allowed access to the internet. That meant they needed to wait until they were released to put in an application and then face a five-week wait for funds. Those under thirty-five would only be eligible for enough housing benefit to pay for a room in shared accommodation. That might not be suitable for various reasons, including the safety of other occupants.

So, no council housing and a five-week wait for benefits. That left people outside the prison gates with just £46 to keep them for at least a month.[74] And yet, they were expected not to fall back into a life of crime. Stuart often felt like he was fighting a never-ending battle just to keep these people alive. And it was getting worse. More and more often, people were being let out of prison straight into homelessness. The number of people leaving prison and immediately sleeping rough had multiplied twenty-seven times, up from ninety-six people in 2016–17 to 2,690 in 2017–18.* In some areas charities were handing out tents to people at the prison gates.

---

*   Even more people might have had a bed for the night but then faced home-lessness: 15 per cent of all people released from prison in 2017–18 were forced straight into some form of homelessness.

Just then Pottsy came barrelling into the room, a rucksack slung on his back. He was wearing camouflage trousers and a branded Firetrap T-shirt.

'All right, Stu!' Pottsy boomed. 'I was just coming to tell you she was on the way,' he said, chuckling and pointing at me.

'You all right, mate?' asked Stuart, jovially.

'I'm good. I've left the baby at home. He's sleeping now, so the missus can get a bit of rest.'

The two talked like old friends. Stuart had been there to help Pottsy when he came out of prison after doing the three-month stretch for criminal damage.

'I haven't used this place for a while but I used to be here all the time, when I was having problems with work,' Pottsy remembered. 'The system isn't working. There's a revolving door like there's always been.'

Pottsy had tried to help stop that, in his own way. A year or so ago he had banded together with other former prisoners and set up a group called 'Breaking the Cycle'. 'If you've not been there, you don't know how to get out of the hole,' he told me.

A simple, A4 leaflet advertised their aims:

- Been caught in the cycle of offending?
- Passionate about people getting the real support they need on release?
- Do you know how services could improve?
- Ready to use your experience to make a difference?

Together, they visited Risley prison and were shown round the prison's visitor centre. Pottsy and his new colleagues had plenty to say about how the facilities could be improved to better support family visits. Their suggestions ranged from allowing Skype video messaging between prisoners and their children to simply reducing the £3.50 price of sandwiches in the visitor centre.

At Wymott Prison they met with staff to feed back on what more could be done to support prisoners on release. 'Prevention is better than the cure,' Pottsy had tried to explain to the staff. 'Better than picking up the pieces afterwards.' But the feedback fell on deaf ears. After a few months he ran out of steam and the group slowly disbanded. Pottsy focused back on the squats.

I said my goodbyes to Stuart as Pottsy guided me downstairs and outside, to the garage out the back of the centre. It had been done up recently but was still a small space, just room for a table in the centre, a fridge and counter tops to prepare food.

Many of the residents of the squat used the place as somewhere to hang out and get a decent breakfast. There in the corner was Daniel, the sandy-haired guy I'd met the day before. I had bumped into him on my walk earlier that morning but, after asking if he was heading in the same direction, he explained quite matter-of-factly that he was actually off on his way to score. It had been 9 a.m.

Now, an hour or so later, his skin was sallow and he was perspiring slightly, despite the cold. His eyes bored into me – tiny pinprick pupils, high on cocaine. He'd also scored some heroin for later. He was talking a mile a minute, aggrieved that the government was spending so much on putting him in prison, and meanwhile was cutting funding for the substance-abuse support he thought he needed to stay clear of crime.

'The system's fundamentally flawed, all of it, the mental health system, the justice system, you know what I mean? It costs them sixty-, seventy-thousand quid a year to keep me inside. I could go do an armed robbery now: it'd cost them half a million quid for the sentence, and yet I can't get detox cos there ain't the funding. They don't see the big picture.'

Like Pottsy, Daniel – a self-confessed 'one man crime wave' – had been in and out of prison for years. Life inside was tough, but nothing compared to the chaos of the outside world. Out here you were left on your own. It was only now, in the squat, that he was experiencing anything like support. But still drugs were everywhere and his habit dictated his path. When the addiction came rattling, it brought with it wild plans for ways to make money quick.

Daniel told me he was ready for detox, though his current state suggested otherwise. 'I'm up for it, you know, I am. I asked them to sort it out but they said it's a ten-week wait to the first appointment! Ten weeks! I can't wait for that. I'd do better going back to prison – you know, get banged up and sorted out there.'

As I left he called after me, joking, 'Hey love, you don't fancy getting beaten up, do ya? Help me out?' I quickened my step. I had a horrible feeling the revolving door of prison hadn't stopped swinging for Daniel just yet. Sometimes the only thing to stop it was a death.

CHAPTER 24

Sanctity and miracles

After leaving Pottsy and the group in the flat, I made my way up to Glasgow. I wanted to find out more about the impact of this prison-to-streets cycle, not just on those living it but on their loved ones too. I wanted to meet Antoinette Kirkland.

I had first come across the pretty, sparkly eyed woman in a photograph in a Scottish newspaper. She was appealing to the public for answers: she wanted to know how her brother, Ian, had died. She hadn't heard anything from him for eight months until a friend directed her to a newspaper heading: a homeless man had been found dead. Her brother.

We had spoken at length over the phone, but I had travelled up, arriving on a dark October afternoon, because Antoinette was taking her search for answers further. She was planning to spend the night sleeping rough, to try and better understand the life her brother had led.

So it was, on one bitterly cold Saturday evening, that I found myself following Antoinette and three of her friends down Glasgow's Sauchiehall Street, dodging the crowds – and their audaciously bare skin – out for some nightlife. Among the mini-skirts and short shirtsleeves, our sad group stood out. The friends were lugging with them sleeping bags and thick coats, the night dark and freezing already. They were joining others, part of a charity event to raise money and awareness of rough-sleeping in the city.

Antoinette wasn't sure what to expect but, as we made our way to the meeting point, we were greeted by a large hoard of people sitting down, framed by the rectangular glow of a Sainsbury's shop window. Dozens had come out to take up the challenge. They pooled in puffa-jacketed groups, handing round biscuits with forced camaraderie. There were so many people out that Antoinette and her friends had to edge on down the road to find a relatively sheltered spot under the overhang of a roof, the entrance to an upmarket designer clothes store.

As they settled down for the night, nestled in thick sleeping bags, I glanced around the cold, dark street. My hands were turning blue already; the women had a long night ahead of them.

A few hours earlier I had met them at Antoinette's friend's flat, where it felt more like preparations for a night on the town than a solemn memorial. Michelle, Antoinette's oldest friend, was meticulously straightening her black shoulder-length hair while Antoinette coddled the tiny chihuahua that danced around our feet.

'Ian preferred jail,' Antoinette remembered with a sigh. 'Inside, he said, he knew whether he was coming or going, there were three square meals a day. He ran a wee shop – you know, in jail terms – a wee business.'

Her brother Ian had been in and out of prison for most of his life. At thirty-nine years old, Ian's life had been an incessant cycle of crime and prison-time. Addicted to drugs, including heroin, Ian had done some terrible things: armed robberies, mugging old ladies. But inside prison he always appeared to sort himself out. There was drug detox there and counselling.

'He'd always come out looking so healthy,' Antoinette told me. But as soon as he was out and back in Renfrew, where he had grown up, he was 'like a kid in a sweet shop; he just didn't have the self-control. He just felt like he was plopped back in. I can't remember him getting any help. I just don't think the support is there.'

In the outside world, Ian didn't want to be around the other addicts in the methadone clinics. Instead he tried to go cold turkey, locking himself in Antoinette's spare room to exorcise the poison himself. But despite the sweat and tears, it hadn't lasted.

There had been moments when it seemed like he had changed, Antoinette recalled, Michelle nodding her agreement. Back in 2017, as he walked out of the prison gates, Ian was determined things wouldn't be the same as before. A few weeks later and he was telling his mum and sister the good news: he had managed to secure a job with House of Fraser, cleaning the store overnight. This was it – this was his clean break.

For three weeks he was full of energy, his sister remembered. Every day he'd wake up and get on the bus, whisking him along the M8 motorway and into the city centre. He'd sit low in the seat; he complained that people were staring at him, judging his thin frame. He had never felt quite comfortable in his skin.

But all that was forgotten once he was in the store. With the doors closed and the place empty, he lost himself in the cleaning – wiping down surfaces, buffing the floor. As if the messiness of his life could be worked out with bleach and rag-cloths.

It didn't last. One day Ian was called in to a meeting with the manager. His work references had been followed up – the police check had come back. Ian had failed to mention, when he applied, that he had a rap sheet as long as his arm: mostly for shoplifting offences. He was fired on the spot. That did it

– he gave up. 'He was just like, "Fuck it",' his sister said. Ashamed, he left his mother's house, where he'd been staying, and disappeared.

It was only now that Antoinette was starting to put the pieces together of what happened next, like some awful jigsaw puzzle. Her appeals in the local paper and on Facebook had prompted a slew of responses from people who had seen Ian in recent months, more than 130 of them in all. From going through each of these, it was possible to get a sense of what had happened after he disappeared.

'I've met this guy. We bought him a burger and coffee – that was a few months ago – outside Glasgow Central. We encouraged him to go to a shelter as it was at night and he was on his own. He said he would go . . . Sorry for your loss,' wrote one woman.

'I spoke to this boy on 21 August. I gave him a few cigarettes. I remember it was on Argyle Street next to the card shop,' wrote another.

'Think I've seen him too. On Buchanan St against the black stone at the subway. I remember saying to my son, "That's somebody's son." Roughly 14/15 Aug,' said a woman.

'Used to see him on Queen St quite often on my way to work in the morning, always seemed like a decent guy to say hello to, such a shame,' wrote a man.

For a few weeks, Antoinette deduced, Ian had been sleeping rough and begging in Glasgow city centre. People saw him there, pale and drawn, his skinny frame swamped in ill-fitting jeans and a waterproof anorak top. He had propped up a jokey sign reading 'The ex-wife had a better lawyer', though he had never married.

But then Ian disappeared from his usual begging spot. He had gone to Paisley, a town just a ten-minute train ride from the city. It was August by then and warm enough to sleep outside, the sun dipping late in the evening. On the evening of 30 August, a Thursday like any other, he found an alcove, a dark, grassy area flanked on one side by the dirty white-washed walls of a Domino's takeaway shop. He had a stash of food – crisps, cold meat and pork pies. I visited that same spot later. The hum of the busy junction in front of the grassy area played like white noise.

From where he sat, perched between bushes and a spindly young tree, Ian would have been able to see the outstretched arm of the bronze statue of St Mirin brandishing a shepherd's crook and cross, as if holding back some great evil. As the evening light dropped, a spotlight at the base of the statue cast a long beam up at the words inscribed in the blond sandstone: '. . . At length, full of sanctity and miracles, he slept in the Lord at Paisley.'

Sanctity and miracles. There was not much of those about these days.

Ian died just five miles away from his family's house. Later, in the morgue, Antoinette was struck by how thin her big brother's arms were, how soft his hair was. She stroked it gently, lost, confused as to how her brother, once so full of life, had ended up like this. An autopsy later failed to find any discernible cause for his death. It was recorded as 'causes unknown'. That had left Antoinette reeling, trying to find the positive. 'He just went to sleep and never woke up. We'll never know why. We're thinking he just gave up.'

In the weeks and months after Ian's death, Antoinette had been struggling to make sense of it all. But there was one beacon in the gloom. One of the messages that had popped up after her Facebook appeal. The message from Steph.

A cheery blonde woman, Steph lived in Paisley, the town

where Ian had come to die. News of his death had shaken her. There weren't many people sleeping rough in the town – it had always felt like something that went on in Glasgow or the other big cities – but now, here it was, on her doorstep. Suddenly she couldn't help but see poverty and need wherever she went. 'I never saw anything in Paisley until I started to look and then it was everywhere, but you know you can go about and just never see it.'

Now she was seeing it, Steph decided she needed to act. She banded together some friends, negotiated use of a storage shed, loaded a car with food and set off to put on a soup-kitchen meal for the vulnerable of the town. 'I read about Ian's death in the newspaper and remember thinking how tragic it was. I'd been thinking about doing something for some months but that spurred me on. It just really saddened me, reading about Antoinette and her wanting to know what had happened to her brother. I wish our organization had been available to him, I really do,' she told me.

We had met at a cafe inside a shopping centre, me a little worn out from all my train travel and her a ball of energy, juggling talking with me with expertly keeping an eye on her fidgeting toddler son who was moving the food around his plate, bored. She was clearly used to multitasking: as well as looking after her young son, she was working as a carer, and now she had grand plans for a big Christmas meal for the homeless of the town. She had held four soup-kitchen events so far and had already learnt a great deal.

'I've heard some horrific stories in the last few months,' she said, smiling sadly, as she helped her little boy with his toast and his butter-smeared hands. 'In Glasgow you see a lot of ex-servicemen. One man was telling me that he'd served in the army and had come back with claustrophobia and PTSD, he'd lost his wife through that trauma, and now his kids refused to speak to him because of his alcoholism. I've spoken to single mums that have barely eaten – just beans on toast for three days – so they can feed their kids. Others still have homes but it's just a shell, no gas or electricity.'

After making contact on Facebook, Steph had invited Antoinette to come out to see the soup kitchen in action. 'She came along to the very first soup-kitchen night. I wanted it to be in honour of Ian. At that event, with everyone that came along, we had lots of conversations about Ian.'

Antoinette had been touched by Steph's work. The idea that her brother's death had prompted something good, something pure, was a real comfort to her. The two women, united by a man one had never met, were now good friends.

'She is such a lovely woman,' smiled Steph. 'It's like we were meant to meet.'

Leaving Steph in the shopping centre, I wound my way through streets as grey as the winter sky above them, lost in thought. Ian, unlike Pottsy, should have had things easier. The Scottish system was much better when it came to homeless provision, and had even been described as 'possibly the strongest legal framework in the world in relation to protecting people from homelessness'.[75]

And yet, many people in Scotland, as in the rest of the UK, were still leaving prison with nowhere to go. (Across the UK 15 per cent of men and 13 per cent of women in prisons listed 'no fixed abode' as their accommodation status when leaving prison.)[76] Those that did go to their local council for help were often placed in hostels or bed and breakfasts, too often surrounded by other prison-leavers battling the same temptations.

Despite the strong policies, in Glasgow, where Ian had

spent most of the time he was sleeping rough, the numbers of those on the street were rising. And with them so too was the number of those dying homeless. I had counted at least thirty-eight people who had died homeless in Glasgow that year alone.

I took Ian's last trip in reverse, travelling back from Paisley to Glasgow, the grand, high ceilings of Glasgow Central station greeting me, the many people begging around the entrances a stark welcome to the city. A twenty-minute walk east from the station was the Lodging House Mission, a grand, grey-stone former church. There I watched as staff and volunteers battled against the tide of deaths. I arrived that day as they doled out the last of the lunchtime fare: beef stew and mashed potatoes. The homeless of Glasgow could convene here seven days a week for three square meals. The building was also being used as a winter shelter and every evening mattresses were laid out across the echoing hall. In a large room upstairs, a space where the high vaulted ceiling still arched to the heavens, thin duvets were airing out.

Angela Vance was showing me around. She was a no-nonsense support worker who helped run the services there. 'A large part of my job is just holding people, just keeping them safe and here for another day,' she explained as she showed me into a storeroom packed with food supplies.

Angela cut a sombre figure. 'You're in black again,' one of the volunteers joked as she passed by. 'Aye, I always am,' she replied, sadly, 'because how many funerals do I go to?' Angela was trying to keep people alive, but it was an uphill battle.

She was hearing day in and day out about the struggles of those coming out of prison. Universal Credit had been rolled out in Glasgow three days previously and in that time she had already seen five men who had left prison and come to the centre. 'It's really hitting me just now,' she said. 'It just went to full-service. They were saying it won't affect you too much because it is only new claims, but the amount of new claims I've got . . . It's a nightmare.'

Those five men were facing weeks of waiting until they saw any funds. 'The guys are saying, "I have to apply for job seeker's allowance." I say, "No, that doesn't exist now, you have to apply for this." They're like, "But I don't want that," and they just get so upset.'

I checked back in with Antoinette a few days later. Their night sleeping out raised money for a local homelessness charity. It also gave Antoinette a better understanding of the life her brother had been living, of how desperate he must have been to spend his nights the same way. There were some rude comments that night, she told me, insults shouted by drunken passers-by. But Antoinette and her group huddled down together in their sleeping bags and focused on keeping warm. Her friends who were with her that night had known Ian too. They had watched him struggle. 'I'm not ashamed of him,' Antoinette said. 'I could never be ashamed of him.' She only wished he had been able to break the cycle. To make it out alive.

People like Ian were lost in a swirl of prison and drugs. Some might argue that we don't owe violent criminals anything – indeed some of those on my list who died homeless had perpetrated terrible, violent crimes. But most would agree that poverty and desperation are often drivers of crime, that supporting someone on release from prison is a sensible and long-term strategy to protect not just that person, but society, from the chances of them re-offending.[77] Many of those desperate to turn their lives around were instead released from prison with a budget equivalent to £1.30 a day[78] and no roof over their heads. The consequences of that were tragically predictable.

But maybe there was a light at the end of the tunnel. Maybe Glasgow could be the key to it all. I had not travelled there just to find out about more deaths. I was there to learn about the solution too.

PART FOUR

Change

Glasgow was ahead of the game compared to many UK cities. It was an early adopter of the Housing First model – a pilot had been run there between 2010 and 2013 – and the results had been impressive.[79] The majority of the twenty-two people supported had managed to stay in their homes.

The brainchild of New York expert Sam Tsemberis, Housing First is a practice that has been credited with eradicating rough-sleeping in Finland and dramatically reducing it in the Netherlands.

The principle is simple; while those experiencing homelessness often have a range of complex needs, one of them is simple to fix – the need for safe, secure, long-term accommodation. Previously the assumption has been people cannot handle the responsibility of a home until they have dealt with their other issues, so they are often offered temporary places to stay while they engage in treatment for their problems, the idea being that they prove themselves before they get a house. Housing First flips this by housing the person immediately, thus eliminating the 'homeless' label and all the stigma that goes with it.

The success of the pilot in Glasgow meant the rest of the UK was toying with implementing it elsewhere. The Scottish government was rolling out 800 tenancies across Edinburgh, Glasgow, Aberdeen, Dundee and Stirling over two years. In

England, pilots were underway in Liverpool, Manchester and the West Midlands, and the Welsh government was getting in on the action too, funding ten pilot projects.

But it was still early days outside Scotland. I was keen to understand just how the process worked, and so I headed to a city that had been taking part in Housing First for years: Amsterdam.

In her sunlit, open-plan office in Amsterdam, Valerie Boogaard was busy. When I arrived she was scrambling to get a document signed off so she shepherded me into a small, glass-panelled room, plain except for a solitary yellow balloon slowly deflating on the floor. From another room the sounds of pop songs played on the radio.

'There's cake in here, Valerie,' a colleague called through the open door. Valerie looked up from her work smiling. 'Leftovers from a little party,' she explained to me, seeing my quizzical face.

Valerie was all energy. Originally from Spain, the dark-eyed, curly haired lady has had quite a career. She trained as a psychologist and worked for years with Médicins Sans Frontières, travelling to Mozambique, Zambia, Zimbabwe and Bangladesh, where she encountered people experiencing all kinds of trauma. But it was in Amsterdam, where she settled with her Dutch husband, that she had found her true calling. 'I see things here that are ten times harder than anything I saw in Africa,' she told me.

Now she was working for a homeless organization called Discus, a group that oversaw much of the Housing First work in the city.

The theory was simple, Valerie explained, you prioritize getting someone into secure, permanent housing and, once there, address their needs holistically, providing support as and when needed. 'They become a citizen again, just like you or me,' she said, smiling.

While everywhere else in Europe was seeing a huge rise in homelessness, the Netherlands was doing better than most.[80] Much of that was thanks to work in the big cities, especially Amsterdam.

On her very first day, Valerie had been tasked with showing one of Discus' clients to his new home. A colleague had filmed the event and Valerie pulled up the video on her laptop. It showed Joop, a lanky, grey-haired man who had multiple issues and had been homeless for some time. As Valerie opened the door to the flat he was being given she beamed with pride. Joop's eyes filled with tears. 'Woooooow,' he gasped, barely audible, as his arms reached out briefly to embrace the space. 'We made it.'

'Do you like it?' Valerie asked, standing happily in the living room. But Joop couldn't reply. He just raised a thumb, overcome, then pinched the bridge of his nose in a futile attempt to stop the tears. 'I'm crying,' he laughed as he wandered around the large, bright room, taking in the kitchen for the first time.

'I felt like Father Christmas,' Valerie remembered.

The rent for the property came from a pot handed to local councils from central government. It was paid into a 'social bank', one specifically for those registered with the council, and staff there divvied up the funds to pay the rent and bills, as well as working out repayment plans for the fines many rough-sleepers had accumulated over the years.

'People typically have up to six thousand euros in debt from things like getting tickets for sleeping in the streets. They don't have to pay them until they are housed but then they end up paying about thirty euros a month to pay them off. So you know, after all that, we see people get about thirty to fifty euros a week,' Valerie said.

'That's not all that much for food, clothes, everything else,' I chipped in.

'No, and then you know if someone has an addiction that can be forty euros on that, but you know we believe clients should make their own decisions about what that money gets spent on.'

Valerie had been using the model for ten years already but her enthusiasm for it had not waned in the slightest. 'When I started, in 2008, we had just six workers. Then in 2010 things just blew up,' she said, beaming, the friendship bracelet on her wrist slipping up her forearm as she gestured. A research project by Radboud University had evaluated the project's progress, looking at the cases of 100 people that had been offered Housing First flats. The results were striking; 93 per cent were still in their houses a year later. That success rate was enough to win over the government and the local council. Now, of the 186,000 social homes held in the capital, 30 per cent were handed over to the Housing First model.

But Valerie wasn't content to stop there. She penned a phrase: 'It can be different', a reminder that whatever the current reality, things can get better. It was a philosophy to think big, keep pushing. And so she had been working on ways to make the experience even more positive for those coming out of homelessness. She wanted to make it a party.

Yazip was frustrated. He'd been given a Housing First flat through Discus earlier that year but it hadn't worked out. He was still getting support through the social worker programme and was attending the occupational therapy they had set up: working on a construction site.

He was there, in the office block of the property his crew were working on, when his social worker dropped by. It wasn't unusual; she often popped in for a chat. But then something out of the window caught his eye. The fluttering of white where there should have been only sky. A video documented what happened next. Yazip stood and walked to the window. There, hoisted from one of the building site's cranes, was a large white sheet painted with: 'Yazip: A New Beginning.' Below the black block letters was a cardboard box covered in streamers. Inside was the key to his new flat.

'We want to make it like a surprise party every time,' Valerie explained. It had been her idea to turn the handing over of keys into a celebratory event. So she would set up these elaborate meetings, signs hung from cranes, keys handed out of the blue in envelopes. They led their clients to flats filled with bunting and alcohol-free champagne. Treats to make it feel like a real win.

That's not the only innovative step Valerie constructed. Each person in the Housing First programme got a personal mentor, a social worker responsible for between seven and nine people each. They visited as often or as little as was necessary, but a minimum of once a week. Valerie had turned matching up social workers with clients into a fine art.

'We basically developed a system that recognized six learning styles,' she explained. 'There's Teacher, Mother, Creative, Policing, Conflict Avoider and Buddy.' In their job interviews, social workers, who didn't need any formal qualifications, were asked questions like 'Your best friend has been being beaten up by her boyfriend for ten years. She comes to you on a Friday night and has another black eye. What do you do?'

'You can tell a lot from a person's answer to that,' Valerie said. 'So the person that says I'd make the tea and give them a hug then spend the night worrying about them, we'd class as the Mothering style. The person that says, "I'd tell them if you continue to go back to him our friendship is over", well, that is more the Policing persona. Or the person who explains, "It's your decision but here are the consequences", that's the Teacher.'

The 'clients' too were given a say in the type of support worker they needed. 'So we'll ask them things like, "If you had a partner, what kind of person would you like them to be?" Or "Imagine you go to a party and there is a room full of people. What kind of person would you want to go talk to?"'

Through that alchemy, she and her team had matched more than 400 clients with support workers. And the success rate of the programme had remained high – there were around 82 per cent of people still in their own homes after the first year.

As I left Valerie in her office in Amsterdam I felt a sense of optimism for the first time in many months. This model worked. Indeed, creator of the Housing First theory, Sam Tsemberis, once said: 'Homelessness is not like cancer or Alzheimer's disease. We have a cure for homelessness; it's quite simple. The thing that's lacking is the political will.'

Political will – and funding.

The problem was the second didn't necessarily work without the first. In the UK, people were turning to Housing First as a panacea, and in doing so ignoring the contextual support services that were needed to make it a success.

In Scotland rumours had started that the investment in Housing First would lead to cuts to established homeless outreach programmes. That it would become an either–or situation. In Glasgow alone, many night shelters and support services were worried about their future in the face of proposed cuts of £2.6 million to existing homeless provision, which could lead to the loss of a hundred emergency and supported housing beds.

In Derry, Northern Ireland, the city had trialled a Housing First scheme but I had heard that months later some of those who had been housed were back in emergency shelters. The charity that ran the service nonetheless saw it as a huge achievement, with 72 per cent of the people helped still in their residence a year on.[81] But others warned that the 'wrap-around' services that were needed weren't available, so people were given a place to stay but the welfare, health and substance-abuse schemes in the community weren't always there to keep them in the properties.[82]

Leaving Amsterdam, I had felt buoyed with hope that there was a tried and tested solution. But housing doesn't work in a vacuum. It took energy, a well-funded support system and, crucially, the spare accommodation to put it into action. The UK had a long, long way to go before this method could prevent more needless deaths there.

Back in the UK, I was still trying to get my head around the Housing First model. In a way, the closest example I had seen was the squat in Manchester: a place where people had a safe roof over their heads, a lock on their bedroom door, and a place where those working in the self-made shelter were pushing to provide a holistic support programme.

Weeks after moving in, Stacie was flourishing there. She had decorated her room with knick-knacks and pictures, and Kion the dog was still protectively patrolling the hallways. The team in the squat had been stepping up, welcoming in whichever newcomer came through the door, and their presence had made quite the impression. Pottsy was taking calls from local police officers, Citizens Advice and firefighters.

'We've got a vulnerable lady that needs to get out of this relationship,' a police officer told Pottsy over the phone one day. 'Have you got any room at your shelter?' Trafford fire service called, asking if there was room for the rough-sleepers near their station. Another day it was the custody officer from the Swinton police office enquiring if they had space for a woman who had been discharged from a mental health institution and had nowhere to go. The answer was yes.

Jannah, one of the people helping to organize the place, had helped to get Stacie on a Construction Skills Certification Scheme and she was excited to be following in the footsteps of her father, who had been a freelance builder. On her first day in class she had quickly put straight the man who had commented with surprise on seeing a woman on the course. They soon realized Stacie was serious.

Life had some kind of normalcy at last. Study, cleaning, helping out others in the squat. Stacie felt useful and driven. But it wouldn't last. She arrived back at the building from a day in the classroom to see Pottsy's and Jannah's worried faces. There had been official-looking men round measuring for shutters on the windows. It looked like they were going to be kicked out and illegally evicted. Stacie's heart sank. If this place closed down she didn't know where she'd go.

She'd been talking to housing officers about finding somewhere permanent and one of them had told her she could be the first to take up a 'dog pod' option with the city's 'Bed Every Night Scheme', a policy designed to house homeless people over the winter. The idea was she'd be given a space that allowed Kion to stay too. But days later she had been told the pod wasn't possible after all, so they were offering to put Kion in a kennel and her in a B & B. 'I told 'em I can't do that, he's just a puppy, he won't eat without me, he'll starve to death.' She'd never been away from that dog and she wasn't about to start now.

Besides, she had watched how others from the squat had floundered after going into the council-provided options. Mark, an alcoholic, had been doing OK at the squat, but in the regimented, crowded conditions of a dry hostel he was spiralling. And she was worrying about Sam, an eighteen-year-old boy who had ended up in the squat after leaving care. As soon as he'd become an adult he'd been put in temporary accommodation with no support and had struggled. Homelessness was horrifyingly common for those leaving the care system; one study showed nearly a third of

care-leavers had become homeless at some point within the
first two years after going it alone.[83] In Scotland, a guy who
had grown up in the care system told me of his dismay at
the double standards in legal responsibility: 'You grow up in
care then the state is basically your parent, so what kind of
neglect is it for that parent to then make you homeless as
soon as you're an adult?'

At the squat Stacie could look after Sam but she worried,
now that he was moving to the hostel, how he would cope
there, when expected to make adult decisions alone.

If the squat was shut down, what would happen to old
Phil or the Romanians Raul and Christina? They wouldn't be
allowed into the official shelters as they didn't qualify because
of their immigration status.

The group waited nervously for the bailiffs to show, but in
the end their fate was sealed with a whimper, not a bang. No
forced eviction, but a letter under the door. They were being
taken to court.

Inside the Manchester Civil Justice Centre, up on the fifth
floor, the winter sun streamed through the large glass panels
that made up one side of the building, helping us forget the
freezing cold outside.

In the waiting area, outside Courtroom 24, a small group
had gathered. Stacie had curled her red hair into tight ringlets
for the court case. She and several others from the shelter
crowded round Kathleen Cosgrove, their recently appointed
housing lawyer. A few metres away, a slick, well-dressed
woman was flicking through pages in a folder. Ms Fane, the
lawyer for the NHS, the landlord of the building, looked cool
and efficient. The group weren't sure how this was going to
go. 'We're hoping for an adjournment today,' a volunteer from

the centre told me. 'That way we can try and get legal aid and get a proper defence.'

Inside the courtroom, Deputy District Judge Thexton took his place behind a light-wood desk. Stacie sat in the back row, directly behind her lawyer. At the back of the room, a long row of chairs against the wall was nearly full, consisting mostly of residents of the squat. Nervously they sat and fidgeted, all except one man with a bushy beard, a guy I remembered from a rambling and conspiracy-theory-laden lecture he'd delivered to me at the Salford Unemployed Centre breakfast club. He had stretched out his legs, his head slumped forward onto his chest, and was quietly sleeping away.

The lawyer for NHS Properties Services Ltd was the first to make her arguments. 'We say we are entitled to possession and that this is a straightforward claim,' she announced, her voice confident and clear. 'We have an immediate right to possession. They are trespassers in the traditional sense. All we have to do is show legal title to the property, which we have done. The council has stated this is not a suitable place to sleep and there is an offer of accommodation for the residents from the council.'

At this Jannah glanced down the row of desks to Stacie, who silently shook her head in disbelief.

'Six people have been offered or accepted offers of alternate accommodation, the others have not come forward,' the NHS lawyer said matter-of-factly. The residents on the back row bristled. Stacie put her finger to her lips quickly, silencing another member of the group who was about to speak out in protest.

'It is unnecessary for them to be occupying this premises,' the NHS's lawyer went on. 'It is a very straightforward matter.'

Judge Thexton sat rather impassively during this whole speech. He had barely spoken yet, except to welcome the court.

A white man with black hair flecked with grey, he had an inscrutable gaze that could have belied either calm wisdom or boredom. He was alone at the front of the room, with no court clerk. There was just thirty minutes allotted for the hearing and he seemed to be in no mood to waste time.

When the time came for the residents' legal team to put forward their arguments, Stacie held her breath. Their lawyer, Kathleen Cosgrove, stood up slowly, brushing her dark-blonde hair off her face. She'd had barely any time to prepare and was on shaky ground. Changes to legal aid, introduced in 2012, had removed its support for trespassers, and without funds the squatters had struggled to find a lawyer to take on the case. Kathleen was doing this pro bono, but had only come aboard recently. She too had been hoping for an adjournment today, and wearily shuffled her papers when she realized this was going to be the one chance to lay out the arguments.

She started by refuting the idea there were ample alternate options for those in the building. '"Bed Every Night – well that's just a slogan,"' she exclaimed. 'There are some mattresses in church halls, some bed and breakfasts outside the borough, but all those are subject to certain criteria. In reality there is no guarantee that there's a bed every night.'

'This isn't a defence, it's a statement,' said Judge Thexton, firmly. The back row stiffened. It was becoming more and more clear whose arguments he favoured and it didn't look good for them.

'Sir, I am doing my best at short notice and with no funding,' Kathleen replied defensively. 'I'm not a substitute for a proper public defence. This centre was set up to provide life-saving shelter,' she went on, slightly rattled. 'They are seeking to be open at least to the end of the cold weather in March. The hardship of being evicted would be exceptional and profound' – she was getting into a rhythm now – 'and the shelter has given them not just support but warmth. There is a significant risk that they'll end up street-homeless again. This is a human rights issue.' Stacie had balled up a tissue in her fist. She was holding back tears.

The judge glanced at the clock. He had heard enough. 'This case comes back to one simple fact,' he announced to the room. 'All the claimant has to do is prove they have immediate right to the property. The defendants themselves have no proprietary interests in this property. They are trespassers.'

Stacie stared wide-eyed. A fellow resident had put his head in his hands and was quietly crying.

'One matter I'm willing to consider is whether or not I should allow seven days until eviction, given the weather conditions,' he mused. He paused for a second and then decided no, the eviction would happen on Monday. The group had just three days to get out. Stacie wasn't there to hear the end of the hearing; she had already grabbed her coat and fled the room.

Outside in the cold, Stacie was trying and failing to hold back her tears. A reporting crew from Channel 4 News had been following the story and were interviewing her. 'I literally don't know where we're going to go,' she told the camera, her voice shaky, 'and they've not given us any time. They've given us the weekend and no organizations are open at the weekend. So we've literally got tomorrow to try and find accommodation for fifteen people. I have no answers right now,' she continued, her face crumpling as the tears started flowing again.

Around her the group of residents embraced each other tightly, wiping away tears. The bushy-bearded man who had slept through most of the proceedings had pulled out a thermos of hot tea from the folds of his clothing and was offering the cup round to the group. It was bitterly cold, below zero, and I couldn't feel my fingers.

I hugged Stacie goodbye and walked to the train station, fuming. How could this be right, that the one thing keeping these people warm and safe was being taken away from them? My entire adult life I had thought there was a safety net designed to stop you falling, but over the past year I had learnt time and time again that this was an illusion. The only safety net was the one people were making for themselves, those stepping up to take control of the situation to save each other. And yet here was a judge saying those attempts were futile. Stacie and the group would be kicked out.

There are an estimated 12,000 people living in squats in Great Britain. Some of these squats are likely dangerous, perhaps squalid, but in Manchester the team had worked hard to make the disused doctor's surgery a safe and pleasant place to live. They had decked out the living room with a pool table and sofas, people had their own rooms with locks on the doors, they had looked out for each other and self-regulated where and how drink and drugs were allowed. Pottsy, no longer homeless himself, had known how to help because he had lived it himself. (He once told me how a former drug support officer had wound him up by giving unhelpful advice when he was rattling for crack cocaine: 'I was like, "You don't know mate, you've never been here, so why should I listen to you?"')

The group had appealed the ruling, which bought them some time, but the appeal failed. Months later, on a Wednesday morning, the bailiffs came with stab vests and dogs. Photographs taken on that day show Stacie grim-faced, her arms wrapped around her furry grey coat. Beneath the coat she was wearing one of the T-shirts the group had emblazoned with bold print that read: 'Homelessness Kills'.

The men from the Sheriff's Office went about their business, tearing down the banners and boarding up the doors.

It was a blow, but they'd managed to move most of the residents out already, many into another of Pottsy's squats nearby. 'At least we kept it through the winter,' Stacie said. 'We've saved lives here. That's something.' And as she watched the men pack up their things, she was proud.

CHAPTER 27

Beginning, again

People become homeless every day, Aisha* knew that. She just never expected it would happen to her.

Things had been going wrong for a while. Aisha had arrived from Somalia ten years ago, fleeing the violence and chaos of Mogadishu, and it had taken some time for her to acclimatize to the UK – she still felt a chill even in the height of summer, and while she now spoke English fairly fluently, she was still working on her reading and writing. So even now, in her mid-thirties, her manner made her seem much younger than her age. Her appearance made her seem younger, too: she had a babyish round face that was always tightly cloaked in her hijab, her nails often painted shiny pink or peach.

She dreamt of becoming a nurse. But that dream was still some way off. For a while she had worked as a cleaner around London, in office blocks in the city. But making enough money to live in this expensive city was hard – she couldn't manage to make the rent for even the most basic studio flat.

Instead, she had been staying with her cousin in her two-bed flat in east London, but the place was cramped, her cousin's three children were growing every day and Aisha, who shared a bedroom with them, had come to realize her presence was a burden on the family. That November, as winter drew in, her cousin had told her she had to go, so Aisha packed up her meagre possessions into a suitcase and set off.

The split had been tough and her cousin wasn't answering Aisha's calls or replying to any of the Facebook messages Aisha sent. Aisha didn't know what to do. Bewildered, she headed to the council offices to see if they had any advice. She had been on their council house waiting list for a while, but so far nothing appropriate had turned up. One place they had showed her was a shared flat where she would be the only woman among five men. Her case worker had been cross when she had turned it down but she knew she just wouldn't feel safe there. They had shown her another place, a clean, simple flat in Finchley, and she had said yes straight away, but that had been weeks ago and she hadn't heard anything back. She was beginning to despair. She didn't have kids, she wasn't ill, she was hardly 'priority need' and the council seemed in no rush to accommodate her.

But Aisha was not giving up quite yet. Some days she would arrive at the council building at 8 a.m. and make her way to the housing department as soon as it opened. When the lady on reception admonished her, pointing out she didn't have an appointment, Aisha stood her ground. 'I told her, "I don't care. I am waiting here until someone sees me."' Hours later, at 2 p.m., a housing officer had come out into the waiting room and handed her a piece of paper – an address of another housing office. Aisha dragged her bag there and told her story again. A man asked her question after question, and finally gave her the address of a church shelter.

She arrived at 7 p.m. It was very dark by then and the wind was icy. It turned out the shelter, which was a makeshift affair in a church hall, didn't open for another hour. Aisha huddled in the dark with her things until finally the doors opened. She had a place for the night.

That winter, churches across the country opened their doors to the homeless, but in many places they worked on a rotating basis – each shelter was open only for one night a week. Which is how Aisha found herself on a grim carousel tour of the east London borough of Waltham Forest; from Chingford she'd moved to Walthamstow, then Leyton the next night and then to Leytonstone the next.

Already she had learnt that some shelters were better than others, and she dreaded the days when certain ones would come around. In Leytonstone, the church's heater had broken so staff had brought in a handful of portable electric heaters. But when the staff said goodnight, leaving the people there to sleep, they took the heaters with them, telling Aisha it was against health and safety to leave them. That night Aisha lay shivering on the thin mat, covered in old clean sheets. She remembered how her feet were so cold they seemed to scream at her. She couldn't sleep.

In the mornings, Aisha would peruse the breakfast offerings and store away things in her bag for later – a few slices of white bread, boiled eggs or a green apple all tucked away in her handbag. She had to be out of the hall by 8 a.m. and the next shelter did not open until that evening, so she had to kill time until then. Sometimes she would head to a day centre run by St Mungo's to use the shower there (there was nothing but the toilet sink to wash in at the churches).

The library had become her sanctuary; she could hole up there and read romance and historical novels, trying to improve her reading skills while staying warm. When I went to meet her there one day, the place was full of people she knew from the shelter, some trying to apply for jobs on the computers, which were free to use. One man napped quietly on a hard-backed chair, his rucksack at his feet. The library was Aisha's safe space, somewhere free and warm where people wouldn't look at her strangely and the staff smiled hello. Watching Aisha there, my mind jolted back to Jayne and the library in

Stafford – she too had whiled away days in its warm safety. But it was also there she had tried to kill herself almost a whole year ago.

Other than the library, Aisha was becoming an expert on the places she could go that didn't involve spending too much money. Sometimes she would find a cafe and try to make a small portion of fried chicken and chips last as long as possible. For a £1.50 meal she could wait until her feet warmed up a little. Then it was on, out into the cold.

Constantly moving was taking its toll. Her arms ached from dragging her heavy wheelie suitcase behind her. In those early days she had got lost more than once. One afternoon, confused, she had stopped a woman at the side of the road to ask the way. Her phone battery had died and she had been out looking for one of the shelters since 4 p.m. She glanced at her watch – it was almost 8 p.m. The shelter would be serving dinner soon and she was hungry. The metal chain of her shoulder bag was digging into her. She still remembered how touched she'd been when, rather than waving her away, the lady had walked with her two blocks before pointing her in the right direction. Those little moments of kindness stood out in those days. But mostly it was hard knocks.

A few weeks into the tour of Waltham Forest, Aisha found herself caught off guard, frozen and blinking at a bank's ATM screen. She had come to check her balance, hoping the benefit payment she was expecting had arrived, and was horrified at the measly figure before her.

Worried, she rushed inside the bank. The teller brought up the information on her screen and lethargically started listing places Aisha had made purchases: Superdrug, a newsagent, and so on. Aisha stopped her, frustrated – she wanted to know what money had come in to her account, not out of it. The bank teller squinted at the screen: £26 from the Jobcentre.

Aisha stared blankly at the bank employee. £26? She had been expecting £317 in Universal Credit. She didn't understand.

In a panic, she dragged her suitcase along Walthamstow high street, her handbag and shoulder bag slipping down her arms as she went. Inside the stuffy Jobcentre reception she waited anxiously until her name was called.

The lady on the desk looked bored as her fingers tapped Aisha's name into the system. 'Ah yes, here it is: £26. It says you've been sanctioned for not applying for enough jobs,' she told her.

Aisha was dumbfounded. She had been applying for jobs, and she had found one that looked perfect. Walking down the street she had seen a poster reading: 'Help Wanted – Care Assistant'. It appeared to be the perfect first step towards her dream of becoming a nurse. She had filled in the forms and had an interview, and it had all been positive. She had told the manager she was looking to work part time so she could study at college too, and he had responded positively. But there was a snag: she needed to undergo a DBS criminal record check as well as providing her National Insurance Number, passport and three months' worth of council tax bills. The DBS check cost £65 and she had to stump up the money for that herself.

She didn't know where she was going to get a spare £65, and she didn't have the council tax bills – she had been sofa-surfing with her cousin and then had spent the last three weeks in church hall winter shelters. Still, undeterred, she was working to get the other papers together and find the money to pay for the DBS check.

But according to the Jobcentre that wasn't enough; she was

expected to prove she had spent thirty-five hours a week looking for a job. As punishment, her benefits were being docked for the month. I later read that UN Special Rapporteur Philip Alston had compared the withholding of benefits and constant slog of job-searching as akin to a Victorian workhouse. 'I think breaking rocks has some similarity to the thirty-five hours of job search [required per week to receive Universal Credit] for people who have been out of work for months or years,' he told journalists. 'They have to go through the motions but it is completely useless. That seems to me to be very similar to the approach in the old-style workhouse. The underlying mentality is that we are going to make the place sufficiently unpleasant that you really won't want to be here.'[84]

When the lady in the Jobcentre had told Aisha she had been sanctioned, she didn't know what to do. It was December, she'd had just £33 in her account yesterday, now, with this £26 she had £59 to her name, and that was supposed to last a month. £1.90 a day. Feeling a wave of panic rise up, she stood up and made to storm out, enraged, dragging her suitcase behind her.

'Hey, wait!' yelled the support officer, stopping Aisha in her tracks and attracting the attention of the entire Jobcentre. She had forgotten her handbag. Her dramatic exit ruined, Aisha made her way back to the desk, sheepishly taking the bag from the woman's outstretched hands. It had her wallet and passport in. She'd have been lost without it.

Despairing, she made her way back onto the high street. With a budget of less than £2 a day, she wasn't sure where to go or what to do. She walked around, dragging her bags with her, until the night shelter opened at 8 p.m.

CHAPTER 28

Goodbye

Back in Brighton, Alfie lay in his bed, flanked by other residents of Martlets nursing home. He hadn't given up on the dream of getting back to his own place, but he could feel his strength fading.

And yet, he felt at peace. A few days earlier Pastor Andrew Ramage had come to see him with some good news. He had been messing around online on his phone to kill time on a train up to London, when he found him, there on LinkedIn: Alfie's son.

Excited, Pastor Ramage had pinged off an email to the man and got a reply. He was up for talking to his dad so, over a patchy phone line in a long-distance call from his son's new home in the Middle East, Alfie heard his boy's voice again. He heard of his great achievements – he had joined the army and was doing well in his career. He had a loving partner, a successful job.

The joy that conversation had brought to Alfie hummed in him still, warming his bones. It strengthened something in him, a final resolve. He had talked to the staff at Martlets and to Sara, the homelessness support worker, reminding them that a judge had ruled that he should be allowed back into his flat, the landlord had no choice, and they were the only ones keeping him away. They relented; Alfie knew what he wanted. So he was moved back to the flat near the sea, a social worker would visit each day and Sara would drop by whenever she could. The old man had won. He was home.

Sitting in the flat with Alfie, Sara had helped him make a playlist of songs he loved. The old man gawped in wonder at the ease with which she managed to find and download them from the internet. He'd found some old, bedraggled speakers on the streets and managed to get them working, so the pair sat and listened to tune after tune.

One song, an upbeat Mexican tune by Flaco Jimenez called 'Ay Te Dejo En San Antonio', particularly took his fancy. 'I have no idea what they're saying,' Alfie told Sara, 'but it sounds like they're having a party.'

Sipping coffee made from a coffee-maker that Alfie had found on the streets, the carer and her ward talked like old friends. 'He'd tell me stories of all the places he'd been, of when he'd been up to the early hours, dancing on the tables, all that sort of stuff,' Sara recalled. 'He described those parties like "the lower deck of the *Titanic*". He was just full of joy.'

Alfie would sit happily, by the window, watching the world go by.

One Wednesday both Pastor Ramage and Sara had been to visit. Pastor Ramage had been sent across the road for cigarettes and milk, noting as he went the various cigarette packets littering the flat. Sara put money on the electric meter, made Alfie some more coffee and sat a while, chatting. 'It's so lovely to see you,' Alfie told Sara, 'so lovely to hear this music.'

Sara left him there, sitting by the speaker and watching the blue seaside sky. Perhaps he was thinking of the many places he had slept through the years: the cold garages, the shop doorways, the friends' sofas and the bug-infested hostel beds.

Now he was exactly where he wanted to be. Frail and warm and home at last.

A few hours later, Alfie died.

I was at work when I got the email from Pastor Ramage, passing on the sad news. I had feared the worst but it still hit hard. 'You should come to the funeral,' he wrote.

Weeks later I was stepping out of a taxi, squinting my eyes against the bright sunshine. The taxi driver had insisted on driving me right up to the doors of the crematorium. 'Most people ask to just drop them at the gates but I warn them about this: it is a bit of a hike,' he said, nodding at the steep hill. The grounds surrounding the old, grey church building, with its grandiose spire, were lush and verdant. Old gravestones poked out through the new plant life.

I took my seat as pallbearers carried Alfie's cardboard coffin into the small chapel (he had joked to Pastor Ramage, 'Just get a big Amazon box and stick me in that'). Alfie's trademark tweed bucket hat was placed carefully on the top. Pink Floyd's 'Wish You Were Here' played through the speakers.

Twenty or so people slotted themselves carefully into the pews. Sara was there, of course, and friends from Alfie's life on the streets. So too was Alfie's ex-partner, the mother of his son. She told a bittersweet story of how, despite the two men barely knowing each other, Alfie's son still took after his father – they even danced the same way, bopping from one leg to another, lost in the music.

Pastor Ramage took his place at the pulpit, nodding a little hello to me as he scanned the room. 'On every chair there is an order of service and inside you'll find a small card, which is blank on one side. On there you can write any messages or anything you wanted to say to Alfie but didn't get a chance, and then there'll be a part of the service where they'll be collected in his hat; they'll go with him during the cremation. So what you write will go with him into eternity, so . . . no pressure,' he joked.

I picked up the card hesitantly.

I had been to too many funerals this year already. Jayne's. Fabian's. But this one felt different. While I felt I had come to know the others, this was the first time I had met the person who had died. I wasn't there to report. (I haven't written about Alfie until now.) I was there because I liked Alfie. I had really enjoyed our time together, and I was sorry we hadn't had more of it. I picked up my pen and wrote him a message. I said thank you and goodbye.

'Usually in the sermon, the pastor will stand up and give a calm, comforting quote from the Bible, something about God's plan and how he has Alfie now, or wax lyrical about how he was a saint among men, absolutely perfect. I thought about that, I really did – this is about the fifth draft of this, because each time it just sounded too poncy,' Pastor Ramage told the congregation. 'And that's not what Alfie wanted. The last thing he said to me was "No fuss, no bother." He wanted it simple, and in fact I think he'd actually be amazed at how many people showed up.

'So instead of some soothing, comforting old cobblers, I thought I'd just share some words about the real person I knew,' the pastor continued. 'Alfie had a less than stellar start to life, not to mention the cancer later, but despite that he didn't end up bitter and hateful, he didn't end up cursing the world' – he shook his fist at the sky jokingly – 'howling at God at the injustice of it all. No, he ended up just being Alfie: quite funny, cheeky, always asking you for a fag, chain smoking. The most common word I've heard when we talk about him is polite, a real gentleman.

'I want to leave you with part of a discussion Alfie and I had – this was just before he passed away. I can't remember the exact words he used but he told me he'd lived his life his way, both the good and the bad, and he'd leave it in the same manner, in the place of his choosing and without fuss, without bother.'

I smiled at that. Of all the awful deaths I had heard about this year – the illness, the cold, the violence – this one was different. Alfie had found redemption; he had found his way home.

In the pew in front of me, Sara bent her head and shed a tear. She was proud of Alfie, she told me later, glad that he had managed to do things his way. 'It was very important to him that he died at home. It was kind of like winning the battle,' said Sara.

We left, the service playing out with the upbeat chords of the Mexican tune Alfie had said sounded like a party. And Sara made her way home, to a flat adorned with the odd assortment of trinkets and gifts that the man with nothing had given his friend.

I woke early in a strange bed. I still hadn't got used to the time difference and yet today I was due to fly home. I was out in Bowling Green, Kentucky, USA, famous only for being the site of a fictional massacre, erroneously cited by Trump's favourite, Kellyanne Conway, as an example of terrorist infiltration. I was there for a cross-border visit that had been part of a journalistic grant I had received for community storytelling. I didn't want to be there. It wasn't the place so much as the fact that that week, of all weeks, was when the findings of our count were finally being published. At long last we had a year's worth of data on homeless people's deaths.

I had spent the past weeks combing through the data meticulously, weeding out duplicate names, anonymizing people that needed to be kept hidden, chasing down any last leads. I had spent months travelling to Manchester, Glasgow, Brighton, Northampton, swapping one grey urban landscape for another, watching the countryside tilting below me from the windows of high-speed trains. And I had been leading a group of journalists from local publications across the UK, too, scores of them who had dug into the data we had found and had questions of their own to ask. This was it. This is what I had been working for over a whole year.

I looked up from my laptop screen and rubbed my tired eyes. I had checked out of the hotel room and was killing time in the hotel lobby, trying to make a rapidly cooling coffee last as long as I could. The minutes were ticking by; 12.17 p.m. in Kentucky meant it was 6.17 p.m. in London. Not long now until the 7 o'clock news. My fingers itched over the computer keyboard. Jittery with nerves, I pulled up the database once more, scanning the list of now-familiar names.

I tried not to get too emotional, aware of how strange my glassy-eyed tension must appear to the hotel staff, who were giving me occasional sidelong glances. Our count was about to reveal the first-ever national figure for those who had died homeless: 449 people's lives logged. Their ages ranged from eighteen to ninety-four years old. Some were found in doorways in the hot summer months, others in tents hidden in the undergrowth. Some were sent, terminally ill, to dingy hostels, while others died in squats and hospitals. Some lay dead months before anyone found them. One man's body showed signs of prolonged starvation. At last the world had a figure, had their names. They couldn't be ignored anymore.

Finally the hour came. Channel 4 News covered the findings at the top of the show with a twenty-minute segment. David Tovey, the artist, had been invited into the television studio to give his reaction to the figures. Seeing him there, nervous and thin in his flat cap, I was hit by an overwhelming sense of pride. He had survived when so many hadn't; he was the perfect person to share his thoughts on our findings. 'I see guys on the streets just asking for someone to talk to,' he told the news presenter. 'You know, we all have the ability to stop and actually talk to somebody, except we have this fear to talk to homeless people, we seem to dehumanize them . . . and that's why there are so many deaths on the streets. I ended up on the streets because there wasn't the help there. When you're a single male you're less likely to be helped.'

Matt Downie, a policy officer from Crisis, was there too,

sitting next to David. Over the past couple of months I'd called Matt so often I'm sure he got sick of my name flashing on his mobile screen. He had been invaluable in helping me navigate the strange complexities of the homelessness system. 'These numbers are beyond appalling. It's a national disgrace,' he said. 'We need to take the numbers and take the lessons learnt from it, and make sure this never happens again.'

From my seat hundreds of miles away, I watched as the story landed and people began to speak out. 'These figures are nothing short of a national scandal,' tweeted one charity CEO. 'I am deeply saddened and shocked beyond belief to hear of the deaths of all these individuals,' added another.

Andy Burnham, Mayor of Manchester, the man who oversaw Stacie and Pottsy's patch, said the number of those dying homeless was 'nothing short of a humanitarian crisis'. Scottish Labour called the scale of deaths in Scotland 'horrifying'.

And then the next day, after I touched down jet-lagged and exhausted in London, I flicked on the TV to see the then Secretary of State for Housing, James Brokenshire, pale-faced and blinking, telling Channel 4 News he had found the number of dead 'utterly shocking . . . It does not reflect the modern Britain that I know that we are, that we need to be,' he said. 'That's why I think it is so important we understand what has caused those deaths.'

But then, as often happens with the news cycle, things moved on. The news became swamped once more with talk of Brexit, football, political spin. Not long after, Chancellor Philip Hammond stood up in parliament and announced that the era of austerity 'is finally coming to an end'. The end of austerity. As if things were over and suddenly all would be well again.

But sleeping bags still littered the streets. The queues

outside the soup kitchens and food banks were as long as ever. In the woods near my flat, the detritus of cans and blankets proved people were living there, camped out in the bushes. It was still all around us. And yet people stopped talking about homelessness. The outcry that had surrounded our work on homeless deaths faded out.

It was hard not to feel dejected. Could nobody see things couldn't go on like this? Did nobody care?

A few weeks later I was heading into central London feeling rather numb. As I walked through the bustling crowds around Leicester Square, my head was full of stories and names, the lives of those I'd come to know over the last year. Both those living and those dead walked with me like Dickensian ghosts.

I was on my way to the annual memorial service to remember those who had died homeless in London that year, held at St Martin-in-the-Fields church, a grand white building which stands just off Trafalgar Square.

As I entered the church I was shocked. After going to small, quiet funerals all over the country, trying to piece together what each death had in common, here I was in a huge space full of people who cared. The place was packed with hundreds of people. They were all here to commemorate the dead.

I felt the tension in my shoulders easing slightly. Sitting in the cool, still air of the church I noticed the strangest sensation of awakening creeping over me. For months I had been working away at this puzzle, this attempt to get to a definitive number of those that died, but I realized now that the project had turned into much more than that. I was used to keeping a certain journalistic distance from my investigations – you need it to be able to do the job – but there in the church all the sadness and horror of what I had been researching washed over me. The awful details of Fabian's blood-soaked death, the desperate tragedy of Jayne slumped in a doorway, the decades-long grief of her mother Pam, the loneliness of Richard, gasping for air in his tiny hostel room. It was too much.

One by one selected guests walked to the front to read a list of names, 165 in total. Lee, Mary, Pawel, Robert . . . I recognized many of them. The names kept going, minute after minute. I sat on the pew and cried.

As my tears fell, a song played: a composition by musician Gavin Bryars that sampled the mournful singing of a man who was sleeping rough in 1971, repeating the refrain 'Jesus' blood never failed me yet', over and over. Dabbing my eyes, I joined the long, snaking queue of people making their way to the altar, where, instead of Holy Communion, we were given a card with the name of one of the dead and were asked to hold them in our thoughts that year.

I returned to my seat and added the name to my mental list of those I wanted to remember. I was still trembling some time later, as I made my way out of the church and back into the world.

Three days later I still had the slip of card with the man's name tucked in my purse, as I stepped off the train at Clacton-on-Sea.

The sadness and frustration I had been feeling earlier had dissipated slightly and given way to a kind of tentative optimism. For months I had been looking into how the UK could have swung from the virtual disappearance of rough-sleeping in the early 2000s to a meteoric rise in almost two decades since. I had set off hoping to find the definitive clause, the exact policy decision which had resulted in this outcome, and had hoped that by doing so I could perhaps come close to finding the solution. But what the life and death of each person I had looked into had told me was that there was no single cause, but rather a myriad combination of shrunken budgets and reduced services. Death by a thousand cuts, literally. People were falling into homelessness with a horrifying regularity because the support services that should have caught them had been cut away.

In the early days of my research I had come across the often-bandied-around phrase that 'many are just one paycheck away from homelessness', but I realized now that this was hugely oversimplifying the situation. Childhood trauma and poverty had appeared time and time again in the stories I had investigated. Care-leaving and prison discharge were known to be key moments when people slipped into homelessness and yet there were no structural buffers in place to stop that happening. The services that could have addressed the various issues that often push people into vulnerability were no longer there. Mental health services were so stretched that even those on the brink of suicide were deemed not to be in crisis enough to access support. Drug and alcohol services said they wouldn't treat people without their mental health being seen to first, and vice versa. The beleaguered NHS was now advising doctors that they may need to turf homeless people back onto the streets. Shelters and refuges were running on shoestrings and were turning away those with the most complex needs. Those cuts had happened slowly, insidiously, over a decade or more. We didn't see them coming. If you don't need to access those services yourself, how would you know they were no longer there?

The homelessness epidemic was not simply the result of hundreds, thousands, of people making bad choices in life. It was the consequence of rising inequality and the systematic decimation of services which had taken place before our very eyes. We had stood by and let it happen, and now we were averting our gaze and ignoring the consequences.

I knew I wasn't the only one who had been thinking about this, and I wanted to test my theory. Which is why I had travelled to the south-east coast of England, hoping to find out if I was on the right track.

The village of Jaywick is perched perilously close to the sea. It is a curious place. In the early twentieth century, the trend for commuter-belt getaways from London had resulted in the construction of the village, originally a seaside resort. The network of squat bungalow houses, many constructed from wooden frames, were laid out along roads designed in the shape of a car radiator grille, a nod to the fact so many of the original residents would drive in from the capital. But progress in the village stalled: the planned-for amenities never materialized, and instead residents were left somewhat isolated in this strange, unnatural village. These days, residents across the area earnt less on average than the general population, and a higher percentage were on benefits – at the local primary school half the children were eligible for free school meals. The area had the worst result in the English deprivation index in both 2010 and 2015.[85] In early November 2018 the UN Special Rapporteur on extreme poverty and human rights, Philip Alston, was on a fact-finding mission to gather evidence on poverty in the UK. There was no better place to look.

As my taxi drove past the scruffy white sea wall that framed the south edge of the town, past an old, clapped-out classic car, I had the strangest sense of being not in the UK but in Havana, Cuba. The glow of the sunset on potholed, cracked streets; the cluster of shuttered houses, paint peeling under the onslaught of sea air.

In the window of one of the houses someone had stuck a

hand-painted sign that read: 'Jaywick Special Needs: libraries, roads, supermarket' – a wishlist presumably in response to the recent investment ploughed into the area by the local council. While the subsequent improvements had been welcomed, there was clearly much more to be done.

Outside a small community centre, Philip Alston was giving interviews to the cameras crowded around him. He looked as far from a UN official as I could imagine: a tall, very slender man, gaunt almost, with high cheekbones and short white hair. He wore a navy puffa jacket and, out of shot of the camera, gripped a blue canvas shopping bag in one hand, as if just out running some errands.

The inside of the community centre was crowded with residents and members of the press. At the front, a trestle table had been adorned with a vase of yellow flowers and a couple of plates of custard cream biscuits.

For the next couple of hours, residents stood one by one and told the crowd of their struggles. There was Jodie,* a young woman who spoke of the difficulties of trying to get a job when she was stigmatized by the place she lived: 'I was put into a bubble called "Jaywick scum". I couldn't even put Jaywick on my CV,' she told the crowd.

Rob,* who was on long-term sickness benefits. Diane,* who was in her fifties and who'd fled seven years of domestic abuse to a refuge. She was battling with mental illness and years earlier her children had been taken into care. She had been asked to leave the refuge after an altercation and ended up in a night shelter.

Erin* in her wheelchair. She and her family were facing a no-fault eviction after ten years in their rental flat and couldn't find another flat that would rent to someone on benefits. 'The council are saying that until we're on the streets they can't help us,' she explained.

On and on the speeches went. Three people said they had attempted suicide because of the stresses of poverty.

Philip Alston took it all in, calm but grave-faced. He scribbled notes in his notebook. When the last speaker finished he took the microphone. 'What we've heard today is very moving,' he told the crowd, who nodded appreciatively. 'We have seen today the faces of poverty and they don't look like what the politicians describe: down-and-out or hopeless.

'Any one of us could get sick, any of us could suffer from mental illness, any of us could become disabled, any of us could have a life-changing event which suddenly transports everything . . . and the role of a civilized community, and one which respects human rights, is to make sure that whoever stumbles is able to help themselves, that they are picked up and can get on with life.'

The crowd whooped and cheered.

Later, Alston produced his official UN report about poverty in the UK. As I read it, I felt a growing sense of recognition. Everything I had been hearing for the last year, the impact of so many different cuts to the safety net, there they all were, laid out in the report.

'The imposition of austerity was an ideological project designed to radically reshape the relationship between the Government and the citizenry,' Alston wrote. 'UK standards of well-being have descended precipitately in a remarkably short period of time, as a result of deliberate policy choices made when many other options were available.

'The Government's "work not welfare" mantra conveys the message that individuals and families can seek charity but that the State will no longer provide the basic social safety net to which all political parties had been committed since 1945.' I paused, thinking of all I had heard about cuts to mental health provision, reduction in addiction support services, the loopholes of benefits.

'It is hard to imagine a recipe better designed to exacerbate inequality and poverty and to undermine the life prospects of many millions,' wrote Alston, taking the words out of my mouth.[86]

The government's reaction to the UN report was denial. The then Work and Pensions Secretary, Amber Rudd, announced she would lodge a formal complaint, claiming the report was politically biased. An official statement said the report was: 'a barely believable documentation of Britain, based on a tiny period of time spent here', complaining that Alston had only spent twelve days on the ground (in reality there were months of research done beforehand and after). But as I read Alston's comments I recognized every single issue raised.

The report felt like vindication, but there was no real pleasure to take from it. The many, many ways the system was failing was overwhelming. There was no single easy solution, other than to reverse a decade's worth of austerity cuts. The realization was somewhat disheartening. I had thought that by coming to understand Richard, or Jayne or Fabian, I could identify the missteps they took, the personal failing that had led to their situation, but the truth was that the ground had crumbled beneath their feet. Their stumbles were magnified, expanded, by the lack of support around them. They were told, 'We're all in this together', and then we turned our backs.

CHAPTER 30

An early Christmas present

So there we were again. December rolled in, gloomy and cold.

Pam, sitting in her cosy living room on the Isle of Wight, was facing the first Christmas without her daughter. In Stafford, Will was still working to feed those in need. In Glasgow, Antoinette was looking for answers about her brother Ian. And in Lowestoft, back where this story began, Jeremy was still asking why his brother died in the snow, metres from his house.

One freezing-cold Tuesday morning I woke to yet another alert among my emails. Forty-three-year-old Gyula Remes had been found dead in the underpass that runs between Westminster tube station and the Houses of Parliament. He had tried to get into a night shelter but they were all full. Another person to die homeless, this time mere metres from the seat of power. MP David Lammy tweeted: 'There is something rotten in Westminster when MPs walk past dying homeless people on their way to work.'

I added Gyula's name to my list and sighed. What more did those in power want? What more potent image of how far wrong we've gone than a man collapsing in the shadow of the grand parliament building?

The UN Special Rapporteur on extreme poverty and human rights had spoken in unflinching terms of the barbarity of the inequality he saw across the country. Members of parliament up and down the land had espoused chastened messages in response to our findings about their constituents who had died homeless. And yet here we were again. The same sorry dance of a moment's outrage forgotten too quickly.

But then everything changed.

Three days after Gyula died, on 21 December, while Christmas shoppers flooded high streets across the country, the Office for National Statistics published their first-ever data on homeless deaths. By comparing our data against death certificates, the ONS had been able to estimate the number of those that died homeless over several years. The ONS's Myer Glickman had watched with a mixture of excitement and trepidation as the figures, which had been checked and rechecked right up to the last minute, went out into the world.

In a press release which soon became screaming headlines all across the country, the official stats were laid out, showing the number of deaths had increased at a horrifying rate, up 24 per cent in just five years. Eighty-four per cent of those who died were men. The mean age at death was forty-four years for men and forty-two years for women (by comparison, in the general population the mean age at death was seventy-six years for men and eighty-one years for women).[87]

The impact of those official figures was extraordinary. Politicians were up in arms; newspapers, radio and TV quoted shocked members of the public and local council officials.

Sitting at my desk in our small office, I blinked back tears. This is what I had been waiting for. Finally, finally there was a national debate happening.

And then in the weeks after I got more good news. Across the country councils were starting to hold reviews into people's deaths. In Leeds, where Fiona Watson had died unnoticed by passers-by. In Brighton and Hove, where Andrew died and Alfie only just made it home. In Oxford and Malvern and

Hackney. All across the country, officials were asking questions about how these people had come to die, trying to work out what lessons could be learnt and how future deaths could be prevented.

And one day I got an excited call from Hugo Sugg, the campaigner who had been pursuing answers to how Cardon Banfield had died. 'I've just been in a meeting with the head of the Safeguarding Adults Board in Worcestershire,' he explained breathlessly, 'and they're going to do one – a review into Cardon's death!'

It turned out there had been three other homeless deaths in Worcester and the surrounding area and the officials there had finally taken heed, and would be looking into whether there were things they could learn from Cardon's and others' fates. The Worcestershire Safeguarding Adults Board confirmed to me they were undertaking a thematic review 'into the care provided to several people who were sleeping rough within the Worcestershire area.' Though as we went to print – nearly five months after they began – the report was still a work in progress.

Still, I was overjoyed. None of this would bring back those who had died, but now we knew the scale of the issue it was harder than ever to look away.

I scrolled through name after name, photo after photo, of the sad list I had collated. I felt like I knew the answer now, but it was more complicated than I could have imagined. There was no quick fix. The country as a whole needed emergency and immediate investment in mental health, substance abuse and homeless-shelter funding. Councils needed additional funds and that funding needed to be ring-fenced and long term, to ensure real answers to local need. The NHS needed to be working in a much more holistic and joined-up way to ensure those on their radar did not fall through the cracks when they were discharged from hospital. The police needed to take a much more compassionate approach to those in their area. And those experiencing homelessness needed to have a say in the treatment they received, needed to be listened to and learnt from.

There was a way back from the epidemic that was all around us, but it would take more than positive words and good intentions. The government was promising to tackle the crisis and had pledged a sizeable pot of money for the task: £1.2 billion to tackle rough-sleeping. But that funding would barely touch the edges of the many different services that had been pared back or lost across the country. And while the Housing First model was proven to work, you needed adequate housing to put people in, and the existing support services in the community to work with people. We needed more houses, more funding and more long-term thinking if we were really going to address the issue.

The scale of need was overwhelming, something so far removed from an individual's responsibility that it was easy to fall into hopelessness. But, I realized, it was too easy to leave all this to the powers above and to brush off any personal responsibility. At the start of this year I had wanted to understand what more I could do to help. So I was agonizing about how I could be of use when I realized the shining example had been in front of me the whole time.

And that is how I found myself peeling potatoes.

It was the day before Christmas and Jon burst into the room carrying six large bunches of pink and purple flowers. 'I just got fleeced for these, but they'll do all right,' he said. The volunteers in the room looked up from the mound of vegetables in front of them. I was working my way through a huge sack of potatoes, running a rather blunt peeler round each one before cutting it in two and throwing it into the biggest saucepan I'd ever seen.

Outside, on Goodge Street, shoppers were dashing around picking up the last of their shopping, but inside this church tucked off the main road volunteers had turned the hall into a night shelter and somehow Jon had negotiated partial use of the small but well-equipped kitchen. It was here that volunteers would be cooking Christmas dinner. I was one of them.

As I washed off the hundredth potato, I happily glanced around the room. We were just half a mile from Sofia House, where Jon had helped set up that emergency squat all those months ago, and now, as the wind whipped up outside, I got a taste of the jolly camaraderie felt by those who had huddled there against the cold. I had started out the year nervous about even speaking to someone who was homeless, unsure of how I could help and instead electing to walk on by. Now here I was, chatting away to the other helpers, many of whom spent their nights in winter shelters or hostels.

What Jon had taught me, more than any of the figures or statistics I'd uncovered, was that one person can make a difference – it just takes knowing where to start. It would be too easy to sit back and wait for the government-needed changes to kick in, I had realized. If it was the Jons and Stephs and Wills of this world keeping people alive while those in power twiddled their thumbs, well then I wanted to be on their side.

The plan was to put on a Streets Kitchen dinner for all those with nowhere to go on Christmas Day. But, like most things Jon conjured up, he was flying by the seat of his pants. 'How many are we cooking for, Jon?' I asked, putting down the peeler and rubbing my knuckles.

'Who knows, one hundred, two hundred? We didn't do anything of that registering shite. You know, if people come, they come,' said Jon as he set music blaring from a small speaker in the corner. I looked at the pile of vegetables still in front of us. It was going to be a long day.

The next day, Jon was exhausted. He'd worked well into the night alongside the other volunteers as they'd peeled, chopped and baked huge sacks of vegetables into a meal. Now he faced the prospect of getting it two-and-a-half miles down the road to the setting for the feast: Islington.

A few weeks earlier he'd got confirmation from council housing officer Diarmaid Ward: he could use the luxurious Islington Assembly Hall for a Streets Kitchen Christmas party.

'It's really annoying,' Jon had joked to me on one of our now-regular phone calls. 'It's becoming harder and harder to hate the council when they keep doing all right things like this!' I smiled, thinking how just a few months ago Jon had been sneaking me into official council projects and now here he was working hand in hand with them.

As Jon was loading trays of food, as flimsy as they were hot, into the backs of volunteers' cars, across town I was bustling away among a group of volunteers setting up tables, hanging fairy lights and baubles, and arranging the flowers Jon had bought earlier onto each table. One woman folded up white paper tablecloths to cut out random shapes, unfolding each one into an intricate snowflake pattern. The regal red velvet curtains and opulent wooden carving around the large stage at the front of the room already lent it a festive vibe.

Just as the volunteers' polite conversations were wavering into silence, Jon burst through the door, hot metal trays in hand. He was wearing, as always, his flat cap and had put on a thick-knit claret red jumper for the occasion. Not quite a modern-day Santa Claus, but this was as festive as he was going to get. Soon he was barking orders to all those standing around.

'Let's get some music on, yeah?

'Right, I need those potatoes heating up and that turkey has to get blasted right now.

'Where's the jugs for gravy?

'OK, we don't start serving until I see one of each thing out on the side, yeah?'

Guests were filing into the hall, past the high-vis-bibbed security men on the gate, their mouths slack at the opulence of the room. A white-haired, gruff man Jon knew from the streets had set up an electric guitar and microphone at the front of the room and was strumming out sad, self-penned songs, much to some of the others' annoyance. 'It's 2018 and the food banks are full,' he sang.

'Come on, this is depressing, give us something Christmassy,' a young man in a beanie hat shouted.

Jon blanched and quickly made his way over to the musician. 'Come on, man, people are here to be cheered up,' he pleaded. 'I hate to do this but I'm going to put some music through the speakers, OK – no hard feelings.' Harrumphing, the musician stood up and stomped outside for a cigarette, grumbling under his breath about the unfairness of it all.

The groups of volunteers pooled, unsure, at the edges of the room. I felt chastened. I imagined many of them, like me, had been prompted into action by the festive season. How many of us would still be here in a few months' time? I recalled a phrase a homeless man had used after a death last Christmas: 'People just care for five minutes.' I was determined that wouldn't be me. Pushing through my shyness, I made my way over to a table where three men were making idle conversation. They looked up and smiled and, beckoning others to join us, I sat down and started to chat, asking how they were, what they had been up to, talking about everything and nothing.

One by one the other volunteers started to relax too, and soon it was unclear who was a guest and who was working, the tables filling with smiling faces and animated conversation.

I paused. Of course these well-meaning folks couldn't solve things alone. A Christmas dinner wasn't going to fix the complex issues many of the guests here were going through. We were going to have to keep fighting for the official funding and institutional support. Still, it was heartening to feel that here, in Islington at least, things were improving.

A little while later, once the food was set out buffet-style on a long trestle table and people were lining up to have their paper plates loaded with turkey and all the trimmings, I looked up to see Diarmaid Ward barrelling into the room. 'Merry Christmas to all!' he called out, his cheeks glowing red from the cold outside. 'You're all doing cracking work!' Diarmaid beamed at the scores of volunteers dotted around the room. Jon smiled politely.

Diarmaid was excited about the year to come. The government had lifted the ban on councils borrowing to build houses. 'Now we're building like crazy,' he said excitedly later on. 'We're planning 550 council homes in the next three years. But, you know, if you borrow you still have to pay it back, so it's not like we can just borrow 'til kingdom come.' I thought back to what he'd told me about the waiting list – 550 homes was good, but there were 13,000 households on the waiting list. What would happen to them?

In the end about forty people or so had turned up to get a hot meal and some company. Jon leant against the wall and breathed a deep sigh. Somehow he had magicked another event into existence. But he was all too aware that once the guests had finished their meals, scraped their plates clean and pulled the last of the crackers, he'd be seeing them out of the door again.

Little did I know that, a day earlier, while I was peeling potatoes, Jon had taken a call he had been waiting for. A call that gave him what he had been searching for for months.

Down in Brighton, Jim Deans was feeling a similar sense of wellbeing.

It had been his friend Wayne's idea. 'Why not turn the bus into a Santa's Grotto, spread some festive cheer?' Jim hadn't needed much persuading. Presents were collected and wrapped with the same inexplicable efficiency that Jim applied to all his work. The bus was garlanded with tinsel and fairy lights and Jim had squeezed his appropriately jolly frame into a red Santa suit and slipped on a fake beard.

They drove the bus down to the clock tower in Brighton city centre, the same spot where months earlier crowds had gathered to reflect on Andrew O'Connell's death. Almost as soon as the bus had been parked up the crowds started to gather, the same hungry faces Jim saw week in, week out.

One by one the city's homeless population stepped up into the grotto of the bus, sat on the bulky back seat next to Jim's pound-store Santa and poured out their hopes and dreams.

Jim was dumbfounded, his open mouth hidden under the fake beard. Here were people who usually spoke only about their most immediate concerns: how they'd eat that day or where they'd get their next fix. Now they were talking not in hours and days but months and years. One lady asked if Jim and his group could do the catering at her wedding next year – 'Your food's always so nice.'

Some spoke so passionately, so freely of their dreams and wishes for the coming year that Jim found himself pulling down his beard. 'I was like, "You do know it's me under here? Not actually Father Christmas,"' he laughed later.

A few weeks after his turn as Santa, Jim's plans fell to pieces. His team of volunteers had finished transforming the bus back from Santa's Grotto into a shelter, and a few people had been staying on it one night, when it caught fire.

Everyone got out safely, but the damage was severe. It seemed the electrics in one of the strip lights had blown, and now the top deck was a charred, blackened mess, sodden with the water the fire brigade had doused it with. Some of the five who had been sleeping there had all their worldly possessions destroyed. It was a devastating blow.

Talking to TV cameras in front of the bus, Jim was sanguine, if tired. 'Some of these guys have lost everything. One guy had everything he owns in this world in one rucksack – his birth certificate . . . He's just got what he's standing in. I haven't heard him complain once,' he sighed.

'We've got to rip everything out and start again,' Jim announced.

Later that day he posted about it on a fundraising page, asking for help. It was an emergency – he needed to buy supplies now. The donations flooded in: nearly £5,000 was raised. Jim got ready to start again.

Aisha spent her Christmas day alongside nearly 200 others in a 'Crisis at Christmas' shelter set up in a high school in north London. She had never been to such a place. I caught up with her there and as we settled down at a table in the hall, she was still a little unsure, tugging her headscarf tight down her rounded cheeks, dappled with small acne scars. She still hadn't taken off her thick jacket and sat with her black, fake-leather handbag pulled close to her on the table in front. This was all still very new. It had been just a few weeks since she'd found herself homeless for the first time.

Tired, she stared blankly out the window, watching a gaggle of doctors and nurses who volunteered at the centre to treat any minor ailments the residents had scurrying across the school playground in their scrubs, a blur of shades of blue. She still hadn't given up on her dream of becoming a nurse, but it seemed a long way off. The job as a healthcare assistant that she'd applied for still hadn't materialized.

The nurses there had been kind. She'd got a flu vaccination and they'd given her some painkillers for her stomach cramps. The first day she had arrived at the centre, Aisha had been suffering. A volunteer had noticed her face crumple with pain as she washed her hands in the high-school students' bathroom. Aisha explained she was having bad period cramps. Concerned, the woman found her a quiet classroom upstairs in the building. They got her a blanket and sat with her as she rested up. They even brought her dinner up on a tray but, feeling stronger, she gratefully took the food and headed back downstairs to join the others in the canteen.

There had been no shortage of food at the centre. There were other luxuries too. The school's changing-room showers were hot and strong, and once washed, Aisha had relished a back massage from a masseuse who was volunteering at the centre. And once she knew there was a place she could take off her headscarf away from men, she had her hair cut not once but twice. The caring touch of the hairdresser as she carefully trimmed the ends of Aisha's dark hair felt like an embrace. Another day, a beautician carefully cleaned off the thick layer of pink varnish on Aisha's fingernails then repainted and buffed them to a glowing peach shine.

Aisha was still thinking of these treats when we met a few days later. The Crisis shelter had shut on 29 December and she was back on the exhausting carousel of transferring from one church hall night shelter to another each night.

That night it was the United Free Church in Leytonstone and Aisha was counting down the hours until it was bedtime. The honey-coloured brick building was hive-like in its labyrinth of angular, connecting rooms. Off to one side of the hall was a small room where the women would sleep. Aisha had chosen one of the beds by the wall, a thin yoga mat with a blue sleeping bag and a too-soft pillow. There were usually five women that stayed in this room but so far only she and two others had shown up. Upstairs the men's sleeping bags were laid out in rows in a larger hall space. Aisha knew that the noise of those in the hall meant she couldn't go to sleep until the men were sent off to bed.

The council had told her they hoped she'd be in a full-time shelter by mid-February. The hostels they had mentioned would be paid for by her benefits, but as soon as she got a job she'd be looking at a charge of £70 a week.

After a long chat I said my goodbyes and, aware of the cold and the dark, opted for a taxi ride home. It cost me £10.13, more than Aisha currently had in her bank account.

A few nights later, on New Year's Eve, Aisha was in Walthamstow church hall. She tried to sleep while other residents cheered and celebrated when the clock hit midnight. 'Happy New Year!' they crowed. Aisha just pulled her sleeping bag up higher.

CHAPTER 32

Start again

The sun rose on New Year's Day, hitting the town of Lowestoft first, warming the cold ground and marking a year and three days since Tony had died in his former backyard. Since that day, hundreds more had suffered the same fate – untimely and preventable deaths while homeless.

But others struggled on.

David the artist had seen in the New Year on Blackfriars Bridge accompanied by his brother and his young family. As they watched the fireworks, David remembered a time, years ago, when he had left the confines of the car he was calling home and walked down to the same spot. He had been lost then, alone, and yet he had snapped a photograph, one of the best he had ever taken: a long-exposure blur of people rushing by, and there in the centre, one man staring straight at him. In the darkness, behind his camera, David had been seen. And in the end, being seen had kept him alive.

In Manchester, Pottsy and the others in the squat had been partying, laughing and drinking, and singing, 'Should auld acquaintance be forgot and never brought to mind?' Stacie, mistiming her commute back from the town centre, was alone on the tram when the clock struck midnight. Even from there the new year looked hopeful. Soon they would be opening up new squats around the town, taking their merry band of friends with them and keeping the people who everyone else had forgotten safe.

Richard woke wheezing in his cold hostel room. At least this year he wasn't in the hospital when the clock struck midnight. He was going to keep complaining, keep pushing. He wasn't going down without a fight.

While the country nursed its hangover, Aisha was outside, slowly walking up and down the shuttered streets. The library wasn't open that day and she had twelve hours to kill before she could get into the next church hall. The winter shelters would stay open for another two months or so, but what then? Somehow, despite the cold, she had managed to stay positive, cheerful almost, strong in the faith that she would find a home soon.

And for one person at least, a happy ending of sorts was in sight.

I spotted Jon as soon as I got off the bus. There he was, fiddling with his phone and smoking a stubby little roll-up, flanked on either side by a bookie's shop and what looked like a pub but had in fact been converted into a mosque.

'How are ya?' Jon called down the road. 'Come and have a look at what we've got here,' he boomed, giving me a warm hug as I arrived. I was excited. For the past couple of weeks I'd been getting breathless calls from Jon, filling me in on grand plans he had.

'See, we have this building,' he explained. 'It's not much now but the landlord, he's up for letting us use it! So we have a space, at last a space!'

As we made our way down the small alley and into the building, I tried my best not to let my smile falter. Jon's enthusiasm was infectious, but it still couldn't paper over the dilapidated scene in front of me. The space was a former glass factory, a long, concrete-floored building with exposed walls and damp-soaked MDF patching parts of the ceiling. I cast my gaze around, wondering what I was missing, but Jon was still going a mile a minute.

'See, we've got space for beds all along here – maybe eight or ten of them – and then we can fit even more in if we need to for bad weather. Then down here, this can be like a chill-out area and we'll have a kitchen there. You know all the things we need. We'll get them.'

'It's a big job,' I ventured.

'Aye, but we've got loads of people backing us on this. I mean, wow, I've had the council saying they're on board. I mean, fuck! And we'll get all the stuff, no worries.'

I shouldn't have doubted him. A few weeks later the building was done up, the old flakey walls had been painted a clean, light blue, the damp ceiling panels removed and, most miraculously of all, covered over by flame-retardant material that one of Jon's friends had managed to scavenge as a donation from the National Theatre; a patch of red carpet had come from the BAFTA awards ceremony.

Trolleys of donated goods flooded in from all corners. Flat-packed wooden 'pods' had been built for those who wanted their privacy. Others favoured camping beds or even blankets on the floor. 'It's whatever people feel comfortable with,' Jon explained. Thirty people, many of them long-term rough-sleepers too suspicious of official hostels, had bedded down there.

This was it – the space Jon had been waiting for. A place without all the formality or stand-offishness of official home-less provision. Somewhere where the most entrenched rough-sleepers could feel comfortable. Part squat, part shelter, but open to all.

And what's more, unlike Sofia House where he'd been fighting 'the man' to get it done, here the council was surprisingly on board. They had been really supportive and were now talking about finding other empty buildings to hand over. 'It's weird – like, they're starting to listen.' I smiled at Jon's bewilderment.

On sofas in the corner of the room, a young man and woman were playing cards. Someone else was making a round of tea using a selection of branded mugs. At night the residents amused themselves with film nights or, once, a karaoke session. Jon dragged in one of his speakers and mics and they set the music running from YouTube. Everyone got a little teary when one shy and retiring guest, who barely spoke English, took the microphone to sing Tracy Chapman's 'Fast Car'.

> I know things will get better
> You'll find work and I'll get promoted
> We'll move out of the shelter
> Buy a bigger house and live in the suburbs.

I watched happily as Jon stood back and looked at the place. He had built it. 'See, my idea is use this as the model. There are buildings all over the country sitting empty. You use this as the guideline and you do the same thing there. Solidarity shelters all over the place,' Jon said, eyes glowing. 'We can do it, you know. I really think we can.'

Looking back on the two years I've spent reporting on home-lessness in the UK, I am struck by an anecdote I heard about statistician Abraham Wald. The story went like this. In the early 1940s, Wald was part of a team of data scientists tasked with using their statistical expertise to improve the United States of America's efforts in the Second World War. The project in hand was an analysis of the bullet holes in fighter jets that returned from action, with the aim of finding where the air force could strategically bolster the plane's armour so as not to add too much weight to the nimble frames.

Studying the bullet holes on the returned fighter jets showed a clear pattern: the planes were being hit on the fuselage and the fuel system but not the engine. Wald's colleagues came to the reasoned conclusion that the patterns showed clearly where the enemy was aiming their fire, and therefore they should strengthen the armour on the fuselage and fuel systems. A sensible conclusion based on the evidence before them.

But Wald disagreed. He realized that it was exactly the data he *did not* have that was the most important. What the studies of the bullet holes had actually shown was where the planes could be hit and still make it home. It was the bullet holes on the missing planes – the ones that had been shot down – that showed where the vulnerable spots really were. You put the armour where there were no holes.

That story stuck with me. I work in investigative journalism and we rely on data – data to show us trends, data to fact-check the prevalent narratives, data to hold people to account. But in many ways what is most interesting is the times when data is not held. Now that might be because no one has thought to collect it (an unknown unknown) or because someone doesn't want it collected (a known unknown). Either way, once I get the scent, I can rarely let it go.

And so in many ways my mission had been to find the planes that weren't coming back: who was it that was dying homeless, unrecorded and uninvestigated. Who were these people who could no longer talk for themselves? What were their stories, and what could we learn from the patterns there?

I was often struck at the many inquests I attended in the course of this project that the dead person has no advocate for them in the proceedings, no one to question the evidence presented, even when it was wrong. At Jayne's inquest I bit my tongue and furrowed my brow as the coroner matter-of-factly summarized how Jayne's baby had died in the last twelve months – not true, it was decades earlier. At the inquest of the man who died crushed in a bin lorry I baulked as one of the workers on the lorry explained how he banged on the side of the bin, listening for anyone to cry out, before emptying it into the lorry. But as the coroner asked a follow-up question the worker repeatedly failed to hear her, clearly being somewhat deaf. There was no one to point out that perhaps the man had indeed cried out but had not been heard.

And then there were so many people who died unknown, buried with paupers' funerals. Many times, the only way families in other countries found out about deaths was if the person's acquaintances went out of their way to track the family down. Meanwhile, people were dying and rotting in tents and no one was looking into this. In the case of Cardon Banfield, who had Hugo Sugg as an advocate, any calls for an exploration of the events leading up to his death were brushed aside.

Something was going very wrong.

In the end we collected more than 800 cases of people dying while homeless in eighteen months. It was a jigsaw, a piecing-together of names and stories as and when we heard them, but sadly it was also undoubtedly an underestimate. Many, many more people will have died without a home.

And yet homelessness continues to rise. The charity Crisis predicts the number of core homeless (rough-sleepers, those in unsuitable temporary accommodation, sofa-surfers), could increase two-and-a-half times by 2041. The only way to stop that, and to stop more people dying homeless, is to get to grips with the myriad causes that plunge people into poverty and homelessness in the first place.

The more I learnt about Jayne, Hamid, Richard, David, Stacie, the more I understood the weak points in the safety net (the missing holes from the planes). I now understand so much more about the multi-faceted nature of the issue that the UK is facing: there is no one cause for homelessness. But there are clear patterns, which I saw time and time again.

It is incontrovertible that more than a decade of austerity measures has cut away the safety net below us. Perhaps those cuts are most acute at the level of local councils, who are responsible for adult social services, substance abuse programmes, child protection, council homes, indeed most of what we think of as the safety net. They have seen their budgets cut by central government by 21 per cent between 2010 and 2019. Those same councils also have to keep the street lights on, the bins collected, the parks open. With a fifth of the budget gone, it is often the things invisible to most people which get cut: the domestic violence refuges, the drugs support services, the help for those in so-called supported housing. The cuts affect councils run by all the major political parties – Labour, Conservative . . . I saw councils of all colours cutting vital, life-saving services.

Those cuts have become so relentless, quiet and consistent that we, as a nation, have somehow come to accept them. Like frogs in slowly boiling water, we have sat and watched as libraries have closed, food banks have opened, and more and more people have found themselves homeless, living in bed and breakfasts, cars, doorways. The newspaper-reporting that has tried to flag some of the cuts has often been a Cassandra-esque warning, clear in its prophesy and yet brushed aside with slogans like 'We're all in this together.' We all begrudgingly accepted that the 2008 global financial crash changed things for everyone, and somehow forgave the banks' bail-out and the following reduction in corporation tax while accepting the myriad cuts that hit our social services.

It is the ensuing poverty and inequality that is the key driver in our rising homeless figures. When I started my research I had heard the much-repeated adage that we are all only a few missed paychecks away from homelessness. It is a neat image, one that makes everyone sit up and think, but the truth is that those who have families with resources they are willing to share, those who have robust enough mental health and who are not surrounded daily by the lure of drink or drugs, those who aren't carrying festering, untreated child-hood trauma – they are the ones who are going to find it easiest to bounce back from a low period.

More often, it is those ground down by the constant pressure of poverty, or those valiantly battling the daily onslaught of mental health issues or substance addictions, who are the ones that will be knocked out by some event, a tipping point like a lost job or a relationship breakdown. For too many, those moments are the point when the downward spiralling speeds up, the problems intensify. And when the safety net fails those people, they die.

The solution to this feels so large and yet so simple that it seems almost laughable to write it down: reverse the decimating austerity cuts of the past decade. The impacts are not irreversible. Pumping funding back into councils, ring-fencing funds for support services, creating sustainable, long-term funding for refuges, supported housing, drug programmes; I imagine things would change incredibly quickly.

Then there is the fact that the UK is in a widespread housing crisis. The sell-off of council properties under Right to Buy has left councils with dwindling housing stock; meanwhile the properties that are being built are rarely affordable. Instead, developers building luxury flats promise a percentage will be affordable and then weasel out of those promises later, presumably lured by the profits that can be made on the high-end units. Meanwhile the properties that are left, that are set aside for social housing, are all too often not fit for purpose: converted office blocks that warehouse vulnerable people, or high-rise tower blocks with fragile fire safety.

The dire lack of affordable properties to buy or rent has pushed up market prices. Housing benefits were frozen in 2016, meaning those benefits now rarely cover costs. It is a clear and simple recipe for homelessness.

So, again, there is the strikingly simple solution, which is to build more houses. Crisis estimate the UK needs 100,500 new social (council) homes each year for the next fifteen years 'to meet the needs of homeless people and people on low incomes – including those at risk of homelessness'. That will take a concerted effort, perhaps subsidies, and a strength of resolve not to bow to market pressures and whittle down the number of actually affordable properties to make more money in the long term.

While more housing is the answer for most, there are some who need extra support to get off the streets. But again, a tried and tested solution already exists: we know that the Housing First model has virtually eradicated rough-sleeping in Finland and has been wildly successful in cities like Amsterdam, or Medicine Hat in Canada. Getting someone into safe, long-term accommodation and providing them with wrap-around care (in the context of well-funded community services) can pull people from the grasp of life on the streets. And while it may seem expensive, it saves money in the long run: the cost of a single person sleeping rough for twelve months is £20,128 in support services, but if there is a successful intervention with Housing First that gets them back into accommodation, that support cost drops to just £1,426.[88]

And then there is the question of how we use what we do know about homelessness, the data we have gathered, to make informed and bold policies that stop it happening in the first place. I think what struck me most in the course of this research was just how preventable homelessness is. We know so clearly where the crisis moments come; we can pick up with great accuracy what the signals are that someone is at risk of homelessness. So why aren't we doing more with that knowledge?

During one interview, in the public cafe of a glitzy private-member's club, Bill, a formerly homeless man, told me he thought this kind of prevention should be easy. Bill had made a fortune inventing a form of technology vital to modern CGI effects in films, but had lost it all through alcoholism and a breakdown, and ended up homeless. Now he was on his way up, had his own place and had kicked his habit. He wanted to find a solution and had come up with a neat idea. 'There's so much big data out there – you know, health stuff – if people are missing paying bills, if they're needing more benefits, all that stuff, you should be able to write an algorithm and predict who's at risk of homelessness.'

An algorithm might seem crude but actually there are many markers which are clear warning signs that someone is heading towards homelessness. An academic study in Scotland showed a clear pattern of visits to a doctor immediately before someone became homeless.[89] Countless studies have shown that adverse childhood experiences correlate with homelessness in later life. Other studies show clear patterns in people become homeless after leaving care, prison or hospital.

That knowledge can be put to use proactively – just look at the project in Australia which worked with young people still in school, identifying who was struggling and in circumstances that put them at risk, and supporting them in their teenage years. That programme managed to reduce youth homelessness by 40 per cent.

The challenge is there. It is up to the political leaders to take the bold action needed. And in some ways they are trying; there have been some forward steps in recent years. As I write this, the UK government seems to be acknowledging the scale of the homelessness crisis. The Homelessness Reduction Act came into force during the course of my research, a legislative framework that strengthens the statutory duty on councils to prevent homelessness for all eligible applicants, including those who do not have 'priority need' or may be considered intentionally homelessness, regardless of whether they have a connection to the local area and could therefore access longer-term support. Prisons and hospitals now have a duty to refer people to the local authority if they are discharged homeless. Unfortunately, referral doesn't mean guaranteed housing and the prevention side of things is too often just about advising people to try the private rental market, even when we know that doesn't work. I heard from more than sixty-five people across England who described how the legislation looked good on paper but wasn't actually making any positive difference in reality.

On top of that, £1.2 billion has been pledged to tackle homelessness and rough-sleeping, and a Rough Sleeping Initiative team has created a strategy to achieve the bold target of halving rough-sleeping numbers by 2020 and eradicating rough-sleeping by 2027. Those kind of targets can work: the focus and political clout given to a similar initiative under New Labour resulted in getting rough-sleeping figures to almost zero. But it has to be noted that that initiative came in the context of funding to councils and other services too. Many people I spoke to worried that the current government's £1.2 billion looked great on paper but in reality is nowhere near filling the gaping hole of cuts over the last decade.

Still, we can take some comfort from the past. We know how to reduce homelessness. We did it before, in the early 2000s. We can learn from cities and countries that have made it work for them. But it takes political will, money and a recognition that there is no single panacea that will fix everything – instead we need consistent and substantial investment in all the various systems that save people's lives.

That is a big ask. So you might be reading this and feeling powerless. But it is up to us to demand these things from our elected representatives. To demand that services which might seem invisible to many, but are lifesaving to some, have a future.

And I have found that there is much I can do as an individual too. It is easy to feel powerless, or to protect yourself by closing your mind off to the humanity of those we see on the streets. When that happens to me I try to remember Dr Lasana Harris' MRI scans and his simple question: 'Do you think they like broccoli or carrots?' Sometimes it is as simple as making eye contact with someone sitting on the streets, and smiling, stopping to have a chat, asking if you can buy them a drink or a sandwich. I can't tell you whether it is wise to give money or not. I had hoped I would come to a clear conclusion but I heard warnings from some that it can fund drugs habits, and admonishments from others that such worries are presumptuous and patronizing, that these are adults who can make up their own minds on what to spend their money on. If you're really worried about that, why not donate to a food bank or help out at a soup kitchen. Ask your local homeless shelter or outreach workers what support they need or how they think you can help. And if you're worried about someone who is sleeping rough in England or Wales you can alert StreetLink – a homelessness charity that connects rough-sleepers with local services – to their whereabouts and they'll go and see if they can help.

For Fabian, Jayne or Hamid there was a moment, maybe several, somewhere in their pasts when the right intervention could have turned things around, could have helped them get clean or stopped the slide into substance abuse, could have addressed the mental health issues early before they took hold, could have kept them safe and warm in a house instead of leaving them adrift on the streets. For Stacie, Aisha and Richard, I hope those moments are coming soon, that they achieve that most basic of human rights, that most instinctual of human desires: a safe, secure home.

About this project

For a year and a half I travelled the country interviewing the family and friends of those who died, attending funerals, scribbling notes at inquests and at criminal trials. I visited Glasgow, Bradford, Edinburgh, Belfast, Brighton, Manchester, Leeds, Northampton, Harlow, Canterbury, Maidstone, Lewes, Stafford, the Isle of Wight, Milton Keynes, Newport and many other towns and cities in my quest to come up with answers about how and why people were dying homeless.

I spent hours shadowing people, undertaking long interviews, meeting them repeatedly over months. Those interactions were recorded and much of the dialogue in this book comes from transcripts of those conversations. I have endeavoured to highlight where I was not physically present for the events described and have based those descriptions on deep research and cross-referenced interviews. Beyond interviews, I obtained reports and vital documents through sources and from Freedom of Information requests. I compiled huge databases of figures on cuts to vital services, also using FOI.

I have changed names where necessary to protect people's privacy. I recognize, of course, that writing about people who have died is an incredibly complicated endeavour and I truly felt the weight of that responsibility. I have tried to reflect the memories of their friends and loved ones but recognize I can give them, the deceased, no opportunity to reply, correct or challenge those memories. I pulled together as much documentation as possible to support the core facts of their histories, but we will never know the whole picture of their thoughts, concerns, hopes.

Other findings in this book are drawn from the important evidence-gathering of many amazing academics and journalists, including Rob Aldridge, Michelle Cornes, Alex Bax, Patrick Greenfield, Michael Yong, Jennifer Williams, Rory Winters, Samir Jeraj, Natalie Bloomer and Karin Godwin, among others. I am indebted to the work of my Bureau of Investigative Journalism colleagues Charles Boutaud, Megan Lucero, Eliza Anyangwe, Rachel Hamada, Gareth Davies, Meirion Jones and editor Rachel Oldroyd.

I was joined on this quest by a network of local journalists who fed names and data into our database. Together they then published more than a hundred local news stories, asking important questions of local authorities. While the national press often missed these deaths, it was the local reporters, so endangered by cuts to their own resources, that did the public-interest work of recording when people were dying while homeless.

So it was together that we called for an official body to log these deaths using #makethemcount. We knew it shouldn't take journalists to do this vital work; we needed the powers that be to sit up and take note. In December, prompted by our work, the Office for National Statistics produced the first-ever official data on homeless deaths.

The project was cited in parliamentary debates, in both the House of Commons and the House of Lords. The work was presented to the All Party Parliamentary Group for Ending Homelessness and shown to the UN Special Rapporteur on extreme poverty and human rights. We also presented it at various expert-led conferences.

James Brokenshire, the Secretary of State for Housing, called our findings 'utterly shocking' and the government's

Rough Sleeping Strategy recommended, for the first time, that homeless deaths be reviewed. Now several councils, including Brighton and Hove, Oxford, Malvern and Leeds have said they will undertake their own reviews into homeless deaths, while others, such as Haringey council, have put in place new protocols to log how and when people die homeless, a move we were told was directly prompted by our work.

The work was also received positively by those working with and for homeless people. Several organizations called it a 'wake-up call'. The *Big Issue* called the work 'pioneering' and said: 'To its huge credit, the Bureau's research extensively looked into the stories of every one of those deaths.' It named the Bureau's 'Bureau Local' team as one of its Top 100 Changemakers for 2019. Crisis UK said: 'It is difficult to overstate the importance of the Dying Homeless Project, which has shed new light on a subject that was ignored for too long.' Our findings were also picked up and used by Comic Relief for Red Nose Day 2019, to help raise vital funds for UK homeless services.

This was a project to get to the truth and to tell stories that were being forgotten – or worse, ignored. I will forever be indebted to the many friends and family of those who died, for trusting me to share their loved ones' stories. This book is dedicated to the memory of each of them.

What can I do?

I hope that after reading these stories you feel many things: anger, frustration, the impetus to help – anything but hopeless. Because the situation is not hopeless. There are any number of things we can do, from the small to the large-scale, that could prevent more people falling into homelessness and dying. Here are a few ideas:

1. Smile. Stop for a chat. The next time you see someone sitting or sleeping on the streets, make eye contact, say hi, ask them how they're doing. It is not on you to solve all their problems, just treating them as human can make a huge difference.
2. Connect people to services that can help them. After saying hello you could check if they'd like you to alert StreetLink of their location. Working only in England and Wales, StreetLink has an app and website where you can enter details of people you have seen and an outreach team will be sent out to check what help they need. Find out more: https://www.streetlink.org.uk/. Or you can phone your local council and ask for their homeless team.
3. Support your local homelessness services. You can find details via Homeless Link: https://www.homeless.org.uk/search-homelessness-services. Get in touch and ask what they need: donations, bedding, volunteers. If you have some spare time, food banks and winter night shelters often need supplies and people to keep running. If you're

confused about who to support, there are many organizations mentioned in this book that always need support: Streets Kitchen; Northampton's Hope Centre; Sussex homeless support CIO; A Helping Hand, Paisley; Lodging House Mission, Glasgow; House of Bread, Stafford; and Manchester's Salford Unemployed and Community Resource Centre.

4. Support national charities that are doing the large-scale support work and the necessary lobbying, like Crisis, Shelter or the Simon Community in London.

5. Write to your local council and MP – ask them what they are doing to prevent homelessness and to support those living homeless. In the past, caring about those experiencing homelessness has hardly been a vote-winner for local or national politicians. Telling them you care about this topic could prompt action.

6. If you see news of someone who has died while homeless, write to your council asking whether there will be a Safeguarding Adult Review (SAR) into the death. You can mark your emails or letters 'For the Attention of the Chair of the Safeguarding Adult Review Board'.

7. Write to the government, demanding action. At the time of writing there is a post called Parliamentary Under Secretary of State (Minister for Local Government and Homelessness) – you should be able to find their email address by searching online.

Acknowledgements

I am eternally grateful to all those who took the time to talk to me for this work, both those whose stories were included and the many, many more whose did not make it into these pages. I have been touched by the grace and openness with which the families of the bereaved have welcomed my enquiries.

Thanks must also go to my partner, Ed Hamilton, for his enduring patience and unwavering support as I attempted to juggle this research around a myriad array of other duties and stresses (not least training our naughty dog and gestating our baby). Thanks too to my colleagues at the Bureau of Investigative Journalism, in particular my editors Rachel Oldroyd and Megan Lucero, for allowing me the space and freedom to develop this research over time. I have cited the work of many amazing journalist colleagues whose research I drew on for this book, including the fantastic Patrick Greenfield, Liam Geraghty, Natalie Bloomer, Samir Jeraj, Jen Williams, Rory Winters and Michael Yong. Matt Downie from Crisis was endlessly helpful in clarifying policy issues and helping me get up to speed with the facts.

I would never have made it this far without the support and expert guidance of Picador's Kris Doyle, Laura Carr and Grace Harrison. Special thanks are due to my agent, Richard Pike, who helped me develop and hone the idea for the book from the vaguest notion to the final product. Alice Milliken and Eli Lee were both rigorous and kind in their fact-checking and editorial guidance. And I'll be eternally grateful to Clare and Tony Fletcher for providing us with a safe home during the chaos of the pandemic.

Finally, thanks to my parents Roisin and Tony, who met working with people experiencing homelessness in Belfast and who taught me to open my eyes and care. All I have done was only possible thanks to you both.

Notes

All URLs correct at the time of going to print.

1   Survey from Shelter in 2016: 'One in three working families only one paycheque away from losing their home' (2016), https://england.shelter.org.uk/media/press_releases/articles/one_paycheque_away

2   Matt Broomfield, 'The Sofia Solidarity Centre Squat Exposed a Housing Crisis Past Breaking Point' (2018), Novara Media, https://novaramedia.com/2018/03/26/the-sofia-solidarity-centre-squat-exposed-a-housing-crisis-past-breaking-point/

3   Martin Burrows, Rob Edgar and Théa Fitch, 'More Than a Statistic: A Peer-Led Consultation with People Experiencing Homelessness for the London Homeless Health Programme' (2016), Groundswell, https://www.healthylondon.org/wp-content/uploads/2017/10/More-than-a-statistic.pdf

4   'History of Homelessness', *Homelessness in the UK*, vol. 262, p. 14, Independence Educational Publishers, https://www.independence.co.uk/pdfs/issuesOnline/Vol.262%20Homelessness%20in%20the%20UK/files/assets/basic-html/page14.html

5 In the first three months of 2018, 25,750 people approached councils across England, saying they were homeless. Just 52 per cent (13,320) were deemed to be 'priority need' and offered housing.

6 In England, the Homelessness Code of Guidance, introduced in 2018, notes that: 'A person who is vulnerable as a result of having been a member of Her Majesty's regular armed forces (a veteran) has a priority need for accommodation.' In 2016, Wales introduced a Code of Guidance to support local authorities in making decisions about veterans and homelessness. The code recommended the relevant council officer take into account the length of time and type of service the person has undertaken when assessing how vulnerable they would be if homeless.

7 The number of veterans suffering mental health issues appeared to rise following the return of personnel from conflicts in Iraq and Afghanistan. The charity Combat Stress reported a growing demand for its services, with 2,400 former servicemen and women treated in one year alone.

8 Edward Kirton-Darling and Helen Carr, 'Homeless Veterans in London: Investigating Housing Responsibilities', University of Kent (2016), https://static.kent.ac.uk/media/news/2016/12/Homeless-Veterans-in-London-Investigating-Housing-Responsibilities.pdf

9 Research by Shelter in 2018 showed that more than a thousand people become homeless every month in the UK – that's more than thirty a day: https://england.shelter.org.uk/media/press_releases articles/320,000_people_in_britain_are_now_homeless,_as_numbers_keep_rising

10   Nearly a quarter of the survivors supported by Women's
      Aid's No Woman Turned Away project who approached their
      local housing team were told they weren't in 'priority need':
      https://www.womensaid.org.uk/research-and-publications/
      nowhere-to-turn-2018/

11   In 2017, Homeless Link's 'Annual Review of Single
      Homelessness Support in England' found that 42 per cent
      of homelessness accommodation projects had turned
      people away because their needs were too complex. Fifty-nine
      per cent said they had turned people away because their
      needs were too high, and 71 per cent had turned someone
      away because they were deemed to be too high-risk:
      https://www.crisis.org.uk/ending-homelessness/the-plan-to-end-
      homelessness-full-version/solutions/chapter-9-the-role-of-housing-
      first-in-ending-homelessness/

12   Richard Partington, 'Construction of homes for social rent
      drops 80% in a decade', *Guardian*, 22 November 2018,
      https://www.theguardian.com/society/2018/nov/22/
      construction-of-homes-for-social-rent-down-80-percent-on-a-
      decade-ago-england-families-waiting-lists

13   Research by Nick Mathiason for the Bureau of Investigative
      Journalism revealed how 'financial viability assessments on
      behalf of a leading housebuilder repeatedly persuaded
      councils that having larger affordable-housing quotas would
      make schemes uneconomic.' 18 September 2013: https://
      www.theguardian.com/society/2013/sep/18/thousands-
      affordable-homes-axed-councils

14   Suzanne Fitzpatrick, Hal Pawson, Glen Gramley et al.,
      'The Homelessness Monitor: England 2019', Crisis (2019),
      https://www.crisis.org.uk/media/240419/the_homelessness_
      monitor_england_2019.pdf

15   Matt Downie (ed.) et al., 'Everybody In: How to End
      Homelessness in Great Britain', Crisis (2018),
      https://www.crisis.org.uk/media/239951/everybody_in_how_
      to_end_homelessness_in_great_britain_2018.pdf

16   Researchers from King's College London mapped medical
      provision across England and identified 123 homeless GP
      services. The research found: 'They were mainly located in
      urban areas where there are concentrations of people who
      are homeless and homeless services. Relatively few such
      health services were found in rural areas. Most of the 35
      largest cities in England and several London boroughs had at
      least one specialist primary health care service. However, in
      more than one-half of London boroughs and a few large
      cities no specialist primary health care service was identified,
      despite these locations having homelessness services.'
      Maureen Crane et al., 'Mapping of specialist primary health
      care services in England for people who are homeless',
      February 2018, https://www.kcl.ac.uk/scwru/res/hrp/hrp-
      studies/HEARTH/HEARTH-study-Mapping-FullReport-2018.
      pdf

17   A quarter of homeless people polled by monitoring group
      Healthwatch Croydon in 2018 said they had struggled to
      register with their GP. 'I was living in a tent and I needed
      ID proof of address, they wouldn't let me register without',
      one person said. https://www.healthwatch.co.uk/news/2018-
      03-23/improving-access-gp-services-people-who-are-homeless

18   A study by University College London found that a third
      of deaths among homeless people are caused by treatable
      conditions, such as tuberculosis and gastric ulcers, which
      can improve with the right care. Robert W. Aldridge et al.,
      'Causes of death among homeless people: a population-based

cross-sectional study of linked hospitalisation and
mortality data in England', 11 March 2019, https://wellcome-
openresearch.org/articles/4-49/v1

19   Matt Precey and Laurence Cawley, 'Inside Harlow's
     Office Block "Human Warehouse" Housing' (2019),
     https://www.bbc.co.uk/news/uk-england-essex-47720887

20   It's not just those already homeless that are affected.
     Across the board, mental health services are stretched.
     Analysis by the Royal College of Psychiatrists found that
     funding for mental health trusts had plummeted since
     2012. Since that time, the responsibility for treating mental
     health issues has been spread out, with funding now
     going to GPs, local councils, private providers and
     charities. The problem was that councils then elected to
     spend less than 1 per cent of their budget on mental
     health: May Bulman, 'Mental Health Trusts Left With
     Less Funding Than 2012 Due to Government Cuts, New
     Analysis Reveals', *Independent*, 21 February 2018,
     https://www.independent.co.uk/news/health/mental-health-
     trusts-uk-funding-government-cuts-royal-college-
     psychiatrists-a8219486.html

21   St Mungo's, 'Stop the Scandal: An Investigation into Mental
     Health and Rough Sleeping' (2016), https://www.mungos.
     org/wp-content/uploads/2017/12/Stop_the_scandal_
     Feb20161.pdf

22   Based on a study in London by St Mungo's: Sarah Marsh
     and Patrick Greenfield, 'Deaths of Mentally Ill Rough
     Sleepers in London Rise Sharply', *Guardian*, 18 June 2018,
     https://www.theguardian.com/society/2018/jun/19/deaths-of-
     mentally-ill-rough-sleepers-in-london-rise-sharply

23   David MacKenzie, 'The Geelong Project: Interim Report 2016–
     2017' (2018), Analysis and Policy Observatory, https://apo.org.
     au/node/133006

24   St Mungo's, 'Stop the Scandal'

25   According to information provided to people who approach
     the council for help, released under the Freedom of
     Information Act: 'Finding Accommodation', What Do They
     Know, Brighton and Hove City Council, https://www.what
     dotheyknow.com/request/532433/response/1279112/attach/
     html/9/Finding%20Accommodation%20Sept%2018.doc.html

26   According to minutes from Brighton and Hove's Health
     & Wellbeing board, 11 September 2018, https://phantom.
     brighton-hove.gov.uk/Published/C00000826/M00008123/
     $$$Minutes.doc.pdf

27   In the first three months of 2018, 25,750 people approached
     councils across England saying they were homeless. Just 52
     per cent of them were deemed to be 'priority need' and
     offered housing.

28   Between April and June 2018, Brighton and Hove council
     saw 343 people approaching them as homeless, and there
     were many more from previous months and years. Initial
     assessments available at https://www.gov.uk/government/
     statistical-data-sets/live-tables-on-homelessness

29   Homeless Link, 'The Future Hostel: The Role of Hostels in
     Helping to End Homelessness' (2018), https://www.homeless.
     org.uk/sites/default/files/site-attachments/The%20Future%20
     Hostel_June%202018.pdf

30   Sarah Marsh and Patrick Greenfield, 'Removal of Homeless
     Camps Trebles as Charities Warn of "Out of Control" Crisis',

Guardian, 17 June 2019, https://www.theguardian.com/
society/2019/jun/17/removal-of-homeless-camps-trebles-as-
charities-warn-of-out-of-control-crisis?CMP=share_btn_tw

31   Stafford – 17.5 per cent of children in poverty (after housing
costs), BASW child poverty survey 2016, https://www.basw.
co.uk/system/files/resources/basw_32630-4_0.pdf

32   According to Staffordshire County Council's 2018 'Stafford:
Locality Profile', 24 out of 100 adults were financially
stressed: https://www.staffordbc.gov.uk/sites/default/files/
cme/DocMan1/Corporate%20Business%20and%20
Partnerships/Stafford-Locality-Profile-2018.pdf

33   St Mungo's, 'Rebuilding Shattered Lives: The Final Report',
https://www.mungos.org/publication/rebuilding-shattered-
lives-final-report/

34   Sacks-Jones also notes: 'Homeless women are often left
with lasting trauma, have poor mental health and some
misuse substances to cope. Their needs are distinct from
men's. Yet most homeless services aren't set up to respond
to women's needs. Hostels are often predominantly used
by men which means they can be intimidating and
unsafe places for women. A gendered approach to
supporting women who are homeless is essential to
helping them rebuild their lives. An important part of
this is to take into account the fact that many homeless
women are mothers, whether or not their children are in
their care.' Katherine Sacks-Jones, 'Motherhood,
Homelessness and Abuse: The Importance of a
Gendered Approach' (2017), http://www.safelives.org.uk/
practice_blog/motherhood-homelessness-and-abuse-
importance-gendered-approach

35   In 2017, Staffordshire County Council reduced the funding
      for drug and alcohol services by 59 per cent. Research by
      Healthwatch Staffordshire found that those cuts had resulted
      in 'unmet need for service users and additional pressures
      placed on other healthcare providers, criminal justice
      agencies, and local authorities': 'Annual Report 2017/18',
      Staffordshire Healthwatch, http://moderngov.staffordshire.
      gov.uk/documents/s111735/Appendix%20A%20for%20
      Healthwatch%20Staffordshire.pdf

36   Staffordshire County Council told me: 'The county council's
      adult safeguarding enquiry team conducted a thorough
      enquiry into the allegations of domestic abuse. This was
      completed in conjunction with other agencies, including
      Staffordshire Police. Jayne was supported throughout the
      process, where we identified all of her issues and actions
      taken in accordance with her wishes. Following this the
      enquiry worker concluded that there was a continued risk
      and following the Staffordshire and Stoke-on-Trent safe-
      guarding policy a safeguarding plan was implemented, with
      Jayne's views and wishes considered throughout. In line
      with our procedures the safeguarding plan was passed to the
      area social work team for ongoing relevant monitoring and
      review. Jayne had an allocated social worker, had been
      accommodated into a supported tenancy with a care plan
      in place as well as the local authority having appointeeship
      for her benefits.'

37   Nathaniel Barker, 'Council's Temporary Accommodation
      Spend Nears £1bn', *Inside Housing*, 31 August 2018,
      https://www.insidehousing.co.uk/news/news/councils-
      temporary-accommodation-spend-nears-1bn-57695

38   According to SafeLives, 'Safe at Home: Homelessness and

domestic abuse' (2018), http://safelives.org.uk/sites/default/files/resources/Safe_at_home_Spotlight_web.pdf

39   One study, from Kent, found that 27 per cent of women who were sleeping rough there had been sexually assaulted or raped while on the streets.

40   According to a response following a Freedom of Information request.

41   Research from Public Health Wales found that 30–40 per cent of people become homeless because of alcohol misuse. An estimated 60 per cent of the homeless population drink alcohol at hazardous and harmful levels: 'Misuse of Alcohol One of the Main Causes of Homelessness' (2015), Health in Wales, https://www.wales.nhs.uk/news/39384

42   Chen X et al., 'Mental Disorders, Comorbidity, and Postrunaway Arrests Among Homeless and Runaway Adolescents' (2006), *Journal of Research on Adolescence*, 16(3), pp. 379–402.

43   In Portugal, heroin use had been extraordinarily high in the 1980s – one in a hundred were using the drug and HIV infections from infected needles were sky-high. But in 2001 the country decriminalized all illicit substances; being found with heroin meant perhaps a small fine or the requirement to talk to officials about ways to get treatment, but no more long prison spells. At the same time, reforms were happening in how services supported and cared for those with addiction issues. Problematic drug use dropped dramatically, as did HIV infection rates.

44   Khalil Hassanally, 'Homeless Mortality Data from East London', *London Journal of Primary Care*, 5 April 2018, pp. 99–102.

45   A BBC investigation found the number of people of no fixed
abode admitted to hospitals for drug addiction increased by
about a quarter between 2014 and 2016: Craig Lewis,
'"Crisis" Warning Over Homeless Addicts Admitted to
Hospital', 6 October 2017, https://www.bbc.co.uk/news/
uk-england-41260042

46   Analysis of death certificates carried out by the Office
for National Statistics found that over half of all deaths
of homeless people in 2017 were due to three factors:
accidents (including drug poisoning), which accounted
for 40 per cent, suicides, which accounted for 13 per
cent, and diseases of the liver, at 9 per cent: https://
www.ons.gov.uk/peoplepopulationandcommunity
/birthsdeathsandmarriages/deaths/bulletins/deathsof
homelesspeopleinenglandandwales/2013to2017

47   Bethan Thomas, 'Homelessness Kills: An Analysis of the
Mortality of Homeless People in Early Twenty-First Century
England' (2019), Crisis, https://www.crisis.org.uk/
media/236799/crisis_homelessness_kills_es2012.pdf

48   The numbers shot up by 52 per cent between 2013 and
2017: Office for National Statistics, 'Deaths of Homeless
People in England and Wales, 2013 to 2017' (2018),
https://www.ons.gov.uk/peoplepopulationandcommunity/
birthsdeathsandmarriages/deaths/bulletins/deathsofhomeless
peopleinenglandandwales/2013to2017#drug-related-deaths-of-
homeless-people-increased-by-52-per-cent-over-five-years

49   'Cuts to Addiction Services in England are "a False Economy"
warns expert', BMJ, 25 May 2017, https://www.bmj.com/
company/newsroom/cuts-to-addiction-services-in-england-are-
a-false-economy-warns-expert/

50 David Rhodes, 'Drug and Alcohol Services Cut by £162m as Deaths Increase', 11 May 2018, BBC News, https://www.bbc.co.uk/news/uk-england-44039996

51 The number of people in alcohol treatment has fallen more than 12 per cent since 2013, according to data provided by the House of Commons Library: Alex Matthews-King, 'Tory Cuts Leave Alcohol Addiction Services at Breaking Point Warns Labour, As Figures Show Record Low in Treatment', *Independent*, 13 September 2018, https://www.independent.co.uk/news/health/addiction-alcohol-drugs-tory-cuts-austerity-rehab-ashworth-labour-corbyn-a8534791.html

52 Often those classified as NRPF have entered the country illegally or their visa allowing them to stay has expired.

53 46 per cent of the 158 people who died in London since 2010 were non-UK nationals, including 28 per cent from Central and Eastern Europe: 'Dying on the Streets: "The Case for Moving Quickly to End Rough Sleeping"' (2018), St Mungo's, https://www.mungos.org/app/uploads/2018/06/Dying-on-the-Streets-Report.pdf

54 Like David, one in four people experiencing homelessness identified as LGBTQ+, and yet crucial LGBTQ+ services were being cut.

55 Civil liberties group the Manifesto Club sent Freedom of Information requests to councils and found an 89 per cent increase in Public Spaces Protection Orders (PSPOs) between 2016 and 2019.

56 Ben Sanders and Francesca Albanese, 'An Examination of the Scale and Impact of Enforcement Interventions on Street

Homeless People in England and Wales' (2017), Crisis, https://www.crisis.org.uk/media/237532/an_examination_of_the_scale_and_impact_of_enforcement_2017.pdf

57   Studies show people sleeping rough are seventeen times more likely to suffer violent attacks than the rest of society. More than one in three have been deliberately hit or kicked, and nearly one in ten have been urinated on. Violent attacks on homeless people tripled between 2013 and 2015. Some were carried out by strangers passing by, some by people with houses. In other cases, like Andrew's, it was other rough-sleepers that perpetrated the violence: Amy Walker, 'Beaten, Harassed, Set Alight: Rough Sleepers Tell of the Horrific Rise in Violence' *Guardian*, 15 December 2018, https://www.theguardian.com/society/2018/dec/15/people-are-dragged-out-of-tents-attacks-on-homeless-soar-up-to-30-percent

58   According to a Freedom of Information response from Brighton and Hove council, it spent £1,710,884 in 2010/11 – the equivalent of £2,154,949.48 in 2018 (when inflation is taken into account). However, by 2018/19 the council was spending just £1,501,242.40 a year, a drop of 30 per cent in real terms.

59   MP Ed Davey had drafted a bill to ensure terminally ill homeless people got the support they needed, and was pushing for it to be ratified in parliament. The bill, if made into law, would mean that if a doctor diagnoses a homeless person with advanced ill health and certifies that they expect that person to die within the next twelve months, then the person would have an automatic legal right to appropriate housing, along with a care package: Ed Davey, 'Terminally Ill Homeless People Are Dying on Our Streets. They Deserve

Dignity Like the Rest of Us', *Independent*, 6 July 2018, https://www.independent.co.uk/voices/homelessness-terminal-illness-death-ed-davey-parliamentary-bill-a8434581.html

60   According to research compiled by Patrick Greenfield and Sarah Marsh at the *Guardian*: Sarah Marsh and Patrick Greenfield, 'Removal of Homeless Camps Trebles as Charities Warn of "Out of Control" Crisis', *Guardian*, 17 June 2019, https://www.theguardian.com/society/2019/jun/17/removal-of-homeless-camps-trebles-as-charities-warn-of-out-of-control-crisis?CMP=share_btn_tw

61   The Royal College of Nursing (RCN) reported: 'growing numbers of nursing staff using food banks' in order to feed themselves and their families, as well as them 'taking on additional jobs and accruing personal debt', https://fullfact.org/economy/how-many-nurses-are-using-foodbanks/

62   Andrew Waugh et al., 'Health and Homelessness in Scotland': 'It was found that health activity increases in the years prior to the homelessness assessment date for people in the EHC, indicating a relationship. The relationship is most clearly seen for health activity that relates to mental health, drugs and alcohol. These issues are likely to be risk factors for homelessness.' The study, based on medical records of 435,853 people who had been in households assessed as homeless or threatened with homelessness between June 2001 and November 2016, found 'increased interactions with health services preceded people becoming homeless' and 'a peak in interactions with health services was seen around the time of the first homelessness assessment.' https://www.gov.scot/publications/health homelessness-scotland/pages/1/

63   From data obtained from eighty-nine NHS trusts in England
     by Patrick Greenfield and Sarah Marsh of the *Guardian*, who
     found the number of discharges from hospital of people
     with no fixed abode rose by 29.8 per cent from 6,748 in
     2014 to 8,758 in 2018: Sarah Marsh and Patrick Greenfield,
     'Removal of Homeless Camps Trebles as Charities Warn of
     "Out of Control" Crisis'

64   More than forty journalists worked on this project and
     contributed names of those who had died homeless.

65   ITV's *Ross Kemp: Living with Homelessness*. Heather Wheeler
     was criticized on the show for an email she had sent where
     she used language offensive to travellers, calling those
     experiencing homelessness in her area 'traditional type old
     tinkers, knife cutters'. Wheeler told ITV the comments were
     an 'error of judgement' and, responding to the count figures,
     said, 'South Derbyshire's data provides a reliable way of
     comparing change over time. But the count of zero did not
     imply that there were no rough sleepers in the constituency
     throughout the year.'

66   The words of Sir David Norgrove in an open letter
     published on the UK Statistics Authority's website:
     https://www.statisticsauthority.gov.uk/correspondence/
     response-on-rough-sleeping-statistics-in-england/

67   CHAIN's data showed that 59 per cent of people seen
     rough-sleeping in the borough of Islington during the
     year were new rough-sleepers. One fifth of the new
     rough-sleepers had come from privately rented
     accommodation. Eighty-two per cent of the total rough-
     sleepers logged were male, 18 per cent were female. Nine
     people seen rough-sleeping in the borough in 2018–19 had

experience of serving in the armed forces, of whom one was a UK national. Time spent in the forces could have been at any point in the person's life, and it is not necessarily the case that the person has recently been discharged: https://data.london.gov.uk/dataset/chain-reports

68 Researchers engaged 269 people experiencing homelessness and found that 62 per cent reported to be currently experiencing physical pain, while 53 per cent were experiencing chronic pain. Almost a quarter had been suffering from physical pain for ten years or more: 'Out of Pain: Breaking the Cycle of Physical Pain and Homelessness', Groundswell, August 2018: https://ground swell.org.uk/what-we-do/peer-research/out-of-pain/

69 Research by Shelter found that more than 33,000 families are holding down a job despite having nowhere stable to live – a figure which has increased by 73 per cent since 2013, when it was 19,000 families. Shelter note that: 'This trend in "working homelessness" is being driven by a combination of expensive private rents, the ongoing freeze on housing benefit, and a chronic lack of social homes.' 'Over Half of Homeless Families in England Are in Work, Shock New Figures Show' (2018), Shelter, https://england.shelter.org.uk/media/press_releases/ articles/over_half_of_homeless_families_in_england_are_ in_work,_shock_new_figures_show

70 '"No DSS": Five Leading Letting Agents Risk Breaking Discrimination Law' (2018), Shelter, https://england.shelter. org.uk/media/press_releases/articles/no_dss_five_leading_ letting_agents_risk_breaking_discrimination_law

71 Jennifer Williams, 'The Deaths They Don't Count', *Manchester Evening News*, 12 August 2018, https://www.

manchestereveningnews.co.uk/news/greater-manchester-news/the-deaths-they-dont-count-15021204

72   'A Safe Home: Breaking the Link Between Homelessness
     and Domestic Abuse', Crisis, 22 August 2018, https://www.
     crisis.org.uk/media/240459/cri0198_domesticabusebill_
     appg_report_2019_aw_web.pdf

73   A Justice Select Committee report from 2017 highlighted
     just how worrying this trend was. 'We find that it is
     unacceptable that any local council has been able to deem
     an individual who has served a custodial sentence as making
     themselves intentionally homeless,' they wrote. 'We call on
     the government to amend its guidance for local authorities
     to make it explicit that an individual who is homeless
     because of having served a custodial sentence should be
     deemed vulnerable for the purposes of the Homelessness
     Reduction Act 2017': https://publications.parliament.uk/pa/
     cm201719/cmselect/cmjust/482/48202.htm

74   Many people experiencing homeless will have had some
     experience with prison. Data from London shows 36 per
     cent of those sleeping rough had served a custodial sentence
     at some point: 'Rough Sleeping Strategy, August 2018',
     Ministry of Housing, Communities and Local Government,
     https://assets.publishing.service.gov.uk/government/uploads/
     system/uploads/attachment_data/file/733421/Rough-
     Sleeping-Strategy_WEB.pdf

75   Isobel Anderson and Regina Serpa, 'The Right to Settled
     Accommodation for Homeless People in Scotland: A Triumph
     of Rational Policy-Making?' (2013), School of Applied Social
     Science, University of Stirling

76   In 2014, more than 900 people were classified as having

'no fixed abode' when released from prison in Scotland: Joe Connolly, 'We Must Recognise the Impact that Homelessness Has on People Leaving Prison', *Holyrood*, 16 November 2017, https://www.holyrood.com/articles/comment/associate-feature-we-must-recognise-impact-homelessness-has-people-leaving-prison

77   Research found that 15 per cent of newly sentenced people in prison reported being homeless before entering custody, with a third of people seen rough-sleeping in London reported serving time in prison. Research by the Ministry of Justice showed that 79 per cent of those who were previously homeless went on to be convicted in the first year after being released. 'Working with Prison Leavers: Resource for Homelessness Services' (2018), Homeless Link, https://www.homeless.org.uk/sites/default/files/site-attachments/Working%20with%20prison%20leavers%20March%202018.pdf

78   Calculation based on a discharge grant of £46 lasting five weeks while Universal Credit is processed.

79   The pilot employed six members of staff, including three peer support workers with a history of homelessness and substance misuse, who supported twenty-two homeless people over a three-year period. The majority of those who took part in the pilot maintained their tenancies continuously and half had been in their home for over two years by the end of the project: Sarah Johnsen, 'Turning Point: Scotland's Housing – First Project Evaluation', 7 February 2014, http://www.turningpointscotland.com/wp-content/uploads/2014/02/TPS-Housing-First-Final-Report.pdf

80   Across Europe, homelessness had been on the rise. Earlier
      in 2018 the European Federation of National Organisations
      Working with the Homeless (FEANTSA) put out its
      annual report, describing the situation in the starkest
      terms: Alice Cuddy, 'This past year has resolutely
      confirmed the existence of another Europe: a Europe
      not merely ignored but also misunderstood, not just
      despised but also forgotten – a Europe of the homeless.
      The homeless population has increased steadily in almost
      all EU countries': https://www.feantsa.org/download/full-
      report-en1029873431323901915.pdf

81   As quoted in the *Derry Journal*: Kevin Mullan, 'Housing
      First Works in Derry and Could Work Down South: DePaul',
      Derry Journal, 7 June 2019, https://www.derryjournal.com/
      business/housing-first-works-in-derry-and-could-work-down-
      south-depaul-1-8952456

82   In charity DePaul's assessment of their practice they
      recognized the same: support for service users with mental
      health issues, substance use, education or physical health
      issues can vary radically: 'Housing First Leading the Way
      Together' (2018), DePaul, https://ie.depaulcharity.org/sites/
      default/files/Depaul%20Housing%20First
      %20Fidelity%20Report%202018_0.pdf

83   'Care leavers' transition to adulthood' (2015),
      Comptroller and Auditor General, National Audit Office,
      https://www.nao.org.uk/wpcontent/uploads/2015/07/
      Care-leavers-transition-to-adulthood.pdf

84   Philip Alston spoke to the *Guardian* following the
      government's rejection of his official report: 'Visit to
      the United Kingdom of Great Britain and Northern
      Ireland. Report of the Special Rapporteur on extreme

poverty and human rights', 23 April 2019,
https://www.theguardian.com/society/2019/may/24/
un-poverty-expert-hits-back-over-uk-ministers-denial-of-facts-
philip-alston and https://undocs.org/A/HRC/41/39/Add.1

85   It returned to that ignominious top spot in 2019. More
     recently the town has gained unwelcome notoriety after an
     old photo of the town's potholed streets was used by
     US congressional candidate Nick Stella as a warning
     against what might happen to the USA under a Democrat
     leadership.

86   'Report of the Special Rapporteur on extreme poverty and
     human rights – Visit to the United Kingdom of Great
     Britain and Northern Ireland', United Nations, General
     Assembly, 23 April 2019, https://undocs.org/A/HRC/41/39/
     Add.1

87   The ONS analysis also found that over half of all deaths of
     homeless people in 2017 were due to drug poisoning, liver
     disease or suicide; drug poisoning alone made up 32 per cent
     of the total. London and the north-west of England had the
     highest mortality of homeless people, both in numbers of
     deaths and per-million-population of the region.

88   'Housing First in the UK and Ireland', Chartered Institute of
     Housing, 21 November 2017, http://www.cih.org/resources/
     PDF/Scotland%20Policy%20Pdfs/Housing%20First/
     CIH0220-PDF-B_Housing%20First_RV_13112017%20
     FINAL.pdf

89   Andrew Waugh, 'Health and Homelessness in Scotland',
     https://www.gov.scot/publications/health-homelessness-
     scotland/pages/1/